SUMMER COOKING

HALL, GEORGE HENRY, *Raspberries on a Cabbage Leaf.* 1889.

SUMMER COOKING

Elizabeth David

Line drawings by ADRIAN DAINTREY

DORLING KINDERSLEY LONDON

A Jill Norman Book

First published by the Museum Press 1955
A revised and enlarged edition published in Penguin Handbooks 1965

This illustrated edition published in 1988 by
Dorling Kindersley Limited
9 Henrietta Street, London WC2E 8PS

British Library Cataloguing in Publication Data

David, Elizabeth, *1913*–
Summer cooking.
1. Cookery
I. Title
641.5'64   TX829

ISBN 0–86318–278–X

Computerset in 13 point Perpetua by DMD,
52 St Clements, Oxford
Colour reproduction by Hong Kong Graphic Arts,
Hong Kong
Printed by Craftprint, Singapore

MORRIS, CEDRIC, *The Corduroy Trousers*, 1961.

CONTENTS

ACKNOWLEDGEMENTS

I am indebted to Messrs Methuen & Co. and to Messrs Constable & Co. for permission to quote passages from T. Earle Welby's *The Dinner Knell* and from Logan Pearsall Smith's *All Trivia* respectively. The editor and publishers of *Harper's Bazaar* have kindly allowed me to reproduce recipes originally published by them, and Messrs Evans Brothers a recipe which first appeared in *The Traveller's Year* by Elizabeth Nicholas. One recipe has been reproduced from my own *Italian Food*, published by Messrs Macdonald & Co.

INTRODUCTION TO THE FIRST EDITION

By summer cookery I do not necessarily mean cold food; although cold dishes are always agreeable in summer, at most meals, however hot the weather, one hot dish is welcome, but it should be a light one, such as a very simply cooked sole, an omelette, a soup of the young vegetables which are in season – something fresh which provides at the same time a change, a new outlook. . . . My object in writing this book has been to provide recipes for just such dishes, with emphasis on two aspects of cookery which are increasingly disregarded: the suitability of certain foods to certain times of the year, and the pleasure of eating the vegetables, fruits, poultry, meat or fish which is in season, therefore at its best, most plentiful, and cheapest.

A couple of years ago an advocate of the tin and the deep freeze wrote to a Sunday newspaper explaining that frozen or tinned vegetables were better than fresh ones, as the 'pick of the crop' goes straight to the factories to be frozen or tinned. Can this be a matter for congratulation? I am not unappreciative of modern marvels, and in its way the deep freeze is an admirable invention, particularly for the United States, where fresh produce has to be transported great distances. Some foods, game, for example, stand up remarkably well to the freezing process, but let us not pretend that frozen green peas and broad beans, strawberries, raspberries, and blackberries are as 'good as fresh'. They may indeed be quite adequate, and are an incontestable blessing to people pressed for time or space, or having to provide meals at very short notice, but is it necessary for those not in such circumstances to eat all this food out of season? Frozen peas seem to have become the almost obligatory accompaniment to every meal, whether in private houses or restaurants; yet how often during the season of fresh peas, which is quite a long one, do we get a dish of those really delicate, fresh, sugary green peas? Is it because the 'pick of the crop' has gone to the factory instead of to the market and we are therefore unable to buy them, or is it because people no longer know how to shell them and cook them and have forgotten what they taste like?

The deep freeze appears to have gained over the minds of the English housewife and restaurant keeper a hypnotic power such as never was

KNIGHT, HAROLD, (1874-1961), *In The Spring.*

exercised by the canning factories. Even leaving out of consideration the fact that the pleasure of rediscovering each season's vegetables and fruits at the appropriate time is thereby blunted, this method of marketing seems to me an extravagant one. As I write, there are lovely little South African pineapples in the greengrocer's down the road for 1s. 6d. each, sweet, juicy oranges at seven for a shilling, yet people are crowding round the deep freeze in the same shop paying four times as much for a few strawberries in a cardboard packet. As soon as strawberries and raspberries are in season they will be clamouring for frozen pineapple and cartons of orange juice.

Then there are those people who in restaurants insist upon ordering a certain dish although some essential ingredient is not in season, and then complain that the truffles were tinned, or the *sole Véronique* made with the wrong kind of grapes. In a London restaurant which claims to serve Provençal food I found *ratatouille* on the menu in February. Upon inquiring how this could be when there are neither pimentos nor aubergines nor courgettes at this time of the year I was informed that it was made with cabbage and tomatoes. The fact that restaurant keepers can and do rely upon the ignorance of the customers is to blame for these absurdities.

Almost as perverse a situation seems to prevail in the choice of suitable dishes for the time of year; anyone who has spent a summer in India will remember the famous New Delhi hotel where oxtail soup, Irish stew and treacle pudding as well as all the routine curries were served all through the summer, with the temperature round about 110 degrees. 'Turtle Soup, plum pudding and champagne for an August Sunday luncheon in a seaside villa would be to say the least, incongruous, but have been experienced,' wrote Lady Jekyll in *Kitchen Essays*. That was in 1922, before ice cream all winter and frozen game all summer had become a matter of routine, and it is hardly surprising that inexperienced cooks and hostesses do not stop to think whether a cassoulet of haricot beans, sausages, pork, and bacon, or an enormous dish of *choucroute garnie* are suitable for a hot summer evening. It would be absurd to pretend that there are not a good many summer days in England when such dishes would be welcome barriers against the cold, but I still think it is rather dull to eat the same food all year round; these heavy foods should be kept for the winter, and cooler, lighter dishes served in the summer; dishes which bring some savour of the garden, the fields, the sea, into the kitchen and the dining-room. It is this kind of food, as well as methods of dealing with the fruits and vegetables and herbs of summer in a manner in which their freshness and flavour may be best appreciated, which I have tried to describe in this book. I have also given a few suggestions and recipes for summer occasions such as picnics and outdoor parties, and for presenting those foods available all the year round in ways appropriate to spring and summer.

London
January 1955

INTRODUCTION TO
THE FIRST PENGUIN
EDITION

As I understand it, summer cooking means the extraction of maximum enjoyment out of the produce which grows in the summer season and is appropriate to it. It means catching at the opportunity of eating fresh food freshly cooked. It means appreciation of treats such as new peas, fresh little carrots, the delicate courgettes now home produced and to me as delicious as the finest asparagus. There are cheap treats such as omelettes flavoured with fresh green chives, chervil, tarragon, parsley; and occasionally there will be an expensive treat such as Cornish lobster, a salmon trout, a freshly boiled and freshly dressed crab, a few heads of purple-sprouting broccoli or a pound of tender little string beans cooked for just seven minutes, to be eaten cold – as a separate course, with an olive oil and lemon dressing – but quickly, almost before they have cooled. An important point, this. To many people, summer food means cold food. That should not mean congealed, over-refrigerated lifeless food. A chicken slow-roasted in the morning, left to cool, and eaten cold at lunch time can be a true treat. Kept until next day it is just a cold chicken. The same applies to salmon, salmon trout, lobster, duck and small joints of meat. Summer cooking implies therefore a sense of immediacy, a capacity to capture the essence of a fleeting moment.

In the summer there is also holiday cooking. That may well mean food cooked in an unfamiliar kitchen equipped, more than likely, in an impersonal and inadequate fashion by the owners of a house, holiday villa, or caravan hired out for the summer. For some, and the numbers are increasing yearly, this temporary Paradise will be situated close to a Mediterranean shore. Food shopping will be done in a general store, or in some chaotic little market where the best produce will be sweet ripe tomatoes, mild onions, olives, and cheese of an undistinguished nature. The eggs, however, will be fresh and the bread authentic. Meals will be primitive – and, so long as one has learned to be adaptable and not to hanker for roast meat and steaks – entirely delicious because perfectly appropriate to the time, the place and the circumstances.

HODGKIN, ELIOT, *Brioches*, 1977.

There will be cheap coarse red wine to drink, and the wise will follow the example of the local people, dilute the wine with ice and have a supply of bottled mineral water as an alternative.

Those who have a mind for outdoor cooking and camping meals will invest in one or two cheap local cooking pots and brew their own soups and rice dishes, or grill their own fish in some secret cove, rather than sit in an overcrowded seashore restaurant eating yet another Spanish Sunday paella, or the steak with chip potatoes and salad dressed with ground-nut oil which has become the standard midday meal throughout tourist France.

The less heroic, lacking the organizing ability and resolution of the outdoor cooking enthusiast, will settle for the car-borne picnic bought in a market, or in Sunday morning shops of small French towns. A bottle of wine from a café, a baguette or two of freshly-baked bread (it would be sad if English travellers new to the continent were all to emulate the lady from the Midlands who wrote to a Leicester newspaper two years ago declaring that she had taken half a dozen large English loaves to France and so had made her family independent of French bread and French bakers), a little parcel of butter, a variety of ready-made salads, olives, slices of sausage and mountain-cured ham from the cooked-food shops; some creamy ewe's milk Banon cheese wrapped in chestnut leaves, a hard, salty grey-coated Valençay, or a long neat little log of Sainte-Maure; a bag of cherries or fresh peaches – all these are crammed into your shopping bag. A last stop to buy a slab of chocolate and a packet of *Petit Beurre*, and you are off. Does it matter very much that by the time you have driven fifty miles and settled on your picnic spot your parcels are a little crumpled, your wine a trifle warm (too late, you remember that had you taken the precaution of wrapping the bottle in several sheets of dampened newspaper it would have been as cool as cucumber), your chocolate beginning to melt? After all, it is summer. You are on holiday. You are in company of your own choosing. The air is clean. You can smell wild fennel and thyme, dry resinous pine needles, the sea. For my part, I ask no greater luxury. Indeed I can think of none.

London, January 1965

NOTE

The quantities given for each recipe are for four persons unless otherwise stated.

FRESH HERBS

HOLMAN-HUNT, WILLIAM, (1827-1910), *Isabella and the Pot of Basil.*

FRESH HERBS

The use of herbs in cooking is so much a matter of tradition, almost of superstition, that the fact that it is also a question of personal taste is overlooked, and experiments are seldom tried; in fact the restriction of this herb to that dish is usually quite arbitrary, and because somebody long ago discovered that basil works some sort of spell with tomatoes, fennel with fish, and rosemary with pork, it occurs to few people to reverse the traditional usage; to take an example, fennel is an excellent complement to pork, adding the sharpness which is supplied in English cookery by apple sauce, while basil enhances almost anything with which it is cooked; for ideas one has only to look to the cooking of other countries to see how much the use of herbs as a flavouring can be varied. In England mint is considered to have an affinity to lamb, new potatoes, and green peas; the French regard the use of mint as a flavouring as yet another sign of English barbarism, and scarcely ever employ it, while all over the Middle East, where the cooking is far from uncivilized, mint is one of the most commonly used of herbs; it goes into soups, sauces, omelettes, salads, purées of dried vegetables and into the sweet cooling mint tea drunk by the Persians and Arabs. In Spain, where the cooking has been much influenced by the Arabs, it is also used in stews and soups; it is usually one of the ingredients of the sweet sour sauces which the Italians like, and which are a legacy from the Romans, and in modern Roman cooking wild mint gives a characteristic flavour to stewed mushrooms and to vegetable soups. The Indians make a fresh chutney from pounded mint, mangoes, onion and chillies, which is an excellent accompaniment to fish and cold meat as well as to curries. Mint is one of the cleanest tasting of herbs and will give a lively tang to many vegetables, carrots, tomatoes, mushrooms, lentils; a little finely chopped mint is good in fish soups and stews, and with braised duck; a cold roast duck served on a bed of freshly picked mint makes a lovely, fresh-smelling summer dish; a few leaves can be added to the orange salad to serve with it. Dried mint is one of the most useful of herbs for the winter, for it greatly enlivens purées and soups of dried peas, haricot beans and lentils. Finely powdered dried mint is a characteristic flavouring of Turkish, Egyptian and Lebanese cooking. It is particularly good in mixtures of tomatoes and aubergines, and with rice dishes cooked in olive oil.

In England basil is one of the traditional herbs for turtle soup, and it is well known that it brings out the flavour of tomato salads and sauces; although it was common at one time in English kitchen gardens it is now extremely hard to lay hands on fresh basil, a state of affairs which should be remedied as fast as possible, for, with its highly aromatic scent, it is one of the most delicious of all herbs. In Provence, in Italy, in Greece, basil grows and is used in great quantities. The Genoese could scarcely exist without their *pesto*, a thick compound of pounded basil, pine nuts, garlic, cheese and olive oil which is used as a sauce for every kind of pasta, for fish, particularly red mullet, and as a flavouring for soups and minestrones. The Niçois have their own version of this sauce called *pistou* which has given its name to the Soupe au Pistou made of french beans, potatoes and macaroni, flavoured with the *pistou* sauce. To the Greeks basil has a special significance, for the legend goes that basil was found growing on the site of the Crucifixion by the Empress Helena, who brought it back from Jerusalem to Greece, since when the plant has flourished all over the Greek world; scarcely a house in Greece is to be seen without its pot of basil in the window. Once you have become a basil addict it is hard to do without it; Mediterranean vegetables such as pimentos and aubergines, garlicky soups and wine-flavoured dishes of beef, salads dressed with the fruity olive oil of Provence or Liguria and all the dishes with tomato sauces need basil as a fish needs water, and there is no substitute.

Of that very English herb sage I have little to say except that, and this is where the question of personal taste comes in, it seems to me to be altogether too blatant, and used far too much; its all-pervading presence in stuffings and sausages is perhaps responsible for the distaste for herbs which many English people feel. The Italians are also very fond of sage, and use it a great deal with veal and with liver; it seems to give a musty rather than a fresh flavour, and I would always substitute mint or basil for sage in any recipe. The same applies to rosemary, which when fresh gives out a powerful oil which penetrates anything cooked with it; in southern France it is used to flavour roast lamb, pork and veal, but should be removed from the dish before it is served, as it is disagreeable to find those spiky little leaves in one's mouth; in Italy rosemary is stuffed in formidable quantities into roast sucking pig, and in the butchers' shops you see joints of pork tied up ready for roasting wreathed round and threaded with rosemary; it looks entrancing, but if you want to taste the meat, use only the smallest quantity, and never put it into stock destined for a consomeé or for a sauce.

Thyme, marjoram and wild marjoram are all good and strong-flavoured herbs which can be used separately or together for robust stews of beef in red wine, for those aromatic country soups in which there are onions, garlic, bacon, wine, cabbage; the *garbures* of south-western France and the minestrones of northern Italy; one or other of these herbs should go into stuffings for chicken, goose and turkey, for pimentos and aubergines, into meat croquettes (accompanied by grated lemon peel), terrines of game, and stews of hare and rabbit; either thyme or marjoram is almost essential to strew in small quantities on mutton, pork and lamb chops and liver to be fried or grilled; wild marjoram is called *origano* in Italy and Spain and is used for any and every dish of veal and pork, for fish and fish soups, and is an essential ingredient of the Neapolitan pizza, that colourful, filling, peasant dish of bread dough baked with tomatoes, anchovies and cheese. The marjoram called *rígani* which grows wild in Greece and Cyprus is a variety which has a more powerful scent; the flowers as well as the leaves are dried and no kebab of mutton, lamb or kid is thinkable without it. Lemon thyme is at its best fresh rather than cooked and is particularly good in a buttery potato purée, and in salads; there are dozens of varieties of thyme each with its particular scent, the best for cooking being perhaps the common thyme which grows wild on the Sussex Downs. A curious thyme which has a scent of caraway seeds is good with roast pork.

Fennel, both the leaves and stalks of the variety which grows rather too easily in English gardens, and the root-bulb of the Florentine fennel which is imported from France and Italy, has many uses besides the sauce for mackerel which is found in all old English cookery books. For the famous Provençal *grillade au fenouil* the sun-dried, brittle stalks of the fennel are used as a bed on which to grill sea-bass (*loup de mer*) or red mullet; there is a Tuscan chicken dish in which the bird is stuffed with thick strips of ham and pieces of fennel bulb and pot-roasted; in Perugia they stuff their sucking pig and pork with fennel leaves and garlic instead of the rosemary prevalent elsewhere in Italy; one of the best of Italian sausages is *finocchiona*, a Florentine pork salame flavoured with fennel seeds; if you like the aniseed taste of fennel use it chopped up raw in soups, particularly iced soups, and in vinaigrette sauces, in rice salads to give the crisp element so necessary to soft foods, in mixed vegetable salads, in fish mayonnaises, in the court-bouillon in which fish is to be poached, in stuffings for baked fish, in chicken salads, and mixed with parsley and juniper berries for a marinade for pork chops which are to be grilled. The leaves of dill are not unlike those of fennel, but the aniseed flavour is less pronounced; it is a herb much used in Scandinavian and Russian cooking, particularly to flavour pickled cucumber and for soups.

Tarragon is essentially a herb of French cookery; *poulet á l'estragon* and *œufs en gelée à l'estragon* are classics of the French kitchen; without tarragon there is no true Sauce Béarnaise; with chives and chervil (which also goes well with carrots, potatoes, and in salads) or parsley it is one of the *fines herbes* for omelettes, sauces, butters, and many dishes of grilled meat and fish. It is a herb to be used with care for its charm lies in its very distinct and odd flavour and too much of it spoils the effect, but a few leaves will give character to many dishes and particularly to smooth foods such as sole cooked in cream, eggs *en cocotte*, cream soups, bisques of shell fish, stewed scallops, potato purées and also to tomato salads. In Italy, tarragon is to be found only in and around Siena, where it is used in the stuffing for globe artichokes, and to flavour green salads. When buying tarragon plants be sure to insist on the true French tarragon. Common tarragon, sometimes called Russian tarragon, has a rank taste and no scent at all.

The routine bouquet garni of French cookery consists of a sprig of thyme, parsley, and a bay leaf (which besides its well-known use in soups and stews and marinades gives a good flavour to béchamel sauce if put with the milk while it is heated, and then removed). Chives, with their delicate onion flavour and brilliant green colouring, are one of the best of summer garnishes for eggs, vegetables, salads and soups. Borage is used by the Genoese to mix with the stuffing for ravioli, and to make fritters; the finely chopped leaves give a delicate cucumber taste to cream cheese, and its use in wine cups is traditional. The Sardinians flavour roast pork with myrtle, the French consider savory (*sarriette*) indispensable as a flavouring for broad beans; lovage, a member of the *Umbelliferae* family, has a peppery leaf with a faint hint of celery and gives an interesting taste to a salad of haricot beans and to fish soups. Among its thousands of uses in the kitchen, parsley is the perfect foil for garlic; the fresh leaves of angelica can be used in salads, while the translucent green stalks have a very strong fresh scent, which when candied give such a delicious flavour and elegant appearance to sweet creams and cream cheese puddings; the leaf of the sweet-scented geranium gives a lovely scent to a lemon water ice and an incomparable flavour when cooked with blackberries for jelly. The fresh leaves of coriander are much used in Oriental, Middle Eastern and Mexican cookery, while the dried seeds are one of the essential ingredients of nearly all curries and Oriental cooking; with their

ANONYMOUS CARAVAGGESQUE ARTIST, (c. 1610) *Still life with Fennel, Cardoon, Radish and a basket of Rochet, Rue and Lettuce.*

slightly burnt orange peel taste they are also good to flavour pork, mutton and venison, and in sauces for coarse fish; they can also be used to flavour milk and cream puddings and junkets. All these herbs and many others, tansy, violets, balm, marigold petals, nasturtium flowers and leaves, pennyroyal, yarrow, costmary, burnet, rocket, sorrel and rue, were familiar ingredients of country cookery all over Europe until the twentieth century brought such a battery of chemical flavourings and synthetic essences that the uses and virtues of fresh plants have almost been forgotten. But when you are accustomed to their presence in food they are as necessary as salt; during the summer months while their flavours are fresh and their leaves green they add enormously to the appearance as well as to the flavour of food.

The quantity in which any given herb is to be used is a matter of taste rather than of rule. Cookery books are full of exhortations to discretion in this matter, but much depends on the herb with which you happen to be dealing, what food it is to flavour, whether the dish in question is to be a long simmered one in which it is the sauce which will be ultimately flavoured with the herbs, or whether the herbs are to go into a stuffing for a bird or meat to be roasted, in which case the aromas will be more concentrated, or again whether the herbs will be cooked only a minute or two as in egg dishes, or not cooked at all, as when they are used to flavour a salad or a herb butter. Whether the herbs are fresh or dried is an important point. The oils in some herbs (rosemary, wild marjoram, sage) are very strong, and when these dry out the flavour is very much less powerful. But in the drying process nearly all herbs (mint is an exception) acquire a certain mustiness, so that although in theory one should be able to use dried herbs more freely than fresh ones, the opposite is in fact generally the case.

Some fresh herbs disperse their aromatic scent very quickly when in contact with heat; a few leaves of fresh tarragon steeped in a hot consommé for 20 minutes will give it a strong flavour, whereas if the tarragon is to flavour a salad considerably more will be necessary. Lemon thyme and marjoram are at their best raw, or only slightly cooked, as in an omelette; the flavour of fennel stalks is brought out by slow cooking; basil has a particular affinity with all dishes in which olive oil is an ingredient, whether cooked or in salads. Knowledge of the right quantities, and of interesting combinations of herbs, can be acquired by using egg dishes, salads and soups as a background. Even if the herbs have been dispensed with a less cautious hand than is usually advised the result will not be a disaster, as it can be when some musty dried herb has completely permeated a roast bird or an expensive piece of meat. You may, on the contrary, have discovered some delicious new combination of tastes, and certainly the use of fresh herbs will be a startling revelation to all those people who know herbs only as something bought in a packet called 'mixed dried herbs', and for which you might just as well substitute sawdust.

It is particularly to the dishes in which fresh herbs are an essential rather than an incidental flavouring that I would like to call attention, for it is this aspect of cookery which is passed over by those writers who enjoin so much caution in the use of herbs. Sometimes it is a good thing to forget that basil, parsley, mint, tarragon, fennel, are all bunched together under the collective word 'herbs' and to remember that the difference between leaf vegetables (sorrel, spinach, lettuce) and herbs is very small, and indeed at one time all these plants were known collectively as 'salad herbs'. Nobody tells you to 'use spinach with caution', and neither can you be 'discreet with the basil' when you are making a *pesto* sauce, because the basil is the essential flavouring (so for that matter is mint in mint sauce).

In a slightly different way, a plain consommé or potato soup can be used as a background for a flavouring of herbs, tarragon being a particularly good one for this purpose. An *omelette aux fines herbes* needs tarragon as well as parsley and chervil. So do many sauces; the delicious *sauce verte* and *sauce ravigote* are two of them; the wonderful Sauce Messine (the recipe is on page 191) is another.

There are many recipes in this book calling for fresh herbs, for they can be enjoyed only in the summer (with the exception of parsley, mint, and the thymes, which go on until Christmas), and for quick reference they are found in the Index listed both under their own names and under the particular herb which is an essential or important ingredient of that dish.

For the dispensing of fresh herbs into salads and soups it is advisable to keep a pair of kitchen scissors handy, and for chopping larger quantities a two-handled, crescent-shaped chopper such as may now be obtained in the larger kitchen stores. Small sturdy wooden bowls complete with a little axe-shaped chopper are also now obtainable in some stores and are invaluable in any kitchen where fresh herbs are frequently in use.

An increasing number of more enterprising independent greengrocery firms are finding that by offering a small supply of fresh herbs in season as well as the more unusual vegetables and salad greens, they can keep their customers happy – and away from the supermarkets. At any rate it does no harm to ask your local greengrocer for such commodities as fresh chives, tarragon and fennel. By creating a demand we may end by getting the supplies we need.

❖ TO KEEP FRESH HERBS ❖

To those who cannot grow their own herbs, the arrival of a country friend bringing fresh garden herbs makes the cooking of summer omelettes, salads and sauces a matter of urgency. Windfall cooking, this, to be done quickly, and the results enjoyed before the country produce loses its pristine freshness. But what is to be done with the surplus? And supposing that circumstances prevent you from making immediate use of fragile chives, chervil, basil, freshly picked mint?

Storage boxes with sealing covers, of the kind which originated with the products called Tupperware, now copied in this country and widely sold at very much less cost than the originals, go far to solving the problem. In the summer of 1963 I kept a large bunch of chervil, the most perishable of all herbs, sealed in one of these boxes and stored in the refrigerator for a fortnight. It emerged in perfect condition. Parsley, basil and tarragon also keep well this way. Chives last a shorter time; fresh fennel leaves are even more fragile.

It is essential when attempting to store herbs and salad-stuffs in plastic boxes, or for that matter in polythene bags, that they should be bone dry when sealed in the boxes; and it goes without saying that the fresher they are when put away the longer they will last.

An alternative short-term method of keeping small quantities of fresh herbs is to make them up immediately into herb butters, or to half-make certain cream or oil-based sauces, store these in small covered pots or plastic containers in the refrigerator and draw on them for flavouring omelettes and other egg dishes and serving with grills as and when the opportunity arises.

Herb butters described in this book are parsley (*maître d'hôtel* butter, page 192), mint (page 193), and basil (page 119). Tarragon and chervil also make delicious fresh herb butters. The former is good with steak (see the recipe on page 119) and chicken, the latter with fish and for stirring into potato and carrot soups. Fennel butter for veal or fish is made like parsley butter.

Mint can be made also into the fresh uncooked mint chutney described on page 194. A little of this mint chutney stirred into thin cream or yoghourt makes an interesting dressing for a salad of shredded lettuce and hard-boiled eggs. As a sandwich filling it is wonderfully refreshing. It can be blended with cream cheese or the yolks of hard-boiled eggs.

Fresh basil is too precious for so much as one leaf to be allowed to go to waste. What cannot be used fresh in a tomato salad, a soup or freshly made sauce can be made, if there is enough, into a *pesto* sauce – the most original and marvellous of all herb sauces – which will keep in the refrigerator for at least a few days, until you have occasion to eat a pasta meal or to make the gnocchi described on page 83. To make *pesto* for keeping, omit the garlic and add it only on the day the sauce is to be eaten. Pounded and uncooked garlic in conjunction with oil or butter tends to give a stale or rancid taste to a sauce or a herb butter.

❖ TO DRY AND STORE HERBS ❖

Tarragon, mint, basil, marjoram, summer savory and the thymes are all good herbs for home drying. Parsley, chives and fennel leaves are not successful. Fennel stalks are at their best when they have dried out naturally, in their own habitat and the heat of a Mediterranean summer. The smaller stems of English fennel can, however, be artificially dried, although they neither keep so well nor retain the aroma of the Mediterranean plant. Rosemary and bay dry out naturally but while they are drying keep the bunches in tall glass jars or in bags.

Herbs for drying should always be picked on a dry day, when they are coming into flower, about mid-July to the beginning of August. Spread them on a newspaper in an airing cupboard, in the plate-warming draw of the cooker or on the rack above it. Protect them from dust and light with muslin or more newspaper. Let them dry slowly. Don't cook out their essential oils by drying them in a heated oven, however fuelled, and that includes microwave.

If you have the storage space, let the leaves and any dried flowerheads remain whole and on the stalks instead of stripping them and crumbling the leaves. Herbs on the stalk retain more of their aromatic qualities and are more useful than powdered herbs. Twigs of thyme are particularly needed for tying into the herb faggot, or bouquet garni, with bay leaves and sometimes other herbs to flavour a stew or a braised meat or poultry dish. Fennel and tarragon stalks are useful for flavouring fish stocks and court-bouillons. Arranged in the cooking-pan underneath pork chops, chicken, lamb and fish to be grilled, or baked in the oven, branches of thyme (wild thyme is especially good), fennel, bay, rosemary and wild marjoram give out their scents and oils as the food is cooked. The result is deliciously aromatic meat or fish tasting and smelling almost as if it had been cooked over a crackling open fire of kindling gathered on some dry southern hillside.

For the storage of dried herbs use glass sweet jars with well-fitting stoppers. Keep them in a cupboard away from the light. An alternative method is to store bunches of dried herbs in little cotton or paper bags, labelled and loosely tied so that they can be easily undone. Stored in this fashion, herbs can be kept all together in a big bowl standing near the cooker, or in a straw bag hanging on the kitchen door or wall. A selection of the herbs most often used, such as bay leaves, fennel stalks and thyme, is then always to hand, but protected from dust, grime, steam and light.

As soon as the new season's herbs are dried and stored, throw away any left over from the previous year. With a few rare exceptions, a year is the maximum period for which aromatic herbs in dried form retain any virtues as far as cooking is concerned.

✧ COMMERCIAL DRIED HERBS ✧

Dried herbs on the stalk, notably wild thyme and fennel twigs imported from Provence, are now sold by many health food stores, delicatessens, and kitchen shops. These herbs retain their aromatic properties far longer (they have more to start with) than do our northern plants.

Dried herbs in jars should be bought in the smallest available quantities. Three-quarters of the dried herbs bought in an excess of enthusiasm by amateur cooks end up in the dustbin because they have been kept too long. Throwing away stale herbs is, it has to be admitted, preferable to throwing them into the food.

Italian dried wild marjoram, called *origano* (all marjorams are origanums) can be bought in many Soho stores. Greek wild marjoram, another variety of the plant, called *rígani*, is particularly aromatic. It is always dried on the stalk, and the flower-heads as well as the leaves are used. It is this version of marjoram, very potently aromatic, which gives the characteristic flavour to Greek lamb kebabs. A little goes a long way, and it keeps remarkably well. (For excellent Greek recipes see *The Home Book of Greek Cookery* by Joyce M. Stubbs, who gives also a list of London shops where Greek specialities can be bought. The book is published in paperback by Faber.)

HORS D'ŒUVRE AND SALADS

MONET, CLAUDE, (1840-1926), *Le Déjeuner.*

HORS D'ŒUVRE
AND SALADS

How one learns to dread the season for salads in England. What becomes of the hearts of the lettuces? What makes an English cook think that beetroot spreading its hideous purple dye over a sardine and a spoonful of tinned baked beans constitutes an hors d'œuvre? Why make the cold salmon, woolly enough anyhow by midsummer, look even less appetizing than it is by serving it on a bed of lettuce leaves apparently rescued from the dustbin? What is the object of spending so much money on cucumbers, tomatoes and lettuces because of their valuable vitamins, and then drowning them in vinegar and chemical salad dressings?

Cookery books are full of instructions as to the making of a plain lettuce salad but it seems to me that there are only three absolutely essential rules to be observed: the lettuce must be very fresh; the vinegar in the dressing must be reduced to the absolute minimum; the dressing must be mixed with the lettuce only at the moment of serving. Wash the lettuce (ideally of course it should not be washed at all, but each leaf wiped with a clean damp cloth) under a running cold tap; don't leave it to soak. Drain it in a wire salad basket, or a colander, or shake it in a clean teacloth in which it can then be hung up to dry; or it can be put, still wrapped in its cloth, into a refrigerator until half an hour before it is to be served (don't put a freshly picked garden lettuce in the refrigerator, but it will do no harm to the average bought lettuce). The salad dressing can be prepared beforehand and when it is time to mix the salad, do it gently, taking your time, and ensuring that each leaf has its proper coating of oil. The most effective way of mixing a green salad is with your hands.

The French dressing most commonly used consists of 3 parts oil to 1 of vinegar, but to my mind this is far too vinegary, and I seldom use less than 6 times as much oil as vinegar. Tarragon-flavoured wine vinegar makes the best dressing. First-class olive oil is of course essential, and given this, the flavour of the lettuce and the oil, with a little salt and garlic, is quite enough to make a perfect salad without any further seasoning. The grotesque prudishness and archness with which garlic is treated in this country has led to the superstition that rubbing the bowl with it before putting the salad in gives sufficient flavour. It depends whether you are going to eat the bowl or the salad. If you like the taste of garlic but don't actually wish to chew the bulb itself, crush it with the point of a knife (there is really no necessity to fuss about with garlic presses and such devices unless you wish to intensify and concentrate the acrid-tasting oils in the garlic instead of dispersing them), put it in the bowl in which the dressing is to be mixed, add the other ingredients and stir vigorously. Leave it to stand for an hour and by that time the garlic will have flavoured the oil, and it can be left behind when the dressing is poured on the salad. A piece of bread or toast, what the French call a *chapon*, can be thoroughly rubbed with garlic, sprinkled with oil, and placed at the bottom of the salad bowl. Put the lettuce on the top and let it stand for a little before mixing it with the dressing. The garlic flavour will be powerful, and the bread will be as delicious as the lettuce.

To keep lettuces fresh wrap them in newspaper and put them in a covered saucepan in a cool larder. Don't remove the outer leaves until the lettuce is to be prepared for the salad. Polythene food bags are also excellent for keeping all greenstuff fresh, whether in the refrigerator or larder. To keep watercress, which so rapidly withers, put it in a deep bowl, and completely cover it with water.

A good many of the salads I have given in this chapter may be served as an hors d'œuvre. It is so very easy to make an attractive first course from vegetables, eggs, prawns, rice, and simple sauces, that it is only a question of taste, imagination, and the most elementary knowledge of cooking to avoid alike the everlasting grapefruit, the woolly melon and the awful little collection of obvious left-overs. The simplest hors d'œuvre are the best, looking clean and fresh; leave those huge spreads of twenty-five different dishes to pretentious restaurants, where as a matter of fact all the dishes taste exactly the same because they are all dressed with the identical over-vinegared sauce. When devising a mixed salad be careful not to overdo the number of ingredients, or chop everything into small pieces, or mash them all up together into one indistinguishable morass; one of the nicest of all country hors d'œuvre is the Genoese one of raw broad beans, rough salame sausage, and salty sheep's milk Sardo cheese; each of these things is served on a separate dish, and each person peels his own beans and cuts his own cheese; if the same ingredients were all mixed up together in a bowl the point would be quite lost. In the same way a salad of tunny fish piled up on haricot beans or french beans dressed with oil has two quite contrasting but compatible flavours, whereas if the tunny fish is mashed up among the beans, the flavours and textures of both are sacrificed, and the appearance of the dish messy as well.

Apart from all the little dishes which can be cheaply made at home there are now so many products on the market which make delicious hors d'œuvre that to anyone who can afford them the first course need be no bother whatever. All the smoked fish, trout, mackerel, buckling, salmon, sturgeon, eel, need no accompaniment other than lemon, and bread and butter; red caviar, which is made from salmon roes, is comparatively cheap, but not sufficiently appreciated; smoked cod's roe pounded into a paste with olive oil and lemon juice is excellent served with hot toast (eaten straight, it is good but disconcertingly sticky). If you are serving salame, buy the best (ask in Italian shops for the kind they call *casalinga*, which is usually better than the mass-produced Milan salame) and have plenty of it, and with it some olives, french bread and good fresh butter. Raw Parma ham with fresh figs is a combination scarcely ever, alas, obtainable in this country, but there is the smoked fillet of ham usually called *filet de Saxe* which is excellent with melon, there is smoked turkey, smoked pork fillet, good quality tunny fish in tins, and for people who can shop in Soho such delightful things as Greek stuffed vine leaves, Calamata olives, spiced, peppery Spanish sausages, Cyprus sausages flavoured with coriander seeds, the Arab *tahina* sauce, and that salty Greek cheese called *fetta* which goes so well with rough wine and olives and plenty of thickly cut coarse bread. With all these things serve inexpensive wines; whether white, rosé or red does not really matter, but any delicate wine would be overpowered by their salty, smoky flavours.

A SUMMER
❖ HORS D'ŒUVRE ❖

A dish of long red radishes, cleaned, but with a little of the green leaves left on, a dish of mixed green and black olives, a plate of raw, round, small whole tomatoes, a dish of hard- (not too hard) boiled eggs cut lengthways and garnished with a bunch of parsley. On the table a pepper mill and a salt mill, lemons and olive oil, butter, and fresh bread. Not very original, perhaps, but how often does one meet with a really fresh and unmessed hors d'œuvre?

EGGS IN ASPIC
⋄ WITH TARRAGON ⋄

One or two eggs, either poached or *mollet*, per person, approximately a coffee-cupful of aspic jelly per egg, a few leaves of tarragon, a small slice of very mild ham per egg.

Put a slice of ham at the bottom of each small china or glass ramekin (large enough for one egg). On top of the ham put the egg. Put a few leaves of tarragon into the melted aspic and let them infuse for an hour. Pour the strained aspic very carefully over the eggs, and when it has nearly set decorate each egg with two fresh tarragon leaves.

Instead of the ham a layer of chicken mousse (page 248) or a little slice of smoked turkey or half a poached fillet of sole, very well strained, can go

underneath the eggs. There is no point in bothering about this dish unless it is made with genuine aspic. Gelatine will not do.

It is, I think, one of the best of summer hors d'œuvre.

⋄ EGGS WITH SKORDALIÁ ⋄

Skordaliá is a Greek garlic mayonnaise. Pound 4 large cloves of garlic in a mortar; stir in the yolk of an egg. Add a little salt and ground black pepper. Stir thoroughly. Add ¼ pint of olive oil, drop by drop at first as for a mayonnaise, more rapidly as the sauce thickens. When the oil is all used up stir in 2 oz. of fresh white breadcrumbs, then 2 oz. of ground almonds, then a little lemon juice, then a handful of finely chopped parsley. This is a sauce which easily curdles, so be prepared to use another egg yolk if necessary, putting into a clean bowl, adding the curdled *skordaliá* spoonful by spoonful until it has thickened again. It is worth the trouble. Serve it in a separate bowl to accompany a dish of halved hard-boiled eggs, quartered raw tomatoes, some black olives and some radishes.

⋄ PÂTÉ OF TUNNY FISH ⋄

Pound the contents of a small tin of tunny fish in a mortar; work in half the weight of the tunny in butter; when the mixture has become a smooth paste season very lightly with a drop of lemon juice and a little black pepper. Turn into a small dish and put in the refrigerator, or a cold larder. Garnish with a few capers and a little parsley or chives. Serve with hot toast.

⋄ SMOKED COD'S ROE PASTE ⋄

Turn the contents of a 6–oz jar of smoked cod's roe paste into a bowl. Over it pour about 4 tablespoons of water. Leave for an hour or two, or overnight if more convenient. The water will soften the roe, making it easier to work, and also de-salting it a little.

Pound a clove of garlic in a marble mortar or wooden bowl. Drain off excess liquid from the cod's roe, which you now pound or mash with the garlic, adding, gradually, about 4 tablespoons of olive oil, the juice of half a lemon, and 2 to 3 tablespoons of cold water.

The paste should be of the consistency of thick cream. If you prefer it thicker or find it too salt, add the crumb of a thick slice of white bread first softened in water and squeezed dry. A tablespoon or two of mashed potato serves the same purpose.

This cod's roe paste is served chilled, in a small bowl or shallow dish. Fresh bread or thin dry toast goes with it.

✧ FRENCH BEAN AND PRAWN ✧ SALAD

Season cooked french beans (whole, or cut in half across, but not lengthways) with olive oil and lemon. Arrange them in a mound, and on top put peeled prawns, also seasoned with oil and lemon. Garnish with halves of hard-boiled eggs. Serve as an hors d'œuvre.

✧ MAURITIAN PRAWN ✧ CHUTNEY

4 oz of peeled prawns, a green or red pimento or half a small hot green or red chilli pepper, olive oil, salt, cayenne, green ginger or ground ginger, lemon or fresh lime juice, 4 spring onions.

Pound the peeled prawns in a mortar with the chopped spring onions. Add the pimento or chilli, chopped very finely. Stir in enough olive oil (about 3 or 4 tablespoons) little by little, to make the mixture into a thick paste. Add a pinch of ground ginger, or a teaspoonful of grated green ginger, and, if mild peppers have been used, a scrap of cayenne. Squeeze in the juice of a fresh lime if available, or of half a lemon, and salt if necessary.

Although this is a chutney to be served with curries, it makes a delicious hors d'œuvre served with hard-boiled eggs, or just with toast.

✧ MACKEREL WITH ✧ GREEN SAUCE

Poached mackerel, when cold, and served as an hors d'œuvre with a green, or vinaigrette sauce (pages 189 and 191) poured over.

✧ MACKEREL WITH ✧
SORREL PURÉE

Cold fillets of mackerel on a bed of sorrel purée (pages 168 and 169). Garnish with chopped parsley or tarragon, and capers.

HORS D'ŒUVRE OF
✧ MUSHROOMS, CUCUMBERS ✧
AND FRENCH BEANS

½ lb of mushrooms, ½ lb of french beans, half a cucumber, olive oil, garlic, lemon, salt, black pepper.

Cook the prepared french beans in a little salted water in the usual way. Take care not to overcook them. Strain them, and while still hot season with olive oil and a little lemon juice. Wash the mushrooms, cut them into thinnish slices, put them into a dish with the cucumber, unpeeled, cut into little squares; season with ground black pepper, a little chopped garlic, plenty of olive oil and lemon juice. A little while before serving sprinkle with salt and pile this mixture on top of the french beans, in a shallow dish. Garnish if you like with hard-boiled eggs, or radishes, or shelled prawns.

TOMATOES
✧ WITH HORSERADISH ✧
MAYONNAISE

Cut the tomatoes in half; scoop out the insides, sprinkle them with salt, and turn them upside-down to drain. Fill with a horseradish mayonnaise (page 188) and serve as an hors d'œuvre or as an accompaniment to roast or grilled chicken, or cold beef, or tongue.

✧ HAM AND SAUSAGES ✧

An equal number of Frankfurter sausages and thin slices of ham, butter. Wrap each sausage in a slice of ham (when obtainable raw Parma, Bayonne or

MELENDEZ, LUIS, (1716-1780), *Still Life with Ham, Cheese and Vegetables.*

Westphalian ham is best, but cooked will do). Arrange them on a long dish, with a pat of fresh cold butter on each. Particularly nice for a quick luncheon, or for a car or train picnic.

✦ *PAN BAGNA 1* ✦

'Pan Bagna is simply a slice of *pain de ménage* moistened with good Niçois olive oil (sometimes the bread is rubbed with garlic) covered with fillets of anchovy, slices of tomatoes, capers and gherkins; vinegar is optional. It is rare that a game of *boules* in the country (and every one knows how addicted the Niçois are to this sport) comes to an end without having been interrupted for a few bottles of Bellet and a Pan Bagna.'
From *La Cuisine à Nice*, H. Heyraud, *circa* 1923.

⬦ *PAN BAGNA 2* ⬦

For four people:
¼ lb black olives, ½ lb tomatoes, a celery heart, 2 oz of mushrooms, 1 artichoke, a small tin of anchovies in oil, olive oil.

'Cut a long pound loaf of French bread in half, right through. Soak these two halves first in a little salt water then in olive oil. When the bread is well impregnated, on one half put slices of tomato, small pieces of the cooked artichoke heart, slices of the mushrooms (cooked as for *champignons à la grecque*, page 40), the celery heart cut into small strips, then the stoned black olives and a few fillets of anchovies. Cover with the second half of the loaf, put a fairly heavy weight on the top for half an hour.
   'Cut into thick slices before serving.'
Recipe from *Recettes et Paysages: Sud-Est et Mediterranée*

⬦ *PAN BAGNA 3* ⬦

'A large round, flat country loaf, ½ litre (about ¾ pint) of olive oil, anchovies, fillets of salt herring, rounds of tomato, green and black olives, a lettuce.

'Cut the loaf through the centre into two rounds. Put it on a dish and cover with olive oil. Leave to marinate for an hour. Strain off the oil, spread one half with all the ingredients; cover with the other half of the loaf. Put on a dish with a weight on top. Serve the next day, cut into slices, on an hors d'œuvre dish.'

⬦ *CRAB AND RICE SALAD* ⬦

The claw meat of a large crab (the soft meat from the body can be used for soup), 2 cupfuls of boiled rice, a green or sweet red pepper, garlic, half a dozen black olives, lemon, olive oil, nutmeg, a few walnuts, 3 or 4 raw mushrooms, lemon.

Season the boiled rice while it is still warm with nutmeg, lemon juice, and enough olive oil to make it moist but not sodden. Stir into it the crab cut into squares, the stoned olives, the raw pepper cut into strips, the raw sliced mushrooms, the chopped garlic. Strew the chopped walnuts on the top.

⬦ *CHAMPIGNONS À LA* ⬦
GRECQUE

Bring to the boil the following mixture: ¼ pint water, juice of half a lemon, ½ coffee-cupful olive oil, sprig of thyme, a bayleaf and a piece of celery tied together, ground black pepper, a little salt, a dozen coriander seeds. When boiling put in ½ lb very small white mushrooms washed but not peeled. Simmer 5 minutes. Serve cold as hors d'œuvre, with a little of their stock and a little fresh oil.

⬦ *GLOBE ARTICHOKES* ⬦

If the artichokes are to be served in the ordinary way, boiled, one for each person, buy the large cone-shaped ones, with very close leaves. Wash them and boil them in salted water, with a little lemon juice added, for about half an hour.

Serve them cold with oil and lemon, or hot with *sauce hollandaise, maltaise, mousseline*, or simply melted butter.

⬦ *ARTICHOKE HEARTS, SAUCE* ⬦
MALTAISE

The artichokes can either be cooked as above, and the leaves and chokes then removed, or they can be prepared as follows: Pare off all the outer leaves, cut the remainder right down to within half an inch of the choke, and boil them for about 20 minutes. When cold, remove the rest of the leaves and the choke, fill with a *sauce maltaise* (page 185) and serve cold.

⬦ *AVOCADO PEARS* ⬦

Avocado pears from South Africa, Israel and Madeira are now imported nearly all the year round. They vary considerably both in quality and price. Generally speaking the green variety seem to be better than the red, although not invariably so. They are, I think, at their best served alone, as a first course, with nothing but a dressing of salt, pepper, oil and lemon. Some people like to stuff them with mixtures of mayonnaise, ham or even lobster, which to my mind diminishes their flavour, and makes them sickly. In Jamaica they are sometimes served with a dressing of rum and fresh lime juice.

Sir Francis Colchester Wemyss, writing in *Pleasures of the Table*, advocates cold salt beef as the ideal meat with which to serve an avocado salad. They are also excellent with smoked turkey (see below).

In the West Indies they make a soup from avocados and in Mexican cooking avocados also go into sauces, soups and into stuffings for turkey and red peppers, and into mixed salads, and are also used as a garnish for meat hashes and stews.

When avocados are to be served as an hors d'œuvre cut them in half lengthways, take out the stone, and fill up the cavities with the prepared dressing. Get them ready only just before they are needed, as the flesh tends to turn black when they are left standing for any length of time. Avocados are very filling and a half for each person is usually enough.

⟡ *SMOKED TURKEY* ⟡

Smoked turkey, comparatively new to this country, makes an excellent hors d'œuvre. Serve it cut into thin slices, brown and white meat mixed, quite plain.

⟡ *SMOKED TURKEY SALAD* ⟡

Boil ½ lb of previously soaked small dried green flageolet beans for 2–2½ hours; drain them, season with salt, pepper and olive oil; on top of them put a ¼ lb of raw sliced mushrooms dressed with olive oil, pepper and a very little garlic, and over these arrange a cupful of smoked turkey cut into fillets; garnish with halves of hard-boiled eggs, and serve as an hors d'œuvre.

This is a charming summery-looking salad, pale green, cream, pink and yellow. The flageolet beans are a perfect combination with the turkey, but if you can't get them, make the salad with rice instead, or with green peas.

⟡ *RILLETTES* ⟡

1½–2 lb of belly of pork with a good proportion of lean to fat, a clove of garlic, a sprig of fresh thyme or marjoram, salt, pepper, a pinch of mace.

Remove bones and rind from the meat, and cut it into small cubes. Put these into a thick pan with the chopped garlic, the herbs and seasoning. Cook on a very low flame, or in the slowest possible oven for 1½ hours, until the pieces of pork are quite soft without being fried, and swimming in their own fat. Place a wide sieve over a bowl, and pour the meat into the sieve so that the fat drips through to the basin. When the meat has cooled, pull it into shreds, using two forks. If you cannot manage this, chop the meat. But unless you are making rillettes in a large quantity, try to avoid using the electric blender. It gives the meat too compact and smooth a texture. Pack the rillettes into small earthenware or china pots, and seal them with their own fat. Cover with greaseproof paper or foil. Rillettes will keep for weeks, and make an excellent stand-by for an hors d'œuvre. Serve them with bread and white wine.

⋄ CHICKEN LIVER PÂTÉ ⋄

½–1 lb of chicken livers, or duck, turkey, chicken and goose liver mixed, butter, brandy, port, garlic, thyme.

Clean the livers carefully, making sure that the little bag containing the bile is removed; also pare off any parts of the livers which look greenish, as they will give a bitter taste to the pâté. Melt 1 oz of butter in a frying pan; put in the livers, whole, and let them cook gently for about 5 minutes. They must remain pink inside. Take them from the pan and put them into a marble mortar. To the butter in the pan add 2 tablespoonfuls of brandy and let it bubble; then 2 tablespoons of port or madeira, and cook another minute. Add half a clove of garlic, salt, ground black pepper and a small pinch of thyme to the livers and pound them to a paste; pour in the butter mixture from the pan, and 2 oz of fresh butter. When all is thoroughly amalgamated and reduced to a paste, put it into an earthenware terrine in which it will come to within ½ inch of the top. In a clean pan melt some pure pork, duck or goose dripping, or butter. Pour it through a strainer on to the pâté; there should be enough to form a covering about ¼ of an inch thick, so that the pâté is completely sealed. When the fat has set, cover with a piece of foil and the lid of the terrine. Store in the larder or refrigerator. The pâté should not be eaten until two or three days after it has been made, and as long as it is airtight will keep a week or two in the larder and several weeks in a refrigerator. Serve it very cold, in the terrine, with toast. This is a rich pâté, and butter is not necessary with it. 1 lb of chicken livers makes enough pâté for eight to ten people.

✧ *TERRINE OF RABBIT* ✧

A rabbit weighing about 1 lb when skinned and cleaned, 1 lb of belly of pork, ¼ lb of fat bacon, thyme, pepper, juniper berries, a little lemon peel, 2 tablespoons of brandy, mace, garlic, a bayleaf.

Have the rabbit cut into pieces, and simmer it in a little water for 20–30 minutes. When cold, take all the flesh off the bones, and chop it on a board with the pork (uncooked), 2 or 3 cloves of garlic, a good sprinkling of fresh thyme, about 8 juniper berries and a small strip of lemon peel. (If you have not a double-handled chopper, which makes this operation very easy, the meat will have to be put through a coarse mincer, but chopping is infinitely preferable.) Season the mixture fairly highly with ground black pepper, salt and mace. Stir in the brandy. Line the bottom of a fairly large terrine, or 2 or 3 small ones with little strips of bacon. Put in the meat mixture. Put a bayleaf on top, and cover with another layer of strips of bacon.

Steam, covered, in a slow oven for 1½–2½ hours, according to the size of the terrines. When they come out of the oven put a piece of greaseproof paper over the terrines, lay a fairly heavy weight on top of them and leave them overnight.

Next day, the terrines can either be filled up with home-made aspic jelly, or simply sealed with pork fat. They are good either way, and make an excellent and inexpensive hors d'œuvre.

✧ *TERRINE OF PIGEONS* ✧

3 pigeons, 1 lb of fat pork, ¼ lb of bacon, garlic, 6 juniper berries, 2 tablespoons each of port and brandy, thyme or marjoram.

Proceed exactly as for the terrine of rabbit above and cook for about the same length of time.

Another method is to reserve the breasts of the pigeons cut in small fillets, to add about 2 oz of chicken liver pâté to the rest of the chopped pigeon and pork meat mixture, and arrange the fillets and the chopped mixture in alternate layers. Cook as before.

⋄ PORK AND LIVER ⋄ PÂTÉ

This is the simplest household recipe for a *terrine de foie de porc* on a small scale.

> Ingredients are 1 lb of pig's liver, 6 oz of belly of fresh pork, 1 oz of back pork fat cut into small strips, seasonings of 1 heaped teaspoon of salt, 6 to 10 crushed peppercorns, ¼ of a small clove of garlic finely chopped, and one tablespoon each of white wine and brandy.

Mince the liver and the pork, minus skin and bone (or get your butcher to do it for you). Mix the two very thoroughly together, add the seasonings, wine and brandy (substitute whisky if you have no brandy or wine available, or for that matter, gin, rum or dry vermouth), and if you have time let the mixture stand for an hour or two to give the various flavours a chance to blend.

Pack into a pint terrine, arrange the strips of pork fat in a criss-cross pattern across the top, stand the terrine in a baking tin half-filled with water, cover the terrine, cook in a very moderate oven, gas No. 3, 330°F, for an hour. Then leave it uncovered for a final 10 to 15 minutes.

Leave the pâté to get quite cold before putting it away. It is at its best about two to three days after it has been cooked.

If you don't want to eat the pâté for a few days, seal it completely with just melted pure pork lard (you will need about 3 oz), cover with foil, and it will keep a week to ten days in a cool larder.

Serve it very cold (preferably in its own dish) as a first course, with French bread or toast and butter. It will serve four to six people or even more, depending upon whether it is the only first dish or part of a mixed hors d'œuvre.

Those who find the taste and texture of liver on the rich and cloying side can alter the proportions of the ingredients as follows: ½ lb of pig's liver to 1¼ lb of fresh pork meat.

✧ RATATOUILLE ✧
EN SALADE

Ratatouille is the well-known Provençal mixture of southern vegetables stewed in oil. When it is to be served cold, it is cooked with the vegetables cut up very small and with the addition of garlic and coriander seeds. For a dish of cold ratatouille for four people if it is to be served as a separate dish, or for eight if it is to be one of the constituents of an hors d'œuvre, you need 2 onions, 2 aubergines, 2 large red pimentos, 4 ripe tomatoes, 2 cloves of garlic, a dozen coriander seeds, parsley and olive oil.

Chop the onions fairly small and put them to stew in a sauté pan or deep frying-pan in half a tumbler of olive oil. In the meantime cut the aubergines, leaving on their skins, into ½-inch squares and put them, sprinkled with coarse salt, into a colander, so that some of the water drains away from them. When the onions have cooked about 10 minutes and are beginning to get soft (but not fried) add the aubergines, and then the pimentos, also cut into small pieces. Cover the pan and let them simmer for 30 to 40 minutes. Now add the chopped tomatoes, the garlic and the coriander seeds. Continue cooking until the tomatoes have melted. Should the oil dry up, add a little more, remembering that the juice from the tomatoes will also make the ratatouille more liquid, and the final result must not be too mushy. When cold, garnish it with chopped parsley or basil. Drain off any excess of oil before serving.

✧ MUSHROOM SALAD ✧

½ lb of mushrooms, olive oil, lemon juice, garlic, parsley, salt and pepper.

Buy if possible the larger rather shaggy-looking variety of mushrooms. Wash them but do not peel them. Cut them in thinnish slices, leaving the stalks on. Put them in a bowl, squeeze lemon juice over them, stir in a little chopped garlic, season with ground black pepper, and pour a good deal of olive oil over them. Immediately before serving salt them and add more olive oil, as you will find they have absorbed the first lot. Sprinkle with parsley, or, if you have it, basil, or a mixture of fresh marjoram and lemon thyme.

This is an expensive salad to make, as mushrooms absorb an enormous quantity of oil, but it is extremely popular, and particularly good with grilled or roast chicken. Variations can be made by mixing the mushrooms with a few strips of raw fennel or with a cupful of cooked green peas.

For an hors d'œuvre, mix the mushrooms with large cooked prawns.

⋄ SALADE NIÇOISE ⋄

There is no precise recipe for a salad niçoise. It usually contains lettuce hearts, black olives, hard-boiled eggs, anchovies, and sometimes tunny fish. There should be garlic in the dressing.

In *La Cuisine à Nice*, Lucien Heyraud gives a salade niçoise composed of young globe artichokes cut in quarters, black olives, raw pimento, quarters of tomato, and anchovy fillets. There are, however, as many versions of it as there are cooks in Provence, but in whatever way it is interpreted it should be a simple and rather crude country salad. The ingredients should be put in the bowl with each category kept separate, in large pieces, nicely arranged so that the salad looks colourful and fresh. The dressing should be mixed in at the table.

⋄ SPICED RICE SALAD ⋄

6–8 oz rice, a piece of green ginger* or dried ginger root, a handful of mixed raisins and currants, a shallot, coriander seeds, nutmeg, olive oil, lemon, almonds or pine nuts, 3 or 4 fresh or dried apricots.

Boil the rice with the ginger in salted water for 14–15 minutes; drain very carefully; remove the ginger; while still warm season the rice with black pepper, grated nutmeg, half a teaspoon of pounded coriander seeds, a little lemon juice, and the shallot cut into fine rounds; stir in enough olive oil to make the rice moist but not mushy, then add the raisins and currants, previously simmered a few minutes in water to make them swell, then drained, and the apricots, raw, if fresh ones are being used, soaked and lightly cooked if they are dried.

Garnish with roasted almonds or pine nuts.

* For a method of storing green ginger root see page 239.

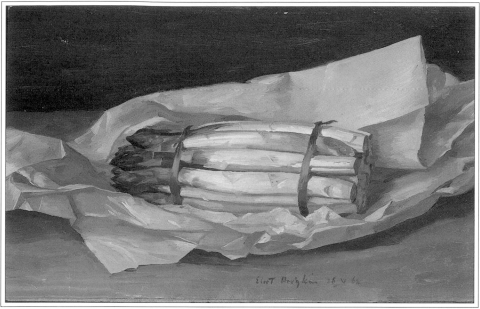

HODGKIN, ELIOT, *Asparagus*, 1962.

✧ *TOMATO SALAD* ✧

Slice the tomatoes into thick rounds and arrange them on a large flat dish. Season with ground black pepper, and strew over them plenty of chopped fresh herbs, tarragon, chives, basil, parsley, whatever is available, and a little garlic. Just before serving sprinkle with salt and olive oil. Made in this way a tomato salad is fresh and crisp and aromatic; it is the salting and dressing of tomatoes several hours before they are to be served which makes them water and clammy, although it has to be admitted that all the precautions in the world can do little to make commercially grown English and Channel Island tomatoes anything but mushy and tasteless.

✧ *PIMENTO SALAD* ✧

Grill the pimentos until the skins turn black and will flake off. This takes about 20 minutes under a gas grill, the pimentos being turned as soon as one

47

side is done. When they have cooled a little, peel off the skin, take out the seeds, wash the pimentos under the cold tap, cut them into strips and dress with olive oil, lemon juice, chopped garlic and parsley.

⋄ PIMENTOS STUFFED ⋄
WITH PRAWNS

Grill and skin 3 or 4 large red or yellow pimentos in the way described in the preceding recipe. Cut each pimento into three or four wide strips.

Have ready a prawn chutney mixture as described on page 36. Put a small spoonful of this mixture on each strip of pimento, and roll it up into the shape of a sausage. Pour a little olive oil and lemon juice over. Arrange on a bed of watercress or shredded lettuce on a long dish. This makes a very beautiful and very excellent hors d'œuvre. Instead of prawns, tunny fish can be used as a basis for the stuffing, either spiced in the same way as the prawn chutney, or simply mixed with a little butter, as for tunny fish pâté (page 35).

⋄ CUCUMBER AND CHIVE ⋄
SALAD

A cucumber, a few chives, and for the dressing a small cupful of cream, a teaspoonful of sugar, olive oil, salt and pepper, a teaspoonful of tarragon vinegar.

Slice the pared cucumber paper thin (with the special instrument which the French call a *mandoline* or *coupe-julienne*, and which can now be bought in London shops, this is a matter of less than a minute). Sprinkle coarse salt over the cucumber and leave it in a colander to drain for half an hour. If necessary, rinse them to get rid of excess salt. Drain them well.

Mix the sugar and vinegar together, then add the cream, pepper and salt. Add about 2 tablespoons of olive oil and the chopped chives, and pour the dressing over the cucumber in a shallow dish.

A plain cucumber salad with no dressing at all other than a few drops each of olive oil and tarragon vinegar is equally delicious.

SALAD OF
✧ RIDGE CUCUMBERS ✧

The short, fat ridge cucumbers which come on the market in the late summer are usually cheap. They make delicious salads but are neglected because their appearance is rough and unfamiliar, and because people think they are suitable only for pickling.

To prepare ridge cucumbers for salad, peel them (use a potato parer), cut them in short lengths, and, still using the potato parer, scoop out the central seeds. Then slice and salt the cucumbers as described in the foregoing recipe. They may need a little sugar in the seasoning. When in good condition these cucumbers really need no dressing or sauce other than salt and sugar, a sprinkling of chives when you have them, and perhaps a very few drops of olive oil and tarragon vinegar.

✧ CUCUMBER SAMBAL ✧

Cut a cucumber into thin strips an inch long; with them mix a teaspoon of finely chopped onion, one of green chilli, one of parsley. Moisten with a dessertspoon of vinegar mixed with sugar, olive oil, salt and pepper.

Serve with cold meat, or the spiced chicken on page 141.

✧ SALADE LORRAINE ✧

Dandelions, shallots, garlic, chives, olive oil, pepper, salt, bacon, wine vinegar.

Mix the cleaned dandelions in a bowl with a little chopped shallot, garlic, chives, ground pepper and a very little salt. Add enough olive oil to moisten the salad.

Cut the bacon in small dice, fry it, and pour it hot with its fat over the salad; in the frying-pan heat a tablespoon or so of wine vinegar, and stir into the salad. The system of adding hot fried bacon to salads is typical of Alsace and Lorraine cookery; it is also German. It is applied also to raw shredded cabbage, to potato salad, and to curly endive or chicory.

SALAD OF BROAD BEANS,
⟡ CUCUMBER AND ORANGES ⟡

½ lb of small new raw broad beans, ½ a cucumber, 2 oranges, a few radishes.

Shell the beans, cut the unpeeled cucumber into small squares, the oranges into quarters, and the radishes into thin rounds.

Mix them with a vinaigrette sauce made with an egg (see page 191). Good with cold duck.

⟡ SALADE ESPAGNOLE ⟡

Sliced boiled potatoes, mixed with oil and lemon, salt and pepper, and a little chopped shallot. Cover completely with slices of tomato; garnish with fine rings of raw green peppers.

⟡ POTATO SALAD ⟡

Opinions differ about the making of potato salad. My own method is to boil waxy potatoes in their skins, taking care that they are not overdone. As soon as they can be handled, peel and slice them, and season them with salt and pepper and chopped chives or the green top of an onion. While they are still warm pour over them a freshly made mayonnaise thinned with a little milk, and mix them carefully so that each slice receives its coating of mayonnaise without being broken. On the top of the salad strew a good handful of chopped parsley and mint mixed together.

⟡ LAITUE À LA CRÈME ⟡

A salad for people who cannot take olive oil. Make a cream dressing in the following way: mix together in a cup half a teaspoon of made English mustard, a teaspoon of sugar, 2 teaspoons of tarragon vinegar, half a crushed clove of garlic (this *can* be left out) and the yolk of a hard-boiled egg. Stir in a teacupful of fresh cream.

Pour the dressing, very cold, over the crisp hearts of cos lettuces, and over the salad sprinkle the chopped white of the egg. Serve very cold. A very beautiful summery-looking salad. If you have fresh tarragon or chives add some, chopped, to the dressing, which should not be made too long in advance. The vinegar sours the cream and may make it too solid for pouring. If this happens thin it with a few drops of water or milk.

⋄ LETTUCE AND ALMOND ⋄
SALAD

Another salad without oil.

The best lettuce for this one is the crisp curly kind known as Iceland or Arctic Prince of Webb's lettuce. The heart of a cos lettuce can also be used.

In the bottom of the salad bowl put the quarters of two oranges. (To prepare oranges for salad, cut them in half lengthways, then into quarters. It is then very easy to cut the pulp from the skin with a sharp knife.) On top of the oranges put the lettuce, then a few roasted, salted almonds. Sprinkle with a very little sugar.

At the last moment pour over a dressing consisting of a piece of butter melted with a scrap of garlic and a squeeze of lemon juice, and mix the orange, lettuce and almonds together as you pour the dressing over.

Goes particularly well with chicken dishes.

⋄ LAITUE AU JUS ⋄

Cold crisp lettuce with the rich gravy from a roast poured over it, hot. Exquisite with the hot meat or bird, especially if it has been cooked in butter and flavoured with garlic and wine.

Dandelions or Batavian endive can also be used for this salad.

⋄ LENTIL SALAD ⋄

Stewed lentils, lentil soup, lentils and bacon are filling winter dishes. They also make a first-class salad for the early summer, before the lettuces and new vegetables have started; the flavour of good olive oil combined with lentils is excellent.

Soak 6 to 8 oz of brown lentils in cold water for an hour or two. Any pieces of grit which they may contain will then have come to the top and can be removed. Cook the lentils, covered with fresh water, for an hour to an hour and a half. Strain them, stir in a few finely cut rounds of raw onion and plenty of olive oil. See that the seasoning is right and when the salad is cold garnish it with quarters of hard-boiled egg.

❖ AUBERGINE PURÉE ❖

Grill or bake 4 aubergines until their skins crack and will peel easily. Sieve the peeled aubergines, mix them with 2 or 3 tablespoons of yoghourt, the same of olive oil, salt, pepper, lemon juice. Garnish with a few very thin slices of raw onion and chopped mint leaves. This is a Near Eastern dish which is intended to be served as an hors d'œuvre with bread, or with meat, in the same manner as a chutney.

❖ AUBERGINE CHUTNEY ❖

Boil 2 aubergines in their skins; leave them to get cold. Peel them and put the pulp through a food mill. Stir a crushed clove of garlic into the purée, add a little minced onion, green chilli and grated green ginger, and season with salt, pepper and lemon juice.

❖ PURÉE OF HARICOT BEANS ❖

Cook ½ lb of previously soaked white haricot beans in plenty of water. When they are very tender pour off the liquid and sieve the beans. To the resulting purée add two tablespoons of olive oil and two of chopped mint. Serve cold.

SOUPS

HARRIS, EDWIN, *His First Catch*, 1888.

SOUPS

A soup is often the only hot dish to be served at a summer dinner; it is also, unless at a long dinner at which hors d'œuvre are served, the first dish, so it is important that it should be very good, attractive, light, well seasoned, promising even more delicious things to come. The pulses and dried vegetables, the cabbage and bacon and haricot beans which make the warming, comforting soups of winter are replaced in the summer by green peas, french beans, new carrots, spring onions; in France there would be the sorrel which makes one of the most delicious and refreshing of country soups; in Italy consommés with a garnish of little egg and breadcrumb *gnocchi*, or broths thickened with eggs and cheese take the place of heavy dishes of pasta. In the days of the Tsars Russian cooking was famous for its luxury, and the summer soups the Russians liked were acid-flavoured with pickled cucumbers, fermented beetroot juice and sour cream; a liquor called kwass, made from buckwheat flour or barley and fermented with yeast, took the place of stock in these soups; little chunks of ice were floated in the soup, and often slices of cold sturgeon or cold salmon, shell fish, or smoked meats were handed round with the soups. The Spaniards have their famous *gazpacho*, compounded of tomatoes, ground red peppers, garlic and cucumber, with ice added; and in Jewish cookery there is an admirable cold beetroot soup thickened with eggs.

In England soup appears to be exactly the same summer and winter, except for the occasional appearance of an iced consommé; often alas not sufficiently clarified, of a depressing colour, and the wrong consistency; a good consommé does indeed require patience and application to produce in its first-class form – the only acceptable one – so those who have not much time to devote to cooking would be wiser to stick to fresh vegetable soups which can be made very quickly, thickened at the last minute with eggs and cream, and served either hot or cold.

Cream soups for the summer give plenty of scope for the addition of attractive garnishes in the form of fresh chopped herbs, a few raw broad beans, little squares of salmon for fish soups, grated lemon peel, grated horseradish; the same soups can be served iced, made rather thinner than if they are to be hot; yoghourt can be mixed into them when they are cold, instead of cream. Quartered hard-boiled eggs, diced cucumber, tarragon, fresh mint, raw fennel, little strips of ham, squares of highly spiced Spanish sausages are additions which go to make a cream soup interesting.

In warm weather never leave unstrained stock standing overnight; the onion is liable to turn it sour. If the stock is to be kept, it should in any case be boiled up every day. If stored in a refrigerator keep it in a covered bowl or jar, or it will freeze, and then turn watery.

POTAGE PRINTANIÈRE ◇

Make a potato soup with 1 lb potatoes cooked in about 2 pints of water. Sieve, and season the resulting purée with salt and pepper and a scrap of nutmeg. Add ½ cupful of hot milk. In this purée cook gently a handful of shelled green peas, and half a dozen very small carrots cut into dice.

Before serving, stir in some chopped parsley or chives and a nice lump of butter.

◇ POTATO AND CHERVIL SOUP ◇

½ lb of potatoes, 1 oz of butter, 1 pint of water, ¼ pint of milk, seasonings of salt and nutmeg, 2 oz of double cream, a heaped tablespoon of fresh chervil cut with scissors.

Cut the peeled potatoes into small strips or dice. Melt the butter in a heavy soup pot. Put in the potatoes, let them cook extremely gently in the butter for about 10 minutes until they are beginning to soften. They must not brown. Sprinkle them with a little salt and a grating of nutmeg. Pour in the water. Cover the pot. Let the potatoes simmer for 20 to 25 minutes. Sieve them through the mouli, preferably twice. Return the purée to the rinsed-out pan. Add the milk, first brought to the boil in another pan. (This point is important.) Taste for seasoning. Before serving stir in the chervil and the cream. Quantities given make three good helpings.

For all its primitive simplicity this is a very excellent and light little summer soup. It should be on the thin side, but creamy and white. The flavour of the chervil with the potatoes is very subtle. For those who cannot get this useful and delicate herb, the same soup can be made using watercress or ordinary cress or chives. Be careful not to overdo the herbs, whichever you use. It is the few green flecks and the contrast of tastes which make the charm of the soup.

✧ BROAD BEAN SOUP 1 ✧

1 lb of young broad beans, 2 potatoes, a little milk or cream, 1 leek, butter.

The beans should be very new ones, so that both beans and pods can be used. Simply cut off the little black piece at the stalk end, and put the beans into a pan with the leek and the potatoes, cut in small pieces. Cover with water, season with a little salt, sugar and pepper, and simmer for about an hour. Strain the beans, keeping aside the liquid. Put them through a sieve (do not attempt this soup unless you have a mouli or food mill, as the pods are not easy to get through an ordinary sieve) and add enough of the water they were cooked in to make a thin purée. Heat it up, add about half a cupful of hot milk or rather less cream, and a small piece of butter before serving.
Enough for six.

✧ BROAD BEAN SOUP 2 ✧

2 lb of broad beans, a few lettuce leaves, 2 or 3 spring onions, 1 pint of light veal or chicken stock, butter.

Boil the broad beans in salted water with the shredded lettuce leaves and onions. Be careful to take them from the fire the minute they are cooked or the skins will turn brown and spoil the colour of the soup. Strain them reserving a small cupful of the water. Sieve them, put the purée into a clean pan and stir in the stock and the water which was reserved. Heat up and before serving stir in a small lump of butter or 2 or 3 tablespoons of cream.

✧ FRESH GREEN PEA ✧
SOUP

A teacupful of shelled green peas, 1 oz of ham, half a small onion, 1½ pints of veal or chicken stock, the juice of a lemon, mint, 2 eggs, 2 oz of cream, butter, salt, pepper, sugar.

Melt the butter; put in the finely chopped onion. Do not let it brown, only soften. Add the ham cut into strips, then the peas. Let them get thoroughly impregnated with the butter. Season with salt, pepper, sugar, and add a little sprig of mint. Pour over hot water just to cover and simmer until the peas are tender. Stir in the boiling cream. Remove from the fire and stir in the eggs beaten up with the lemon juice. Pour the boiling stock over this mixture, stirring all the time, or the soup will curdle. Serve at once. A lovely soup.

❖ CREAM OF GREEN PEAS ❖

3 lb green peas, a few lettuce leaves, a small slice of ham, 2 or 3 spring onions, sugar, salt, pepper, butter.

Put the shelled peas in a pan with all the other ingredients except the butter. Cover with 3 pints of water. Boil until the peas are quite soft and sieve. See that the seasoning is right, heat up and before serving stir in a lump of butter and a scrap of fresh mint into the soup.

A little cream added to the soup while it is heating is an improvement.

❖ SOUP OF PRAWNS AND GREEN PEAS ❖

Add half a teacupful of shelled prawns to the fresh green pea soup described on p. 57 and at the top of this page.

To make a cheaper soup add, instead of prawns, half a dozen soft herring roes poached and cut into strips, or little strips of filleted sole, or rock salmon.

❖ MUSHROOM SOUP ❖

1½ pints of good chicken or meat broth, ¼ lb mushrooms, 2 eggs, 2 oz of cream, fresh mint, butter, lemon juice.

Heat ½ oz of butter in half a teacupful of water with the juice of half a lemon. When the mixture boils put in the mushrooms and cook for 3 or 4 minutes. Season with salt, pepper and a little chopped fresh mint. Add the mushroom mixture gradually to the beaten and strained eggs in a basin; then

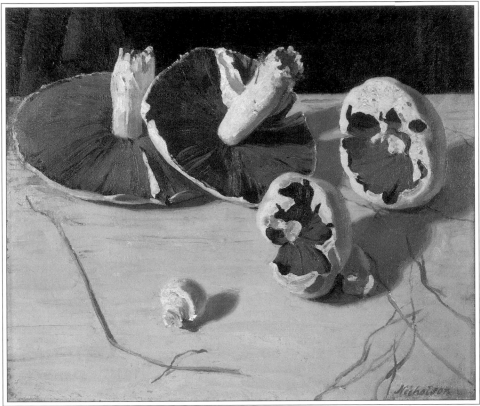

NICHOLSON, WILLIAM (1872-1949), *Mushrooms.*

add the cream, boiled in a separate pan, then the boiling broth. Stir until the soup is amalgamated and reheat but do not boil or the eggs will curdle.

✧ *SOUPE MENERBOISE* ✧

½ lb courgettes (baby marrows), 1 lb tomatoes, 2 onions, several cloves of garlic, 2 small potatoes, a handful of shelled and peeled broad beans, fresh basil, 1½ oz of small pasta or broken-up spaghetti, olive oil, 2 yolks of eggs, Parmesan cheese.

In an earthenware casserole warm a coffee-cupful of olive oil. Into this put the sliced onions and let them melt but not fry. Add the little marrows, unpeeled, and cut into squares (it is best to prepare them an hour before cooking, salt them lightly, and leave them in a colander so that some of the water drains from them). Let them melt in the oil slowly for 10 minutes before adding all but two of the tomatoes, roughly chopped. When these have softened put in the potatoes cut into small squares and pour about 2 pints of hot water over the whole mixture. Simmer gently for 10 minutes until the potatoes are nearly cooked; then add the broad beans, the pasta and seasoning of salt and pepper.

In the meantime grill the remaining tomatoes, remove their skins; in a mortar pound 3 cloves of garlic, then the tomatoes, and a small bunch of basil. Add the yolks of the eggs, so that you have a sauce somewhat resembling a thin mayonnaise. The pasta in the soup being cooked, stir a ladleful of the soup into the sauce, then another. Return the mixture to the pan, and let it heat gently, stirring all the time to prevent the egg curdling. At the last minute stir in two large spoonfuls of grated Parmesan cheese.

A substantial soup for four to six people.

◇ CLEAR BEETROOT ◇
CONSOMMÉ

4 pints of good beef stock, 2 lb of uncooked beetroots, 2 carrots, 2 turnips, cream, vinegar.

Peel the beetroots, cut them into small pieces and simmer them, with the carrots and turnips, in the stock. When they are soft, and the soup a good clear red, strain through a sieve, without pressing the vegetables at all.

When heating up the consommé add about 2 teaspoons of Orléans vinegar, and see that the seasoning is correct. Serve a bowl of cream, either fresh or sour, separately. The quantities given will make four helpings; 4 pints of stock sounds a lot for four people, but a good deal is absorbed during the simmering of the vegetables.

◇ SORREL SOUP ◇

To a sorrel purée made as described on page 168 add gradually 1½ pints of light chicken or veal stock, or half stock and half hot milk. Stir all the time, and serve as soon as the soup is hot.

✧ SORREL AND TOMATO ✧
SOUP

1½ lb of peeled and chopped tomatoes, 1¼ pints of chicken stock, a handful of sorrel leaves, 1 oz of butter.

Melt the tomatoes in the butter until they are soft but not completely disintegrated; five minutes will be long enough. Add the chopped sorrel; give it a stir round, pour over the heated stock, season with salt, pepper and sugar. Serve as soon as the soup is hot; do not overcook, or the tomatoes and sorrel will lose their fresh flavour.

This soup can also be served iced, but do the initial cooking of the tomatoes in olive oil instead of butter.

✧ SORREL AND LENTIL ✧
SOUP

Make a purée with about ¼ lb of brown lentils cooked for 1½–2 hours in about 3 pints of water, adding the salt towards the end of the cooking. Put the lentils through the sieve, add enough of the water in which they were cooked to make a thin purée.

Chop a handful of sorrel leaves (about ¼ lb) fairly finely, cook them in the lentil soup for 10 minutes. Immediately before serving stir in 2 or 3 tablespoons of cream. Enough for four helpings. This is one of the best of the sorrel soups.

✧ WALNUT SOUP ✧

¼ lb shelled walnuts, 1½ pints of meat or chicken stock, ¼ pint of cream, a small clove of garlic, salt, pepper.

Pound the walnuts with a little of the stock and the garlic. Gradually add the rest of the stock. Heat up this mixture, and add to it the cream previously boiled until it has thickened a little. Season with salt and pepper.

Enough for four helpings.

⋄ *TARRAGON SOUP* ⋄

Clear chicken or meat or fish broth, and for each pint of broth about
2 teaspoons of finely chopped fresh tarragon and 1 tablespoon of grated
Parmesan cheese.

Heat the broth very gently with the chopped tarragon, and stir in the cheese
just before serving. Nothing could be simpler, and at the same time more
attractive and original, but if you like, a richer soup can be made with the
addition of cream or eggs, or if you have no good stock to hand a thinnish
potato soup can be used as a background for the tarragon and the cheese, and
is excellent.

⋄ *MARROW FLOWER SOUP* ⋄

In southern France and Italy, the golden yellow flowers of the marrow
are sometimes made into fritters, sometimes stuffed with a rice mixture,
stewed in oil and served cold as an hors d'œuvre. In Mexico, they are
stuffed with pounded beans and fried, and also made into a soup. For those
people who have vegetable gardens, here is the recipe for soup made from
marrow flowers, from the *Mexican Cook Book* by Josefina Velasquez de Leon
(Mexico City, 1947).

2 oz lard, 1 lb marrow flowers, 2 oz butter, 1 oz flour, 2 oz bread, 2 quarts
milk, 1 onion, ½ cup cream, 2 yolks, salt and pepper.

In a tablespoon of lard fry the chopped marrow flowers and onion, season
with salt and pepper. Cover the pan, and let them simmer in their own juice
until they are quite soft. When they are cooked pound them into a paste,
pour the milk over them. Heat up. In another pan melt the butter, stir in the
flour, when it starts to thicken gradually pour in the strained milk and
marrow flower mixture. Stir until all the milk is poured in, and when the
soup has thickened slightly and is very hot, pour it into the soup tureen in
which the yolks and the cream have been beaten up together.

Serve the bread cut into small squares and fried in the rest of the lard.

A pound of marrow flowers is quite a quantity, and the amounts given are
enough for at least eight people, so they can be halved.

PEALE, JAMES, *Vegetables with Yellow Blossoms*, 1828

✧ *FRENCH BEANS AND* ✧
ALMOND SOUP

In about 2½ pints of mild-flavoured stock (chicken is best) cook three-quarters of a pound of french beans, cut into half-inch lengths and with all the strings carefully removed. Have ready two ounces of almonds, skinned, and browned lightly in the oven or with a little butter in a frying pan. Chop them or pound them roughly in a mortar.

See that the beans are sufficiently seasoned with salt, pepper, and a little lemon juice, and stir in the almonds a minute or two before serving. If you want to serve a more luxurious soup, beat up two yolks of eggs with a little of the hot broth, return the mixture to the pan and let it reheat without boiling. Sufficient for four people.

⋄ CRAB SOUP ⋄

A medium-sized cooked crab, ¼ lb of rock salmon or other white fish, a small onion, 2 cloves of garlic, 2 tomatoes, lemon peel, mace, cayenne pepper and black pepper, salt, parsley, 3 tablespoons cream, a small glass of white wine, fresh herbs, 2 tablespoons of rice.

Put the rock salmon into a saucepan with the onion, tomatoes, garlic, a very small piece of lemon peel, salt, pepper, a sprig of parsley and the white wine. Cook for a few minutes until the wine is reduced. Add the rice and pour over 2 pints of water, simmer for 20 minutes, then add all the crab meat, and cook another 5 minutes. Sieve, having first removed the onion and any bones from the fish. Heat up the resulting purée, seasoning with mace and cayenne pepper, and when hot add some fresh herbs such as chives, fennel, marjoram, or lemon thyme, chopped with a little piece of lemon peel. Add the cream just before serving. Enough for four or five.

⋄ WHITE FISH ⋄
SOUP

A large sole, 2 oz peeled cooked prawns, an onion, bayleaf, slice of lemon, lemon juice, pepper, salt, 2 eggs, 2 oz cream, parsley, garlic, a small glass of white wine.

Have the sole filleted and keep the carcass. Put the latter, with the onion, bayleaf, slice of lemon, pepper, salt, garlic, sprig of parsley and the white wine into a pan with two pints of water. Simmer gently for 40 minutes. Strain. Return to clean pan. Put in the fillets. Cook for 10 minutes and sieve. Heat up, add the prawns and the heated cream. In a basin beat the eggs with the juice of half a lemon. Strain this into the soup, and stir vigorously. Do not let the soup boil again.

John Dory, brill or a piece of turbot make a finer-flavoured soup than sole. Halibut, cod and hake can also be used.

✧ COCKLE SOUP ✧

4 pints of cockles, 2 tomatoes, a leek, a piece of celery, 2 potatoes, 2 oz of lean bacon, 1 oz of butter, 2 eggs, lemon juice.

Cook the cleaned cockles* for 10 minutes in about 2½ pints of water. Remove them from the pan and strain the liquid through a muslin.

Melt the butter in a saucepan, and add the bacon, the chopped leek and celery and the peeled and sliced tomatoes. When the vegetables have softened pour over the strained liquid from the cockles, and add the diced potatoes. Simmer until the potatoes are tender, and add the shelled cockles. See that the soup is properly seasoned; thicken it with beaten eggs and lemon juice in which a little of the hot soup has been stirred. Return this mixture to the pan and heat without letting it boil. Serve with rounds of fried French bread.

✧ JELLIED CONSOMMÉ ✧

2 lb of shin of beef, 2 pig's feet, an onion, 2 or 3 carrots, a clove of garlic, a bayleaf, a small piece of lemon peel, 2 tomatoes, salt, pepper, 3 pints of water, 2 tablespoons sherry or port.

Put the beef in one piece at the bottom of the saucepan, then the pig's feet split in halves and washed, the onion, unpeeled (the skin helps to give a golden colour to the consommé), the tomatoes, carrots, bayleaf, garlic and lemon peel seasonings (very little salt to start with). Cover with the water and bring very slowly almost to the boil; if there is any scum skim it off. Keep the liquid barely moving, not boiling, for at least 4 hours; if it doesn't taste strong enough, leave it a little longer. Strain it through a fine sieve and leave until next day. Skim off the fat. The consommé should be clear, golden, and set to a light jelly, much softer than aspic, and if it has not been allowed to boil it will be quite clear, and will not need clarifying.

When every particle of fat has been removed heat it very gently, adding the sherry and a little extra salt if necessary. As it is about to come to the boil turn off the flame, and pour the consommé into a clean bowl to set again. If it

*See page 102.

is kept in the refrigerator, keep it covered, and as far away from the ice trays as possible. Serve in cups. There should be 2 pints of consommé, enough for four large helpings or six smaller onces.

If the consommé has boiled, and turned cloudy, clarify it as described for the aspic jelly on page 194.

If you want to make do with less meat, use a pound and cut it into small pieces, so that it gives the maximum flavour to the consommé; the cooked meat can be used for a tomato sauce.

If you like the consommé to have a slightly gamey taste, use only 1½ lb of beef and substitute a small pigeon for the other half-pound. Do not add strong vegetables like turnips or penetrating herbs such as rosemary or sage to consommés. The beef which has been used for the consommé makes an excellent salad as described on page 122.

⬦ *ZUPPA EBREA* ⬦
(Hebrew soup)

This recipe comes from *Il Gastronomo Educato*, an imaginative and practical book on the subject of civilized eating by Alberto Denti di Pirajno (Editions Neri Pozza, Venice, 1959). The author recalls eating this soup in a Jewish house in Livorno, and recommends it to all his friends – 'baptized christians, circumcized moslems, idolaters or fire-worshippers'.

Peel and chop half a kilo (a little over a pound) of cooked beetroots. Put this beetroot into three pints of salted water, with the addition of a little vinegar. Cook for 20 minutes and put the mixture through a sieve.

In a soup tureen beat three whole eggs, pour the beetroot broth over the eggs, stirring all the time, see that the seasoning is right, press the soup once more through a sieve, and put it on ice until it is perfectly cold.

Serve the soup iced, and for each guest have a bowl or saucer of hot boiled potatoes which have been stirred in a pan with very hot goose fat. The guests take a spoonful of potatoes, mix them with the cold beetroot soup and consume this ambrosia with little sighs of satisfaction.

(The goose fat can be replaced by butter, the juice from a roast, good beef dripping.)

✧ PICKLED CUCUMBER SOUP ✧

½ lb pickled cucumbers, 2 pints of clear meat stock, 2 lumps of sugar, mace, ginger, allspice, pepper, salt, ¼ pint of cream.

Chop the pickled cucumbers and simmer them for 30 minutes in the stock. Put through a sieve. Heat up and add the sugar, a pinch each of mace, ground ginger and allspice, ground black pepper and salt. The soup should have a definitely spiced, oriental flavour about it. Stir in the cream, already boiled in another pan.

Serve iced, garnished with a little chopped fennel, or mint. For a special occasion add a few strips of smoked sturgeon immediately before serving, or prawns, or chopped hard-boiled eggs.

✧ ICED RUSSIAN SOUP ✧

This is a very simplified version of a Russian summer soup called *swekolnik*.

½ lb of the leaves of young beetroots, 4 small beetroots, half a fresh cucumber, 2 or 3 small pickled cucumbers, a few leaves of tarragon, chives, mint, fennel, ¼ pint of cream, salt, pepper, tarragon vinegar.

Wash the beet leaves, remove the stalks. Cook the leaves in a little salted water for a few minutes. Drain, squeeze perfectly dry, chop finely. Put them in a bowl. Cut the cooked beetroots into small squares, salt them, add them to the leaves, and pour in a coffee-cupful of tarragon vinegar. Add the diced fresh and pickled cucumber, and a little of the liquid from the pickle. Pour in the cream.

Put the bowl in the refrigerator, and before serving add the chopped herbs, thin with iced water, and serve with little pieces of ice floating in the soup tureen.

This soup comes out a rather violent pink colour, but is very good on a really hot evening.

✧ GAZPACHO ✧

There are many versions of this Spanish summer soup; the basis of it is chopped tomato, olive oil and garlic, and there may be additions of cucumber, black olives, raw onion, red pepper, herbs, eggs and bread. The following makes a very good and refreshing *gazpacho*.

Chop a pound of raw peeled tomatoes until almost a purée. Stir in a few dice of cucumber, 2 chopped cloves of garlic, a finely sliced spring onion, a dozen stoned black olives, a few strips of green pepper, 3 tablespoons of olive oil, a tablespoon of wine vinegar, salt, pepper, and a pinch of cayenne pepper, a little chopped fresh marjoram, mint or parsley. Keep very cold until it is time to serve the soup, then thin with ½ pint of iced water, add a few cubes of coarse brown bread, and serve with broken-up ice floating in the bowl. A couple of hard-boiled eggs, coarsely chopped, make a good addition.

◇ *ICED HADDOCK SOUP* ◇

Take half a pint of the milk in which smoked haddock has been cooked, and about 2 tablespoons of flaked haddock. Into this mix a quarter pint of yoghourt, and a cupful of cucumber in dill, 2 raw tomatoes, a handful of parsley, 2 small pickled onions, half a fresh cucumber, a tablespoon of capers and a tablespoon of chives or the green part of leeks, all chopped up. Add black pepper but no salt, and a few drops of the vinegar from the pickled cucumber.

To be made some hours before serving, and iced. Two tablespoons of red caviar added to the mixture makes this a soup for a special occasion.

◇ *ICED CREAM SOUPS* ◇

Heat good clear chicken, meat or fish broth and stir in a little thin cream (about 3 tablespoons per half-pint) and a small quantity of very finely chopped parsley, chives, tarragon or whatever herbs are available; add a scrap of grated lemon peel. A thin soup to be drunk iced from large cups.

It is very simple to think of variations on this theme. Thin purées of green peas or french beans, or tomato juice, can be used as a basis. Flavour can be varied with spices: grated green ginger, pounded coriander seeds, a pinch of curry powder, or a little white wine, and instead of lemon peel a little chopped pimento or pounded salt almonds or walnuts.

The important point is to keep the soup thin and light; a thickening of flour would make it pasty and cloying.

EGGS

GILMAN, HAROLD (1876-1919), *The Shopping List*.

EGGS

Eggs provide perhaps the best and most nourishing quickly prepared meal in the world, at quite a small cost; for a luncheon dish an omelette or a couple of eggs baked in cream can scarcely be bettered; a new-laid, boiled egg, with good butter and fresh crusty bread, is every bit as much a treat as any sophisticated dish with a cream and wine sauce.

Although I, for one, never tire of eggs, it *is* dull to have them always cooked in the same way, and in this respect English cookery is curiously restricted; one of the reasons, I fancy, is that so many kitchens lack dishes and utensils in which to cook the *œufs sur le plat*, the *œufs en cocotte* and the egg sauces of which there is such a huge variety in French cooking. These utensils are now freely available in considerable variety, from the remarkably inexpensive Pyrex ramekins or *cocottes* large enough for one egg, to flat, two-handled dishes in earthenware or enamelled cast iron in which 8 to 10 eggs can be cooked and served; these last are particularly useful as they can be used over a direct flame as well as in the oven; but beware, for they retain the heat to such an extent that the eggs go on cooking long after they have been taken from the fire. Perhaps the most useful egg dishes for general use are fireproof porcelain ones, measuring about 5 inches across, intended for 2 eggs; they can be bought at most large stores. Similar shapes are made by the French firm of Le Creuset, in white-lined enamelled cast iron.

As well as a good heavy 10-inch omelette pan for omelettes of 3 or 4 eggs, a small 6-inch heavy aluminium pan is an invaluable asset in any kitchen, and especially for people who often have solitary meals; it is the right size for an omelette of 2 eggs and useful for frying or sautéing a small quantity of onions, bacon, mushrooms or croûtons. The Pyrex flameware frying-pan which goes over direct heat is useful, as it can be used for omelettes, for frying, and for eggs *sur le plat*.

In this chapter are suggestions for a few egg dishes which will vary the usual routine of fried, scrambled, and poached on toast. Variations in the recipes can always be made, but the addition of too many dabs of this and that will spoil them; their charm lies in their simplicity and freshness.

Cold egg dishes will be found in the chapter on hors d'œuvre, and dishes which require whites or yolks only are listed in the index.

⋄ *POACHED EGGS* ⋄

Here is an easy method. Bring a small saucepanful of water to the boil. Add a small spoonful of vinegar. As the water boils remove the pan from the fire and drop in your egg. Count twenty; then with a long handled metal spoon flip the egg so that it rolls over in the water. Leave it in the pan for two or three more minutes according to whether it is a large or small egg and whether you want it well or lightly poached. By this method the white of the egg sets as the egg is put in the water, instead of whirling around. You should have a neat and white veiled poached egg. Provide yourself with a long-handled perforated spoon for getting poached eggs out of the saucepan.

If the eggs are not to be eaten immediately, but to be subjected to a second cooking (see the three following recipes), slip them into a big bowl of cold water.

Small eggs are best for poaching. And they *must* be fresh, although not technically new-laid. The ideal egg for poaching is three to four days old.

ŒUFS POCHÉS ⋄ *À LA PROVENÇALE* ⋄

Cut ½ lb tomatoes into smallish pieces. Heat a little butter or olive oil in a metal egg dish. Put in the tomatoes. Add a chopped clove of garlic, salt and pepper, and a little parsley. When the tomatoes have cooked 5 minutes (they must retain their fresh flavour) add 4 to 6 poached eggs; cover these, but not the tomatoes, with grated Parmesan cheese, and put in a hot oven (gas no. 7 or 8) for 3 minutes, until the cheese has melted.

⋄ *EGGS AND SPINACH* ⋄

½ lb of spinach, 2 eggs, 2 tablespoons of cream and 2 of grated Gruyère or Parmesan for each person. Butter.

Clean and cook the spinach in the usual way. Drain it, and chop it, but not too finely. Arrange it in buttered fireproof egg dishes and heat it gently. Then put two eggs, either poached or *mollets* (eggs put into boiling water and cooked exactly 5 minutes, then shelled), into each dish. Cover with the cream and the cheese. Put in a hot oven for about 3 minutes.

This is a simplified version of the well-known *œufs Florentine*, in which the poached eggs are thickly covered in sauce Mornay (cheese-flavoured béchamel) which is then browned in the oven; a dish which always seems to me rather cloying, but there are those who prefer white sauce to fresh cream.

⬦ *POACHED EGGS IN* ⬦ *CHEESE SOUFFLÉ*

For the soufflé mixture melt ½ oz of butter, stir in a dessertspoonful of flour and add 6 oz (just over ¼ pint) of warmed milk. Season with salt and a little cayenne pepper and ground black pepper. When the sauce has thickened, add, off the fire, the yolk of one egg. Return to the fire and stir for a minute, then add 1 oz of grated Gruyère cheese. When cool, and when you are ready to cook the soufflé, fold in the whipped whites of two eggs.

Have ready, in buttered metal or fireproof egg dishes (about 5 inches diameter), slices of bread fried in butter, or toast, and on top of each a lightly poached egg. Over this pour the soufflé mixture. Put immediately in an oven preheated at the usual temperature you use for cooking soufflés (No. 7 or 8 in a gas oven). Cook for about 6 minutes, and serve at once.

The quantities given are enough for two people.

The first time this recipe was published was, I believe, by Alfred Suzanne in his *Egg Cookery*, 1893. Marcel Boulestin gave a version of it in *The Finer Cooking*, 1937, and a similar dish is now one of the specialities of a London hotel known for good food. The recipe I have given is that of Alfred Suzanne, except that his instructions are to cook the eggs on toast, not fried bread, the eggs ranged on a baking sheet, for 15 minutes.

Another method is to half-fill small soufflé dishes with the soufflé mixture, put the poached egg on top, fill up nearly to the top with the rest of the mixture and cook in a very hot over for 7 to 8 minutes.

Instead of a cheese soufflé, the dish can be made with the crab soufflé mixture described on page 100 and instead of a poached egg a 4-minute *œuf mollet* can be used.

All these little dishes require some practice, but are very attractive when successful.

REMINGTON, MARY, *Prawns on the Kitchen Table*, 1978.

❖ ŒUFS SUR LE PLAT AND ❖
ŒUFS EN COCOTTE

Œufs sur le plat are eggs cooked in butter in a shallow enamel, aluminium, earthenware or fireproof china dish. They can be cooked either on top of the stove or in the oven, but the cooking must always be very gentle, so that the whites remain white and do not get frizzled round the edges. Various sauces can be added to them, or they can be covered with cheese.

Œufs en cocotte are much the same, except that a *cocotte* usually only holds one egg, is deeper than the dishes used for eggs *sur le plat*, and cream is nearly always added to them.

Œufs en cocotte are cooked, covered, in the oven, or on top of the stove with the little dishes standing in a pan of hot water, and a cover over the whole. The addition of a very small amount of chopped tarragon, chives, basil, marjoram or any other herbs you fancy when the cream is poured over them makes these eggs perfectly delicious.

The timing is important, and practice is necessary to get it right, as half a minute too long may ruin them. On no account must the yolks of eggs *en cocotte* be hard, a fact which is not always grasped in this country. They are to be eaten with a spoon.

❖ ŒUFS AU PLAT ❖
AUX BEURRE
D'ESCARGOTS

Prepare a snail butter by pounding 2 oz of butter with 2 cloves of garlic, a shallot, a little salt, ground black pepper, and parsley.

Cook your eggs in butter, in fireproof egg dishes, either on top of the stove or in the oven. A minute or so before they are ready, add a little of the snail butter to each dish; it will just start to melt as you eat the eggs.

Delicious for garlic-eaters and for those who like snails and cannot get them in England.

❖ ŒUFS AU PLAT AUX ❖
ÉCHALOTES

Butter, flour, stock, shallots, white wine, parsley, eggs.

Melt ½ oz of butter, add the same quantity of flour. Stir until it turns golden; add ¼ pint of meat stock, and, when the sauce has thickened, 4 or 5 finely chopped shallots. After 5 minutes add 2 tablespoons of white wine, season with salt and pepper and add a little chopped parsley. Cook another 10 minutes, gently. Pour this sauce over the eggs cooked in butter, in metal egg dishes.

❖ ŒUFS AU PLAT BRESSANE ❖

In each buttered egg dish put a slice of bread fried in butter; over this, pour a tablespoon of heated cream, and then break the eggs very carefully over the bread. Add another 2 tablespoons of the hot cream and cook in a moderate oven for 5 minutes.

If this is to be served as a first dish, one egg is usually enough, as the fried bread makes it fairly filling. Instead of butter, I have sometimes fried the bread in dripping from roast pork, which gives the dish a quite different flavour. If you like garlic, rub the fried bread with a cut clove before putting it into the egg dish.

❖ MOONSHINE ❖

'Break them in a dish, upon some butter and oyl, melted or cold; throw on them a little salt, and set them on a chafing-dish of coals; make not the yolks too hard, and in the doing cover them, and make a sauce for them of an onion cut into round slices, and fried in sweet oyl or butter; then put to them Verjuice, grated nutmeg, a little salt, and so serve them.'
The Accomplisht Cook, Robert May, 1660

Omitting the verjuice (the juice of white grapes), Moonshine is an admirable way of cooking eggs *au plat*. In those days, the dish would have been a pewter plate, It would be unwise, however, to use a treasured old pewter piece for the purpose; it might melt. Kitchen pewter was made from a more heat-resistant alloy than ornamental or serving dishes. It is difficult for a non-expert to distinguish between the various types of pewter.

◇ ŒUFS EN COCOTTE À LA ◇
CRÈME AUX ASPERGES

Pour a little melted butter into each ramekin, put in a few cooked asparagus tips and break an egg into the centre. Add 2 or 3 tablespoons of cream and cook 4 or 5 minutes in a moderate oven.

◇ ŒUEFS EN COCOTTE BERCY ◇

Over each egg broken into a buttered ramekin pour a little sauce Bercy (see page 192). Cook in the oven, or covered on top of the stove.

◇ EGGS EN COCOTTE WITH ◇
LETTUCE AND CREAM

For each person allow 2 tablespoons of lettuce cooked as explained in the recipe for lettuce and egg gratin on page 82, 2 tablespoons of cream mixed with a heaped teaspoon of grated Parmesan, 1 or 2 eggs, a walnut of butter.

Put the cooked lettuce, with a knob of fresh butter, into individual egg ramekins or *cocottes*. Heat gently. Break the eggs into cups. Transfer them to the *cocottes*. Pour the cream and cheese mixture round them. Put small plates or lids over the egg dishes. If these are china or glazed earthenware put them into a shallow pan of water on top of the stove or on a baking sheet in a moderate oven. If they are enamelled cast-iron or enamelled steel use them over direct but very moderate heat.

The eggs will take 4 to 8 minutes to cook, depending upon the type and size of dish used and the degree of heat.

Remove the dishes from the oven or hot-water pan or hot-plate *before* the whites are completely set. By the time they are brought to the table they will be just right. The lettuce, cream and egg combination is a very fresh tasting and original one.

◇ EGGS COOKED IN CREAM ◇ WITH GAME SAUCE

When you have stock from a casserole grouse or partridge, made as described on page 150, boil a little in a saucepan until it is reduced to a syrupy glaze.

In china or metal ramekins, or *cocottes*, melt a little butter. Break two eggs into each, pour fresh cream round the yolks but not over them, cook them for 4 minutes in a moderate oven, then add a dessertspoon of the prepared sauce. Put the dishes back in the oven for another minute. By this time the eggs should be ready, the whites cooked and the yolks still soft.

◇ ŒUFS MOLLETS ◇

Œufs mollets are eggs boiled for 5 minutes, so that the whites are firm and the yolks still slightly runny. Naturally, common sense must be exercised in the cooking of these eggs; if they are very small, cook them a little less, if large a little longer. As soon as they are taken out of the pan, pour a little cold water over them to stop them cooking any more, but they are easier to shell while still warm. This is a process which is perfectly easy as long as it is not attempted in a hurry, with shaking hands. Handle the eggs gently and don't try to peel off the whole shell at once as you can with a hard-boiled egg.

If you have to cook a number of *œufs mollets* at a time, put the eggs into a saucepan and pour the boiling water over them. The incidence of cracked eggs is neither more nor less by this method than when they are put straight into boiling water, but it facilitates the timing (5 minutes from the moment the eggs are covered with the water).

There are also now available metal stands with a handle which will hold 4 eggs, to be lowered into the pan when the water is boiling. With this device (which is a very old one revived) the eggs do not touch the bottom of the pan, and the risk of cracking is almost eliminated.

◇ ŒUFS MOLLETS À LA CRÈME ◇ AUX FINES HERBES

Allow 2 eggs for each person, put them into boiling water, and cook them for exactly 5 minutes. When they have cooled, crack the shells all over, gently,

78

with the back of a knife. They will then be easy to shell. Even so, the operation needs care – and time.

For 8 eggs prepare half a teacupful of chopped fresh herbs, such as basil, chives and parsley, with a scrap of garlic, salt and pepper. Put a piece of butter into a fireproof egg dish, and when it has melted add the eggs, then the herbs, then a cupful of fresh cream. Cook 2 or 3 minutes only, turning the eggs over so that they heat on each side. Serve quickly.

Tarragon is a wonderful herb with this dish, instead of, but not with, basil; a combination of sweet marjoram, lemon thyme, parsley and chives, or a very little of the green part of spring onions, is also very good.

Instead of *œufs mollets*, you can cook your eggs *en cocotte*, having mixed the herbs into the cream before pouring it over the eggs.

⟡ OMELETTE AUX ⟡ FINES HERBES

A great luxury for people who live in towns. Fresh eggs, fresh butter, fresh herbs, what more delicious combination can there be? For an *omelette aux fines herbes* use the same mixtures of herbs as described in the preceding recipe, allowing a large tablespoon of chopped herbs for an omelette of 3 eggs, with a little extra to sprinkle over the omelette before serving. Instead of stirring the herbs into the ready beaten eggs, add them only when the eggs are already in the pan; in this way they will have greater flavour, and there is no risk of little bits sticking to the pan or burning while the omelette is cooking.

TOMATO ⟡ OMELETTE ⟡

For an omelette of 3 or 4 eggs, cook 2 or 3 chopped tomatoes for about two minutes only in butter, adding a little garlic, salt, ground black pepper and some fresh parsley or basil. Add to the omelette when already in the pan.

Provided the tomatoes are cooked just sufficiently to soften them, retaining all their flavour, this makes them one of the nicest of summer omelettes.

❖ *OMELETTE BERRICHONNE* ❖

The white part of a small leek, raw and finely sliced, one shallot, a little mint and a tablespoon of cream, added to the omelette in the pan.

❖ *OMELETTE SAVOYARDE* ❖

A rasher of bacon or a small slice of ham (chopped), a little raw leek, a small diced cooked potato, cooked a minute in butter. Add to the eggs in the pan, cover with two tablespoons of coarsely grated Gruyère cheese.

❖ *KIDNEY OMELETTE* ❖

Cut a cleaned sheep's kidney into dice; sauté it in butter; pour over a tablespoon of port or madeira; let it bubble. Add a teaspoonful of meat glaze, or a dessertspoonful of good stock. When the sauce is thick the kidney mixture is ready to add to the omelette.

❖ *OMELETTE À L'OSEILLE* ❖

One of the nicest of summer omelettes. Wash a handful of sorrel; chop it. Melt it in butter; add salt. In five minutes it is ready to add to the eggs.

❖ *OMELETTE PAYSANNE* ❖

Sorrel, 1 oz ham, a small cooked potato. Cook the sorrel as above (use rather less) add the ham cut in strips, and the potato in dice. Add to the eggs.

❖ *COLD OMELETTES* ❖

A cold omelette makes a most beguiling little summer dish. Country people in Italy, Spain, southern France and Greece take them on picnics, but then they are big, thick, substantial, the diameter of a dinner plate and the thickness of six. For an indoor meal I make very small ordinary rolled omelettes in a 6-inch pan, with one large egg to the omelette or three smaller ones for two. When the eggs are nearly but not quite set, put in one of the following fillings: a dozen tiny raw broad beans and a dessertspoon, no more, of fresh cream; a heaped tablespoon of cream cheese mixed with chopped watercress; one small tomato, raw, but skinned and sliced, and a little chopped parsley.

Turn the omelettes out, neatly rolled, on to a flat dish (I use a worn old meat platter with a border of faded pink flowers that looks just right for the purpose. A small point, but not entirely without importance) and strew a sprinkling of chopped parsley or chives over them.

This is just one way of making an all-the-year-round dish into a specifically summer one. And if you have another plate of thin slices from a cold gammon joint, a brown loaf, a pitcher of cider, some creamy butter, a piece of Lancashire cheese – what more do you need for a midday midsummer meal? But don't cook your little omelettes too long in advance.

For other cold omelette ideas see the chapter entitled 'Improvised Cooking for Holidays', page 255.

MATELOTE
◇ *SANS POISSON* ◇

'You have promised your guests a *matelote*. Like Grouchy at Waterloo, the fish has not arrived. The main body of your well-laid plans is lacking. You have, like Louvois, organized victory, and you are faced with defeat. Visions of Vatel begin to haunt your brain . . . But I am there; the harm will go no further.

'In butter brown two dozen small onions, which you leave whole. Remove them, and to the butter add sufficient flour and water to make a white roux. Then add red wine, a bouquet of parsley, thyme, and bayleaf, a clove, salt and pepper, a large clove of garlic crushed, 3 chopped shallots, the browned onions and a pound and a half of mushrooms. Leave to reduce.

'Prepare a rather firmly cooked omelette; cut into slices into a deep dish, and pour over it your sauce *matelote* after having removed the bouquet of parsley.

'At dinner, recount your anguish and your success; cite the English proverb "Fish must swim thrice – namely, once in the water, once in the sauce, and a third time in wine in the stomach." '

Translated from *Cuisine Messine*, Auricoste de Lazarque, 1909

❖ *LETTUCE AND EGG GRATIN* ❖

Approximately ½ lb of lettuce (i.e. about half an average-sized cabbage lettuce). A béchamel made with 1 oz of butter, 1 tablespoon of flour and ½ pint of milk; 4 to 6 eggs, hard-boiled; ¼ pint of cream; 2 to 4 tablespoons of breadcrumbs; 1 oz of butter.

Wash, drain and slice your lettuce into fine strips. Cook these for about 10 minutes in the melted butter in a heavy covered casserole or saucepan over low heat. Season with salt and a pinch of sugar. Add to the prepared béchamel (see page 186). Shell the eggs, quarter them, and incorporate them into the lettuce sauce. Stir in the cream gently, so as not to break up the eggs. Pour the whole mixture into a shallow two-handled egg dish or gratin dish. Strew with breadcrumbs and the butter in tiny knobs.

Put the dish into a medium hot oven, gas No. 5 or 6, 375–90°F, for 10 minutes, and serve sizzling hot and bubbling. A few triangles of bread fried in clarified butter (see page 151) or even of thin dry toast, arranged round the edge of the dish, make a welcome accompaniment and contrast to the creamy sauce and eggs.

This is a most delicate and subtle dish (it is based on the well-known *œufs à la tripe* or Convent Eggs – but the onions in the old favourite are heavy compared with the lettuce) and one which can be made into a one-dish meal in the most elementary of kitchens and by the least skilled of cooks – provided that the making of the basic béchamel has been mastered.

The dish can, after a little experiment to determine what temperature and timing best suit the dishes you have, be cooked and presented in individual soufflé or egg ramekins, which always look alluring, facilitate service, and ensure that everybody gets his food sizzling from the oven or the grill.

❖ *CHEESE PANCAKES* ❖

Make some thin pancakes, allowing two or three for each person, and using a pancake batter as described on page 83.

For 12 pancakes make a béchamel (see page 186) with 1½ oz of butter, 3 tablespoons of flour, 1¼ pints of warmed milk, salt, pepper and nutmeg.

When it has cooked sufficiently, stir in 2 oz of grated Parmesan. Divide the béchamel into two separate bowls. Into one half stir ¼ lb of Gruyère cheese cut into small squares. Put a tablespoon of this mixture into each pancake. Roll them up. Butter a shallow fireproof dish and spread a layer of the other half of the béchamel on the bottom. Arrange the pancakes on the top, pour a little more of the béchamel over them, then a thin coating of grated Parmesan, then a few knobs of butter. Cook them in a hot oven for 10 minutes, until the dish is browned.

The contrast of the Gruyère cheese with the Parmesan, both in taste and texture, is important. A light white wine accords particularly well with the soft flavour of the Gruyère in this dish.

⋄ PANCAKE BATTER ⋄

Put ¼ lb of flour into a bowl. Add a teaspoon of salt; stir in 1 tablespoonful of olive oil, 1 whole egg, and ¼ pint each of milk and cold water. Stir very thoroughly. Cover, and leave to stand for two or three hours.

Pancake batter in which the liquid consists of half water and half milk makes much lighter and crispier pancakes than one made with milk only.

Quantities given make eight to twelve pancakes according to the size of your pan.

⋄ GNOCCHI ALLA GENOVESE ⋄

This dish is simply an excuse for eating *pesto*, the wonderful Genoese basil sauce.

The preparation of the *gnocchi* is the same as that for *gnocchi à la romaine*, but the final cooking is different, as they are poached instead of gratiné.

For the *gnocchi*: 6 oz of fine semolina, a pint of milk, nutmeg, salt, pepper, 2 oz of grated Parmesan, 2 eggs. Bring the milk to the boil, having seasoned it with salt, pepper and grated nutmeg. Pour in the semolina, and stir until you have a thick, smooth and stiff mass. Add the cheese off the fire and stir in the eggs. Pour the whole mixture into an oiled shallow tin, in one layer about ½ inch thick. Leave to cool for several hours. Cut into small squares, and with floured hands roll each square into a cork shape. Lay these on a floured board until all are ready.

Bring a large pan of salted water to a gentle boil. Drop in the *gnocchi* one by one. Have ready a perforated spoon and a colander and a hot buttered oven dish. As the *gnocchi* rise to the top (3 or 4 minutes) take each one out and drain in the colander. Put them all in the hot buttered dish, put more butter on the top and leave them in the oven for 5 minutes.

The *pesto* sauce (see below) can either be spooned lightly on top of the *gnocchi*, with more butter on top of that, or it can be served separately. A bowl of grated cheese should also be on the table.

⬦ *PESTO* ⬦

A large bunch of fresh basil, garlic, a handful of pine nuts, a handful of grated Sardo or Parmesan cheese, about 2 oz of olive oil.

Pound the basil leaves (there should be about 2 oz when the stalks have been removed) in a mortar with one or two cloves of garlic, a little salt and the pine nuts. Add the cheese. (Sardo cheese is the pungent Sardinian ewe's milk cheese which is exported in large quantities to Genoa to make *pesto*. Parmesan and Sardo are sometimes used in equal quantities; or all Parmesan, which gives a milder flavour.)

When the *pesto* is a thick purée start adding the olive oil, a little at a time. Stir it steadily and see that it is amalgamating with the other ingredients, as the finished sauce should have the consistency of a creamed butter. If made in larger quantities, *pesto* may be stored in jars covered with a layer of olive oil.

This is the famous sauce which is eaten by the Genoese with all kinds of pasta, with *gnocchi* and as a flavouring for soups.

An imitation of this sauce can be made with parsley or sweet marjoram, and although the flavour is totally different, it is still good. Pine nuts are very hard to come by in England, and walnuts can be used instead, or they can be omitted altogether, but the result is a thinner sauce.

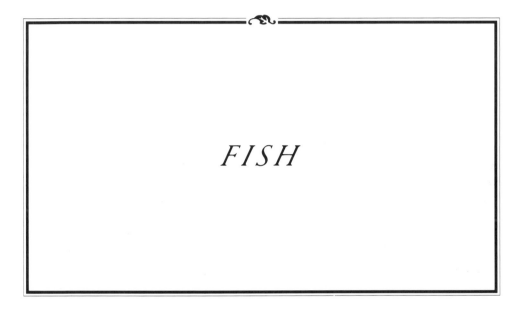

FISH

FORBES, STANHOPE, *Fish Sale on a Cornish Beach*, 1885.

FISH

Boiled salmon with cucumber and mayonnaise is an admirable dish, but anyone visiting this country for the first time and dining out frequently, might well be excused for supposing that salmon is the only fish procurable in England during the whole of the summer. In fact, salmon is at its best in the very early spring; later, it scarcely justifies its high price. Salmon trout, in season all summer until the end of August, is an exquisite fish, and although nearly as expensive as salmon, a small whole one is an occasional possibility for a small household; although again what can possibly induce people to pay something like 14s. a pound for frozen salmon trout which has quite lost its flavour is beyond my comprehension. If it is a cold dish that is needed and there is money to spend, fillets of sole make a very welcome change (see the recipe for soles *à la juive*, page 89) from the eternal salmon. Then there are some excellent lesser-known fish, such as John Dory, sea bream, Cornish bass and grey mullet which are occasionally to be found at the fishmonger's and are comparatively cheap; so it is well worth knowing how to deal with them.

Rock salmon and mackerel make good cheap cold dishes, and red mullet, although more expensive, makes one of the best and most beautiful of summer fish dishes when grilled on a bed of dried fennel stalks. Fresh brown trout fried or grilled and served with plenty of melted butter are a rare treat, but the little rainbow trout usually to be found at the fishmonger's are often rather disapppointing. An interesting sauce, however, does a great deal for them. A grilled herring has always seemed to me one of those cheap luxuries of which there are all too few; herrings are out of season in May and June, but later in the summer they can be enjoyed with fresh herbs and butter and perhaps French mustard instead of pasty mustard sauce. Remember soft herring roes too; with a little ingenuity they make most excellent little dishes, at a very small cost.

There is not much in the way of shell fish in the summer except cockles, although in the Mediterranean mussels are eaten all the year round, but the crustaceans – lobsters, crayfish and crab – are at their best in the summer, and there are prawns and Dublin Bay prawns; with the exception of crabs, these are all very expensive, and with the same exception, are all best served very plain. The difference between Dublin Bay prawns bought alive, cooked at home and eaten at once and the same fish when it has been boiled and recooked, is as the difference between fresh coffee and boiled-up coffee. The frozen ones (called frozen scampi – the word evidently has some magic for the English public) have just a very faint flavour, with what seems to me rather more than a hint of corruption in it. It is odd that this most fragile of sea-creatures should have been singled out for mass deep-freezing, and that it should, in this condition, have gained such a grip on public imagination that demand now far exceeds supplies, which are becoming short.

Crabs are useful for all sorts of soups, salads and soufflés, but a little, unlike other crustaceans of which one needs a lot, goes a long way. Unless you know your fishmonger pretty well, it is not advisable to buy 'dressed' crab from him; it is often mixed with bread, and sometimes not of the first freshness. In the soup chapter there are ideas (which can be varied according to what is available) which may be helpful to those whose families and friends will eat fish only if it is spoon fed to them.

For those who like fish plain grilled, fried, baked or poached, there are the delicious classic French sauces, *hollandaise, maltaise, Bercy, rémoulade*, and a few lesser-known sauces made with herbs, almonds, walnuts, avocado pears, which will often liven up a rather dull fish. Of all vegetables, I think perhaps sorrel is the one which goes best with coarse fish, but in England it is available only to those people who grow it themselves (and at one or two shops in Soho); spinach not being a good substitute, the next best vegetables are tomatoes, and, for more delicate fish, mushrooms, lettuce, courgettes, and watercress cooked a few seconds in butter, then chopped.

⬦ *PAUPIETTES OF SOLE* ⬦
IN LETTUCE LEAVES

4 fillets of sole and the carcass, 2 oz of peeled cooked prawns, 8 lettuce leaves, butter, lemon juice, 2 eggs, nutmeg.

Make a little stock from the carcass of the sole, plus flavouring, vegetables, a piece of lemon peel, a sprig of tarragon, and a couple of tablespoons of white wine, vermouth, or wine vinegar.

Choose 8 good lettuce leaves, not the coarse outside ones, but large enough to roll up. Wash them and blanch them two minutes in boiling salted water, drain them. Season the fillets of sole with salt, pepper and lemon juice. In the centre of each arrange a few prawns, also seasoned; roll up the fillets. Arrange the lettuce leaves overlapping each other two by two, so that you have 4 leaves instead of 8. Put a rolled fillet in the centre of each, and roll the leaves round the fish. Squeeze these rolls in the hand, so that each forms a little parcel, which need not be tied. Grate a little nutmeg on to each paupiette. Melt 1 oz of butter in a small shallow pan. Put the paupiettes in and cook very gently for 30 minutes, with the cover on the pan.

Beat two eggs in a bowl, add about ¼ pint of the strained stock, the juice of half a lemon and a little salt. Remove the paupiettes to the serving dish. Strain the egg and lemon mixture through a sieve into the butter remaining in the pan, and stir very fast until the sauce has thickened and frothed. Pour over the paupiettes and serve at once.

FILETS DE SOLE EN COCOTTE

Fillets of sole folded, cooked in butter in egg dishes with salt, pepper, lemon juice, small chopped mushrooms, parsley.

Allow 2 fillets of sole per person.

SOLES À LA JUIVE

2 large soles, 1 onion, 2 lemons, parsley, bayleaf, pepper, salt, the yolks of four eggs.

Have the soles filleted. With the bones, the onion, a piece of lemon peel, parsley, bayleaf, pepper and salt and 1¼ pints of water, make a court-bouillon. Cook it 15 to 20 minutes, strain, and leave to cool. In this poach the fillets for 10 minutes. Put them in the serving dish. Add a little of the hot court-bouillon to the beaten eggs and lemon juice. Stir to prevent curdling. Return this mixture to the rest of the court-bouillon and heat up, but do not let it boil. Pour over the fillets and serve cold.

✧ *SOLE AU VERT* ✧

Fillets of sole, sorrel, tarragon, chives, parsley, flour, butter, salt and pepper.

Salt and pepper the fillets, dust them with flour, cook in hot butter. When both sides are lightly browned, throw over them a handful of the chopped herbs, in which sorrel should predominate. Add a little more butter and simmer 3 or 4 minutes.

✧ *FILETS DE SOLE VÉRONIQUE* ✧

Wait until the muscat grapes come into season in August to make this dish. No other grapes will really do.

> 8 fillets of sole, a large wineglass of medium-dry white wine, 4 oz cream, 3 teaspoons of flour, 1 oz of butter, ¾ lb of muscat grapes, a little fennel or tarragon if available.

Poach the fillets of sole (seasoned with salt, pepper, and lemon juice) in the white wine with the fennel or tarragon. Meanwhile heat the butter, stir in the flour, and when it has amalgamated add the boiling cream. Season with salt and pepper.

Remove the poached fillets to a narrow oval buttered fireproof dish. Reduce the wine in which they have cooked by a minute's fast boiling, add it to the prepared sauce, and stir until it is the consistency of thick cream. Arrange the peeled and seeded grapes at each end of the dish.

Pour the sauce over the fish, and brown under a very hot grill for about 3 minutes.

✧ *BAR À LA MARSEILLAISE* ✧

Bar or *loup de mer* is one of the most delicate fish of the Mediterranean; grilled on a bed of fennel stalks it makes the famous Provençal *grillade au fenouil*. The bass which come from Cornwall are the English equivalent; they don't appear very often, but are well worthy buying when they do.

> The ingredients for this dish are a bass weighing 2½–3 lb, a coffee-cupful of olive oil, a small glass of dry white wine, a little bouquet of fennel leaves, 2 cloves of garlic, ½ lb of mushrooms, ½ lb of onions, 1 lb of yellow waxy potatoes.

MANET, EDOUARD, (1832-1883), *The Salmon.*

Put the fish in a baking dish, pour over it the oil and wine, cover with the chopped fennel and garlic, round it arrange the sliced onions, mushrooms and thinly sliced potatoes. Season with salt and pepper, add a pint of water and cook in a fairly hot oven for about an hour.

Serve with an aïoli or pimento mayonnaise (see recipe for Rougets à la Provençale, page 92).

◇ BAKED BREAM ◇

Marinate a sea bream for an hour in olive oil and lemon juice, with a bayleaf, parsley, thyme, salt and pepper.

Cook it in an open baking dish in a fairly hot oven so that the skin gets nicely golden and crackling.

Serve with the following sauce: a chopped shallot in a glass of white wine reduced to half; add a coffeespoonful of French mustard, 2 oz of butter, 2 pounded egg yolks, salt, pepper and chopped parsley.

A large grey mullet may be cooked in the same way, but make sure it is very well cleaned, and washed under running water, as these fish sometimes have a slightly muddy taste.

⋄ JOHN DORY ⋄

A fish of alarming aspect, with a very ugly head and good solid white flesh. It is something of a rarity in English fishmongers', but very common in the Mediterranean. In France, it is called *Saint-Pierre*, in Italy, *Pesce San Pietro*. When it does appear in England it is fairly cheap, although there is a good deal of waste as the head is so large.

Have it filleted by the fishmonger; there will be two large triangular fillets which can each be cut into two. The head and carcass make good stock for fish soup. Cook the fillets in a court-bouillon and serve with a green sauce, or a mayonnaise, or on a bed of sorrel purée, or on chopped tomatoes melted in butter.

John Dory can also be cooked in the same way as the Bar or Bass à la Marseillaise (page 90).

⋄ FILLETS OF JOHN DORY ⋄
MARECHIARO

This recipe comes from the Gritti Palace Hotel in Venice, where the *Pesce San Pietro*, or John Dory, is highly esteemed.

Having seasoned and floured your fillets of John Dory, fry them in butter until golden on both sides. Put them in the serving dish and pour over them plenty of bubbling butter, then a sauce made of 4 or 5 tomatoes chopped and cooked with finely sliced onions in butter; garnish the dish with shelled prawns, clams, mussels and chopped parsley.

⋄ ROUGETS À LA PROVENÇALE ⋄

Score large red mullets obliquely, twice, on each side, and paint them with olive oil. Grill them for about 10 minutes on each side and serve with the following sauce, which is a combination of two Provençal sauces, aïoli, and *sauce rouille*: for the aïoli, two large cloves of garlic, pounded in a mortar, two yolks of eggs, a little salt, a third of a pint of olive oil, mixed exactly as for a mayonnaise. For the red part of the sauce, pound the contents of a half-pound tin of red peppers (the roasted ones are best for the purpose, as they are already skinned), or the equivalent in fresh peppers, grilled and skinned, with a teaspoon of paprika; add a teacup of fresh breadcrumbs, softened in water, then pressed dry, to the pounded pimentos. At the last minute amalgamate the two sauces, adding the aïoli gradually to the pimento mixture. Grey mullet may be served in the same way.

❖ TURBOT ❖

Turbot cooked whole, poached, steamed or baked, is such a fine fish that it always seems to me a mistake to fillet it or cut it into steaks, but as such a very large fish is not often practical, and since hardly anybody now possesses a proper turbot kettle for cooking it, here is a method of cooking turbot fillets which keeps the fish moist.

Poach the fillets in milk previously simmered with salt, pepper, nutmeg and fresh green herbs (tarragon or fennel or mint).

Serve the fillets quite plain, accompanied by a *vinaigrette aux œufs* (page 191) or a sauce *à la crème* (page 191) or with a little of the milk in which it has been cooked, strained, thickened with yolk of egg and flavoured with lemon.

❖ COLD STURGEON IN OIL ❖

Recently there have been imports of sturgeon from the Caspian Sea to this country, and it is occasionally to be bought at Harrods and other large stores. It is a magnificent-looking fish, weighing sometimes as much as 100 lb. It is sold in steaks, like salmon, and is about half the price.

Steamed, and seasoned with good olive oil, it makes a good hors d'œuvre.

Have it cut in rather thin slices; season it with salt and pepper and steam it, allowing about 25 minutes for it to cook. While it is still warm, pour some olive oil and a very little lemon juice over it.

Serve it cold.

❖ *FISH KEBABS* ❖

For each person you need a medium-sized mackerel or grey mullet, a rasher of bacon, a little onion, two or three bayleaves, a mushroom. Olive oil, salt, pepper, lemon juice, thyme or marjoram.

Have the backbone removed from the fish; cut each one through into about 6 slices; thread these slices on to skewers, alternating with slices of onion and bacon, with an occasional bayleaf and slice of mushroom. Put the prepared skewers on a dish and season them with salt, ground black pepper, lemon juice and a good sprinkling of thyme or marjoram. Pour olive oil over them and leave them to marinate for an hour or so. Put the skewers under the grill and cook them fairly fast, turning them over from time to time, for 10–12 minutes.

Serve on a long dish (leave the fish on their skewers) on a bed of lemon parsley, or shredded lettuce, garnished with halves of lemon.

Fennel or mint can be used instead of thyme or marjoram.

❖ *MACKEREL WITH SAUCE* ❖ *RÉMOULADE*

Poach the mackerel simply in water to which you add two bayleaves, a few peppercorns, salt, and a slice of lemon. They will take about 12 minutes, cooked gently. Leave them to cool in their juice. Drain carefully and serve on a bed of parsley or watercress, with the *rémoulade* (page 189) served separately.

ROCK SALMON AND ❖ *TUNNY FISH MAYONNAISE* ❖

1½ lb of rock salmon, a lettuce, mayonnaise, a small tin of tunny fish, lemon, cucumber.

Poach the fish in salted water with an onion and a bayleaf for about 15 minutes. Leave to cool, then carefully remove all bones and cartilaginous pieces. Arrange the fillets on a bed of chopped lettuce, and cover it with a mayonnaise into which has been incorporated 3 or 4 oz of pounded tunny fish and the juice of half a lemon.

Surround the dish with rounds of very finely sliced cucumber.

⋄ GRILLED HERRINGS ⋄

A plain grilled herring really fresh is one of the most delicious of fish. Unfortunately by the time herrings reach the shops their flavour is somewhat diminished, but they still make an excellent and cheap luncheon. Have them boned by the fishmonger, and to make them more interesting, buy a few extra soft herring roes, which are sold separately. Salt and pepper the fish, and add an extra roe to each herring. Put a little piece of butter into each fish, close it up and grill them in an oiled dish for about 7 minutes, turning them over half-way through the cooking.

Instead of the traditional mustard sauce, have a pot of French mustard on the table.

⋄ LAITANCES À LA PROVENÇALE

½ lb soft herring roes, flour, butter, parsley, garlic, lemon.

Dust the washed roes lightly with flour. Fry them gently in melted butter. Two minutes on each side should be enough. Sprinkle chopped garlic and parsley over them, cook another half-minute, put them on a hot dish and sprinkle a little lemon juice over them.

FRITTERS OF SOFT ROES, ⋄ MUSHROOMS AND FENNEL ⋄

½ lb of soft roes, ¼ lb of firm mushrooms, a large root-bulb of fennel.

Prepare a frying batter (see below). Slice the washed and well-dried mushrooms into ¼–inch slices, the fennel into 6 or 8 lengthwise pieces. Dip the fennel into the batter and fry in deep, very hot olive oil or fat. Drain on to blotting-paper. Then fry the mushroom slices in the same way; then the soft roes.

Pile up on a dish, sprinkle coarse salt over the fritters, garnish with parsley and lemon.

This is obviously a dish which can be varied according to taste; prawns or Dublin Bay prawns can replace soft roes, celery can replace fennel and so on, but remember to fry the vegetables before the fish.

The smell of deep frying is a very penetrating one, so this method of cooking is not much to be recommended for people who eat in the kitchen.

✧ Frying Batter ✧

4 oz flour, 3 tablespoons of olive oil, ¾ of a tumbler of tepid water, a pinch of salt, the white of one egg.

Mix the flour and the oil to a thick paste, add the water gradually, and the salt. Stir very vigorously until the batter is quite smooth. Leave it for at least 3 hours and before using it stir in the beaten white of the egg.

✧ TO BOIL SALMON AND ✧ OTHER FISH

Meg Dods's recipe for boiling salmon (from the *Cook's & Housewife's Manual*, 1829) is so clear and precise that it cannot be bettered. I have used it with perfect results.

'There are many excellent ways of dressing this favourite fish, but perhaps none equal to plain boiling when well performed. Scale and clean the fish without unnecessary washing or handling, and without cutting it too much open. Have a roomy and well-scoured fish-kettle, and if the salmon be large and thick, when you have placed it on the strainer and in the kettle, fill up and amply cover it with cold spring water, that it may heat gradually. Throw in a handful of salt. Take off the scum carefully, and let the fish boil slowly, allowing twelve minutes to the pound; but it is even more difficult to fix the time fish should boil than the length of time that meat requires. Experience, and those symptoms which the eye of a practised cook alone can discern, must fix the point, and nothing is more disgusting and unwholesome than underdone fish. It may be probed. The minute the boiling of any fish is completed, the fish strainer must be lifted and rested across the pan, to drain the fish. Throw a soft cloth or flannel in several folds over it. It would become

96

soft if permitted to soak in the hot water. Dish on a hot fish-plate under a napkin. Besides the essences to be used at discretion, which are now found on every sideboard of any pretension, shrimp, anchovy, and lobster sauce are served with salmon; also plain melted butter; and where the fish is got fresh and served in what is esteemed by some the greatest perfection – crisp, curdy, and creamy – it is the practice to send in a sauce-tureen of the plain liquor in which it was boiled. Fennel and butter are still heard of for salmon, but are nearly obsolete. Garnish with a fringe of curled green parsley and slices of lemon. The carver must help a slice of thick part with a smaller one of the thin, which is the fattest, and the best-liked by those in the secret. Sliced cucumber is often served with salmon, and indeed with all boiled fish.'

❖ GRILLED SALMON ❖

Have the salmon cut in steaks, each weighing 5 to 6 oz. Season them lightly with salt and pepper, coat them with olive oil, and grill them* under a moderate flame for about 7 minutes, turning them over two or three times and basting with a little more oil. Serve with a *sauce verte* (page 189), or parsley butter to which have been added a little strong yellow Dijon mustard and a scrap of cayenne pepper.

❖ SALMON TROUT ❖

Salmon trout is one of the most delicate of all fishes, and is best cooked very simply and gently, in order that its flavour shall be retained. If you have no fish-kettle, cook it in a baking tin in the oven, in a little salted water, allowing about 15 minutes to the pound in a medium to slow oven.

If to be served cold, let it cool before lifting it out and it will be easier to handle. Serve it on a long dish with a ring of finely sliced and salted cucumber all round it, and, better than *hollandaise*, a *sauce maltaise* (page 185) or *sauce verte* (page 189).

If the fish is too big to go into the baking tin, wrap it up in copiously buttered greaseproof paper and lay it on the bars or on a baking sheet in the

---

*A double grid, in which the fish steaks are enclosed so that you turn the grid rather than the fish, is a great aid to the successful grilling of fish.

GWYNNE-JONES, EMILIE, *Brown River Trout*, 1968.

oven, cooking it rather more gently, and allowing 20 minutes to the pound, and serve it hot straight out of its paper with fresh melted butter, or the same *sauce maltaise* or *sauce messine* (page 191).

If the fish is to be eaten cold, the foil or paper should be oiled rather than buttered.

⋄ TRUITES À LA CRÈME ⋄

Arrange the trout in a shallow pan; cover them with very thinly sliced onions, season with salt and pepper and a sprinkling of fresh herbs. Pour over a glass of white wine and one of water. Poach gently (about 10–12 minutes for small trout). Put them in the serving dish, reduce the cooking liquid to half by fast boiling, add half its volume of boiling cream and pour over the fish through a strainer. Garnish with parsley or tarragon. Can be served hot or cold.

⋄ *L'ANGUILLE* ⋄
AU VERT
(A Belgian Dish)

'Skin, behead and wash some small eels. Cut them in slices 5 centimetres [about 2 inches] long. Put them into a casserole with a good proportion of finely chopped aromatic herbs – sage, mint, savory, sorrel, chervil and parsley. Add a piece of butter, salt and pepper and let the eel and the herbs melt. Cover with a quarter of water to three quarters of white wine.

'The cooking should be carried out at a good pace and for not longer than 10 to 15 minutes, according to the size of the eels. While the eels are cooking prepare the following sauce: 6 yolks of eggs to a kilo [just over 2 lb] of eels, the juice of 3 lemons, 6 tablespoons of cold water, and a few nuts of fresh butter. Having carefully mixed all these ingredients, take the casserole from the fire, giving it several rotating movements as you do so. Incorporate the egg mixture very gradually and gently. Turn the eels and their sauce into a china or earthenware dish and leave to cool. Some people prefer this dish hot or tepid; it is no less delicious.'

Paul Bouillard's recipe

ELIZA ACTON'S
⋄ *LOBSTER SALAD* ⋄

'First prepare a sauce with the coral of a hen lobster, pounded and rubbed through a sieve, and very gradually mixed with a good mayonnaise or remoulade. Next, half fill the bowl or more with small salad herbs, or with young lettuces finely shredded, and arrange upon them spirally, or in a chain, alternate slices of the flesh of a large lobster, or of two middling-sized ones, and some hard-boiled eggs cut thin and evenly. Leave a space in the centre, pour in the sauce, heap lightly some small salad on the top and send the dish immediately to table. The coral of a seasoned lobster may be intermingled with the white flesh of the fish with very good effect.'

From the 1861 edition of *Modern Cookery*, first published in 1845.

This is the recipe I always follow for making lobster salad. It is very successful.

✧ GRATIN DE LANGOUSTINES ✧

For two people:
10–12 Dublin Bay prawns, ¼ pint milk, 1 oz flour, yolks of 2 eggs, 2 oz cream,
butter, grated Gruyère cheese, a tablespoon of brandy, 1 onion, lemon peel.

Shell the cooked prawns. Put the shells and claws into a pan with an onion,
a piece of lemon peel, a glass of water, salt, pepper, and a tablespoon of
brandy and simmer for 10 minutes. Strain the resulting stock.

Make a thick béchamel with a tablespoon of butter, the flour, the warmed
milk. Season it well, let it cook 10–15 minutes. Add 2 or 3 tablespoons of the
prepared fish stock, the cream, and off the fire the well-beaten egg yolks.
Lastly add the prawn tails. Turn into a shallow gratin dish, sprinkle with
grated Gruyère and brown in the top of a very hot oven for about 7 minutes.

All except the final cooking can be done beforehand, but before putting
the mixture into the gratin dish heat it up in a double boiler so that it is
already hot when put into the oven. Otherwise it will have to cook too long
and the eggs may curdle the sauce. Nervous or preoccupied cooks can leave
out the eggs altogether, make a rather thicker béchamel, and use double the
amount of cream.

✧ GRILLED DUBLIN BAY ✧
PRAWNS

To grill scampi or Dublin Bay prawns, cut the tails off the uncooked fish;
wash them in cold water, flatten them out slightly with a rolling pin, paint
their shells with oil and put them, shells nearest the heat, under the grill for
5 or 6 minutes. Serve at once with salt and a little melted butter.

This is worth trying when uncooked Dublin Bay prawns can be obtained;
the flavour is really fresh and enjoyable, but it is no use attempting it with
already cooked or frozen fish. The heads can be used for making stock for a
fish soup, but they should be cooked at once.

✧ CRAB SOUFFLÉ ✧

1 medium-sized cooked crab, ½ pint milk, 3 dessertspoons flour, 2 oz cream,
2 whole eggs and 2 extra whites, 1 oz butter, pepper, cayenne pepper, salt,
nutmeg, 2 oz grated Parmesan.

Make a thick béchamel with the butter, flour and heated milk. Add all the meat extracted from the shell and claws of the crab. Stir in the cheese. Season fairly highly. Add the cream, then the beaten yolks of the eggs. Heat over the flame, stirring all the time, but do not allow to boil after the eggs have been put in. Leave to cool. Immediately before the soufflé is to be cooked stir in the four beaten whites. Fill a buttered soufflé dish with the mixture to within an inch of the top. Put in the top of a No. 8 oven, preheated for at least 10 minutes. Cook for about 15 minutes.

You can nearly always tell when a soufflé is ready by the smell which comes from the oven. Unfortunately the perfect-looking soufflé, with that blown-up crust on the top almost separated from the rest of the dish, is not usually the perfect soufflé inside; by the time the top of the soufflé has risen that much, the inside is usually too dry. So it is best to be content with a slightly less spectacular look and have the inside of the soufflé still a little creamy.

The extra whites in this soufflé make it rise well and quickly, the cream helps it to remain moist.

A nice way to serve a soufflé is to cook it in small dishes, one for each person. Special small soufflé dishes are not necessary. Any little fireproof dishes, about 2 inches deep, will do.

Experiment to find out the correct timing is absolutely essential. Every oven is different and much also depends on the size of the dish. A small soufflé for one person takes about 6 or 7 minutes.

✧ MOUSSE OF CRAB ✧

1 large crab, ⅛ pint (2½ oz) of thick cream, a teacupful of aspic (see page 194), lemon, salt, cayenne pepper, 1 tablespoon of grated Parmesan cheese, the whites of 2 eggs.

Extract all the meat from the body and claws of the cooked crab. Pound it in a mortar with the grated Parmesan (this adds both to consistency and flavour) season with a little salt, a little cayenne pepper, a squeeze of lemon juice. Stir in the melted aspic and the cream. Put in the refrigerator or in a cold place until it is all but set, then fold in the stiffly beaten whites of the eggs. Turn into a soufflé dish just large enough to hold the mousse, so that it is completely filled right up to the top. Leave to set.

This makes a very good creamy mousse, which does not set too hard, so, if the weather is exceptionally hot, use a little more aspic.

A cucumber *sambal* (page 49) goes well with crab mousse.

A salmon mousse made in the same way, allowing a large cupful of cooked salmon, is very successful.

If gelatine instead of home-made aspic is used to set a mousse, melt the powder or gelatine leaves (cut in small pieces) in a teacupful of water in a double saucepan. When cool, strain the resulting liquid into the mousse mixture. For the above quantities, 3 gelatine leaves or a tablespoon of powder should be sufficient.

◇ COCKLES ◇

While mussels are to be found during the winter months at most London fishmongers', cockles are sold only ready cooked and shelled, and that rarely (although some London fishmongers have them once or twice a week). Only on the coast can they be bought in their natural state. The cost and trouble of transport is presumably responsible, for they are excellent little shell fish when cooked in the manner of *moules marinière*, and in summer, when mussels are not sold in England, make a good substitute in sauces and soups.

On the east coast of England and in Scotland and Wales cockles are often eaten for tea, plain boiled. A way of eating them in south Wales is to shell them when they have been boiled, fry them in bacon fat, and serve them on hot buttered toast. An old North of England rhyme mentions 'cocklety pie' and 'musselty cake'. Cocklety pie sounds an excellent dish, consisting of cooked shelled cockles stirred into a white sauce, baked in a dish lined with bread-crumbs and covered with a pie crust.

Cockles live in the sand and must therefore be most carefully washed under a running cold-water tap for about ten minutes; then leave them in cold salted water, changed several times, until there is no more sand. Cockles bought ready cooked are seldom properly cleaned and are also inclined to be over-salted, so before putting them into a soup or stew put them in a colander under a running cold tap for at least an hour. Cockles in their shells can be cooked in a little unsalted water, and as soon as the shells open they are ready. They can also be laid on an iron sheet or griddle, over a flame, and eaten straight from the stove, when they have opened, with bread and butter.

If cockles or mussels are bought the day before they are wanted, keep

WEIGALL, CHARLES HARVEY, *Cockle Women*. c. 1875.

them in a bowl of cold water, in a cool larder, covered with a cloth, over which coarse salt has been sprinkled.

Several Victorian cookery books give recipes for cockles. Here is one from Cassell's *Dictionary of Cookery* (1877).

✧ *COCKLE SAUCE* ✧

'Prepare a gallon of cockles as for boiling. Set them on the fire and when the shells open strain the liquid from them, throw the shells away, and strain the liquid through muslin, to clean it from sand. Stir in a pint of good melted butter (remember this is for a large quantity of cockles) and add a tablespoonful of white pepper.

Stir the sauce over the fire for two or three minutes, but do not let it boil, and serve it with cod or haddock. Sufficient for 4 lb of fish.'

MEAT

COTMAN, FREDERICK GEORGE, *One of the Family*. 1880.

MEAT

Grilled steaks or lamb cutlets with young vegetables make the most delightful of summer meat dishes, but it is not always easy to get the best quality meat which is needed for grills, it is expensive, and in any case few people would want them every day. Home-killed veal and lamb are both at their best during the summer months, and it is worth remembering that joints of both are very much more economical to carve (for so long there was nothing to carve that very few people know anything about this art) if they are boned, trimmed and tied by the butcher, who will do it with the minimum of waste. It is useless to be timid when buying meat; the butcher gives the best service and the best meat to the people who insist on getting exactly what they have asked for.

When buying escalopes of veal, which make very agreeable summer dishes, light, quick to prepare and cook, and susceptible of great variation, see that they are cut from the leg, the bone having been taken out, cut very thin and flattened out for you by the butcher, and when ordering a loin of veal or pork ask for the kidney to be left in. Prime cuts are prime only if expertly cut. An eye has to be kept on your butcher to see that when you have asked for fillet steaks you do not get a badly cut hunk from which there will be a lot of waste. Tournedos are small round steaks cut from what is called the eye of the fillet and they should be at least an inch thick.

Cheaper joints allow for plenty of scope in the matter of flavouring with herbs, wine and spices, and all the vegetables of summer, peas, carrots, little turnips, new potatoes, can be cooked with them.

People who have lived in the East think highly of curries as summer dishes; as every other amateur cook in England has his special recipe for curry I have not included any here, but have given instead two or three Oriental dishes which are deliciously spiced without resembling in any way an English-Indian curry; the flavour of the dishes and the methods by which they are cooked may be new to many people; they also give scope for the compounding of attractive fresh chutneys and sauces to be served with them.

For cold meat dishes my own favourites are the classic *bœuf à la mode* (page 245), a boned loin of pork flavoured with fresh herbs and garlic and cooked so gently that all the flavour and moisture are retained (page 125), and a cold leg or loin of veal (page 117) stuffed with kidneys. Boiled beef can be made into a lovely salad but cold lamb and mutton are best chopped or minced and made into croquettes, or later in the season for the stuffing of aubergines, pimentos and small marrows; fortunately mutton, the least attractive of meats to eat cold, also responds better to re-cooking than any other meat.

⬦ *ÉPAULE DE MOUTON À* ⬦
LA BOURGEOISE

A boned and rolled shoulder (or leg) of mutton, butter or dripping, 2 cupfuls of stock (this can be made from the bones), 1 lb new turnips, 1 lb new carrots, herbs, seasoning, garlic, a little flour.

Put at least one clove of garlic into the meat, season it, and brown it in the butter or dripping, sprinkle with flour, and when this has amalgamated with the fat pour over the heated stock. Add herbs (thyme, bayleaf, marjoram) and the carrots and seasoning, cover the pan and cook very gently either in the oven or on top of the stove for about 2 hours (for a piece of meat weighing 2 lb when boned).

Blanch the peeled turnips in boiling salted water for 5 minutes, cut them in quarters, sauté them in butter and about 15 minutes before serving add them to the meat.

There should be enough sauce left with the meat for the turnips to finish cooking; if there is too much fat, pour it off before adding the turnips.

Potatoes instead of turnips can be used, treated in the same way.

⬦ *GIGOT D'AGNEAU* ⬦
À LA FERMIÈRE

A piece of leg of lamb weighing about 3 lb, a wineglass of white wine and one of stock, ½ lb each of new turnips and carrots, 1½ lb of green peas (weighed before shelling) a dozen or so small new potatoes, 4 oz of cream, 2 oz butter, salt, pepper, sugar.

Melt the butter in a thick pan; put in the meat, let it turn golden all over; pour over the wine and let it bubble a few minutes; add the stock; cover the pan and cook it in a medium oven for 30 minutes; now add the carrots, the turnips, and the potatoes, and five minutes later the peas. Season with salt, pepper, a little sugar. Cook gently for 40 minutes, by which time the meat and all the vegetables should be ready: pour off excess fat, sprinkle the meat and vegetables with flour, stir, and add the boiling cream; see that there is sufficient seasoning and simmer 10 more minutes. If mutton is used instead of lamb cook for an hour at least before adding the vegetables.

⋄ GIGOT D'AGNEAU À ⋄ LA PROVENÇALE

A boned and rolled leg (or shoulder) of lamb, 3 aubergines, 1 lb of tomatoes, ¼ lb of green olives, a teacupful of olive oil, 2 cloves of garlic, parsley, salt, pepper.

Stick a clove of garlic into the meat and roast it in the ordinary way. Cut the unpeeled aubergines into thick slices, salt them and leave them to drain for an hour or two.

Skin the tomatoes, chop the second clove of garlic.

Heat the olive oil in a thick frying pan, and sauté the sliced aubergines. Drain them, put them in the roasting pan with the almost cooked meat and add the stoned olives. In the same frying pan cook the tomatoes, cut into quarters, for 4 or 5 minutes, adding the chopped garlic and salt and pepper. Slice the meat for serving, put the aubergines, tomatoes and olives all round in the serving dish, garnish with chopped parsley.

⋄ LAMB ROASTED WITH ⋄ CORIANDER SEEDS

Make a few incisions in a leg of lamb or mutton and into them put cloves of garlic and crushed coriander seeds – about two tablespoons altogether. Rub the meat with salt and pepper, and roast it in the usual way, adding some potatoes half-way through the cooking. The coriander seeds give a perfectly delicious flavour to the meat. Cut it in thick slices to serve, so that everybody gets some of the garlic and coriander. The meat should be very well done, moist and tender.

⬩ CÔTELETTES D'AGNEAU ⬩
BOULANGÈRE

2 onions, 1 lb new potatoes, a teacupful of good stock, 6 lamb cutlets, butter.

Slice the onions finely, and cut the potatoes into two or four pieces each according to size. Arrange them in a buttered fireproof dish, cover with the stock, season lightly, and cook in a slow oven for about an hour. Now brown the cutlets on each side in butter, and put them in the dish with the potatoes. Cook another 20 minutes.

⬩ LAMB CUTLETS WITH ⬩
MINT BUTTER

Make a mint butter as described on page 193. The quantities given will make enough for eight cutlets. Score the meat lightly on both sides and coat it with the butter. Leave for an hour. Grill the cutlets, first on each side close to the grill, then turn them over twice again, cooking farther away from the flame. They will take about 10 minutes altogether. At the same time, if there is room, grill some half-tomatoes, and serve with some of the butter poured over them.

⬩ NOISETTES D'AGNEAU ⬩
EN BROCHETTES

8 lamb cutlets, 6 rashers of lean bacon, salt and pepper, Béarnaise sauce, butter.

Cut all the meat from the cutlets, so that you have 2 or 3 small rounds of meat from each cutlet. Cut each rasher of bacon into 3 or 4 pieces. On small skewers thread alternate pieces of bacon and meat, starting and finishing with the bacon. Season with salt, pepper and lemon juice, sprinkle over them some chopped fresh marjoram, and grill for 8–10 minutes, turning the skewers round two or three times. Serve on a bed of whole, crisp lettuce leaves, with

HODGKIN, ELIOT, *Garlic*, 1970.

lemon and the Béarnaise sauce, having added to it if you like chopped mint and chives instead of the usual tarragon.

A very excellent luncheon dish.

✧ *POLPETTE OF MUTTON* ✧

Polpette are the Italian version of rissoles or croquettes. In Italy they are usually made with veal, but the recipe also provides one of the best ways of using up cooked mutton or lamb.

Mince ½ lb or so of cooked lamb or mutton with a strip of lemon peel, a clove or two of garlic, a few sprigs of parsley. Mix with a slice of white bread which has been soaked in milk and then squeezed dry. Season with salt, pepper and nutmeg, and stir in 2 eggs. On a floured board form the mixture into little round rissoles no larger than half a crown in diameter. This operation should be performed quickly and with a light hand, or the polpette will be heavy. Roll them lightly in flour and fry them in hot oil or a good clear dripping. Drain them on absorbent kitchen paper. Serve with a salad. If carefully drained, not at all greasy, these little rissoles make very nice picnic food.

FILLET OF VEAL
❖ WITH MUSHROOMS ❖
AND CREAM

A piece of leg of veal weighing about 2 lb when boned and rolled, ½ lb of small mushrooms, 1½ oz butter, ¼ pint of thin cream, a little flour, seasonings, marjoram or thyme, garlic, lemon juice.

Rub the veal with salt, pepper and lemon juice. Melt the butter in a thick braising pan. Put in the meat, let it turn just golden all over, add a clove or two of garlic, some fresh marjoram or thyme, cover the pan and cook on top of the stove or in a gentle oven for 1½ hours. When it is tender, add the mushrooms, whole, and cook 5 minutes. Now sprinkle with flour, stir until the sauce has amalgamated and add the cream, which has been boiled in another pan. Cook very gently for another 5 minutes, and serve on a long, hot dish.

❖ CÔTELETTES DE VEAU ❖
AU VIN BLANC

4 veal cutlets, or escalopes, 2 oz ham, 2 oz bacon, the white parts of a few large spring onions, a glass of white wine, flour, butter.

Season the meat, dust it with flour, brown it lightly in butter. Add the ham and bacon cut into strips and the whole small onions. Cook 2 minutes, pour in the white wine. Cover the pan and simmer for 15 minutes. Take out the cutlets, keep them hot. Scrape up the juices in the pan, add a little more white wine and a small lump of butter. Give a quick stir and pour it over the cutlets.

Escalopes can be cooked in the same way. Ten minutes cooking should be enough.

✧ *ESCALOPES DE VEAU* ✧
À LA CRÈME

Escalopes of veal, butter, cream.

Season the escalopes and brown them gently in butter, turning them over and over. When they are tender move them to a hot dish, quickly add ¼ pint (for 6 escalopes) of boiling cream. Give a quick stir so that the butter, cream and juices in the pan are amalgamated, and pour over the escalopes.

✧ *ESCALOPES DE VEAU* ✧
À LA CRÈME AUX
CHAMPIGNONS

4 escalopes of veal, ½ lb of small mushrooms, butter, cream, garlic, salt and pepper, lemon juice.

Season the escalopes with salt, pepper and lemon juice, and flatten them out a little, not too much. Melt an ounce of butter in a frying pan, brown the meat slightly on each side. Add the thinly sliced mushrooms, a scrap of chopped garlic, salt and pepper. Cover the pan and cook gently for 5–7 minutes, until the mushrooms are done. Transfer to the serving dish. Into the pan, but off the fire, pour ¼ pint of boiling cream. Scrape up the juices in the pan so that they amalgamate with the cream and form a pale coffee-coloured sauce. Stir a few seconds over the flame, and pour over the veal and mushrooms.

✧ *ESCALOPES DE VEAU* ✧
EN AÏLLADE

4 escalopes of veal cut from the leg, 1 lb of tomatoes, olive oil, 4 or 5 cloves of garlic, a handful of dried breadcrumbs, salt, pepper, a bunch of parsley.

Cover the bottom of a thick sauté pan with olive oil. When it is hot (but not boiling) put in the seasoned escalopes. Cook them gently so that they are just golden on each side. Add the skinned and chopped tomatoes and, as soon as they have melted, the breadcrumbs, the chopped garlic and parsley, and cook another 8–10 minutes, by which time most of the oil should be absorbed, and the tomatoes turned to a thick sauce.

⋄ ESCALOPES DE VEAU ⋄ AU FENOUIL

Brown escalopes of veal in pork dripping or butter. Add 2 or 3 spring onions for each escalope; cover the pan and simmer for 7 or 8 minutes. Throw in a handful of finely chopped fennel leaves; stir, add a squeeze of lemon. Excellent.

⋄ ESCALOPES OF ⋄ MINCED VEAL

Veal escalopes, as indeed all prime cuts of veal, have risen to a prohibitive price. Many butchers, however, sell the trimmings of the good-quality joints ready minced, or in cubes as 'pie veal', at very reasonable prices. Out of this veal a number of excellent good-value dishes can be devised. Here is one which can make an alternative to the expensive escalopes proper specified in some of the foregoing recipes.

> 1 lb of minced raw veal, two heaped teaspoons of chopped mixed parsley, shallot and lemon rind. Seasonings of salt, pepper and lemon juice. Flour; 1 egg; 3 tablespoons each of dry white wine, dry vermouth or port, and clear meat stock, *or* if no genuine stock is available, 4 tablespoons of the wine and 2 of plain water. Oil and butter for cooking the escalopes.

Mix the chopped shallot (or tiny onion), parsley and lemon peel with the minced meat. Add several turns of pepper from the mill, a couple of teaspoons of salt, and the juice of half a small lemon. Stir in the well-beaten egg.

Flour a board and your hands. Divide the meat into six or eight portions. Form each into a little round cake about the size of a golf ball, and roll them in flour. Leave them for an hour or so in a cold place. When you are ready to cook the meat, flour a rolling-pin and roll each cake out to a thickness of not

PISSARRO, CAMILLE, *The Market*, 1884.

more than half an inch and approximately the shape of a small escalope, dusting each one with flour as you turn it over.

In a wide frying pan heat two tablespoons each of butter and oil. Put in the escalopes (in an average 10-inch frying pan there will be room only for three or four of the escalopes. They will probably have to be cooked in two batches). Let them cook for a couple of minutes. Turn them over. Both sides should be nicely browned. Turn them again. Now add the wine (only half of it if you are doing two batches); let it bubble a few seconds. Lower the heat, add stock or water. Simmer gently for 7 to 10 minutes. Transfer the escalopes to a hot serving dish and keep them warm in the oven while you pour off the juices into a bowl and cook the second batch of meat in a fresh lot of oil and butter and the rest of the wine and stock; arrange all the cooked escalopes on the serving dish, pour the first lot of juices back into the pan with the second batch, boil them up quickly, and pour them bubbling over the escalopes.

Serve with quarters of lemon round the dish, and if you like, a little chopped parsley on the top.

Freshly cooked leaf spinach or Belgian endives braised in butter are both delicious and refreshing vegetables with this dish, so are small new buttered carrots; but a salad of sliced firm tomatoes or even a bowl of watercress or a plain lettuce salad can take the place of hot vegetables.

⋄ A VEAL AND ⋄
HAM PIE

1½ lb of veal, ½ lb ham, ½ lb bacon, 4 hard-boiled eggs, ¼ lb mushrooms, fresh thyme, parsley, mace, salt, pepper, ½ pint of very good beef or veal stock which will jelly when cold, pastry.

Cut the veal in thin slices about 3½ by 2½ inches. Season with salt, pepper, mace and chopped herbs, lay a rasher of bacon on each slice and roll it up. Arrange these rolls in layers in the buttered pie dish, and over each layer strew more herbs, slices of mushroom, hard-boiled egg and ham, and on top of the final layer put rashers of bacon. Pour in the stock. Cover with pastry and cook in a moderate oven for an hour and a quarter. Can be eaten hot but is best cold.

❖ *VITELLO TONNATO* ❖

This is one of the standard summer dishes of restaurants all over Italy. The following recipe is from an Abruzzesi *trattoria* in Rome, where the *vitello tonnato* was particularly good, although not the classic version.

Make a good cupful of mayonnaise with 2 yolks of eggs, olive oil and lemon juice. Pound or sieve about 2 oz of best-quality tunny fish in oil, and add this to the mayonnaise. Thin slightly with juice from the roast fillet of veal. Cut the cold fillet of veal (which should have been boned before cooking) into slices, and pack it into a deep dish into which it will just fit. Pour the prepared sauce over and leave till next day.

This very delicate *vitello tonnato* is usually eaten as a very light main dish, although in some regions of Italy, notably in Piedmont, it is commonly offered as a first course, or *antipasto*.

❖ *COLD LOIN OF VEAL* ❖
WITH KIDNEYS

2½–3 lb of loin of veal with the kidneys, white wine, carrots, onions, garlic, marjoram or thyme, an extra ¼ lb of veal kidneys or 2 lamb's kidneys.

Have the loin of veal boned, but leave the kidneys. Lay the boned meat out on a board, trim off most of the fat from the kidneys, spike the meat with little pieces of garlic here and there, lay the extra kidneys, trimmed of fat and skinned, on top of the meat, season with salt and pepper, add a sprig of fresh marjoram or thyme, roll the meat up, enclosing the kidneys, and tie into a round. Put it into a braising pan or roasting tin, pour over a glass of white wine and 2 of water. Add 2 or 3 carrots and a small onion, and the bones which were taken from the meat. Cover the pan, and cook in a moderate oven (Regulo 3 or 4) for 2–2½ hours. During the last 15 or 20 minutes of cooking, remove the lid, so that the meat browns.

Take out the meat and leave it to cool. Cook the stock, with the bones, gently for another 30 or 40 minutes. Strain it, leave it to cool. It should set to a jelly. Take off the fat.

To serve, carve the veal into slices, and garnish with squares of the jelly. A truffle, even a tinned one (there are no fresh ones in summer), sliced and put on to the meat before it is rolled up makes this dish even better. Pour the juice from the tin into the sauce during the final cooking.

⋄ *TOURNEDOS BÉARNAISE* ⋄

A tournedos is a small round steak, nearly an inch thick, cut from the fillet and trimmed of all fat. Ask your butcher to cut them from the eye of the fillet. This is the genuine tournedos. A tournedos can be either grilled or fried. If to be fried, first heat a thick frying pan without any fat. When it is very hot put in the seasoned steaks and let them sizzle until the meat is sealed

BELLIS, HUBERT, (1831-1902), *La Côte de Boeuf.*

and brown on one side, then turn them over and brown the other side. Now turn down the flame, put a lump of butter in the pan and cook gently another 2 or 3 minutes, allowing about 5 minutes altogether for a 4-oz steak. If the steak is to be grilled, put it, seasoned, very close to the very hot grill, and brown it on each side. Then move it farther away from the flame, baste it with a little butter, and cook approximately another 3 minutes.

Serve on a very hot dish, garnished with watercress, and the Béarnaise sauce (page 183) separately.

Some cooks contend that steak should be salted only after cooking, as the salt tends to make the juice run. If the pan or grill is really hot before the meat is put to cook the juices are immediately sealed, so that salting it before cooking does no harm, and usually makes for a better flavour.

✧ TOURNEDOS À L'ESTRAGON ✧

Cook small fillet steaks in a little butter in the usual way. When they are browned on both sides, and little beads of juice begin to filter out into the pan, pour over a large tablespoon of madeira or port (for each two fillets). Let them bubble for a little under a minute, stir in a dessertspoonful of chopped tarragon and ½ oz of butter. Put the steaks on the serving dish and pour the sauce over.

✧ TOURNEDOS À LA NIÇOISE ✧

Chop the leaves of a few sprigs of fresh basil and pound it with a small piece of garlic and a little salt; work it into an ounce of butter. Put a portion of this basil butter on top of each grilled or fried fillet steak before serving.

✧ ENTRECÔTE GRILLÉE À ✧ LA MAÎTRE D'HÔTEL

An entrecôte is usually a sirloin steak cut about ½ inch thick, weighing 4 to 6 oz for each person.

Remove skin, gristle, and most of the fat from the steaks. Flatten the steaks out a little, but don't beat them heavily, it spoils the meat. Score the edges lightly with a sharp knife, which will prevent them turning up and hardening during the cooking. Paint the steaks lightly with olive oil. Heat the grill and put the steaks under it, close to the flame, and cook on each side for a minute, then remove the grid a little farther away from the flame, and cook about 2 minutes more on each side. One minute per ounce is about the right timing to get a ½-inch steak grilled *à point*; if you want them well done leave them an extra minute. Put the steaks on the prepared hot dish on which you have already placed the maître d'hôtel butter (see page 192). It is the juice from the meat combined with the butter, just melting, which makes this very simple sauce so good. Salt and pepper the steaks only when they are ready to serve.

❖ *ENTRECÔTE BERCY* ❖

Cook the entrecôtes as for the above recipe, and when they are ready on the serving dish, with a bunch of watercress at each end, pour over them the sauce Bercy (page 192).

❖ *LE BŒUF À LA BORDELAISE* ❖

Pour 2 glasses of white wine over a piece of round of beef weighing about 3 lb. Add thyme, bayleaf, peppercorns, a sliced onion and clove of garlic. Leave it to marinate for 12 hours. Remove the beef next day, wipe it with a cloth, season with salt and put into a roasting pan with good dripping; cook it fairly slowly, basting from time to time.

In the meantime make a sauce by stirring 2 tablespoons of flour into an ounce of hot butter, then adding the heated and strained marinade; let it cook 15 minutes. When the beef is ready, put it on the serving dish, drain off the fat in the pan, add a little water to the remaining juice and pour this into the prepared sauce, which is strained if necessary, and served separately.

❖ *DAUBE À LA CORSOISE* ❖

2 lb of rolled rib or round of beef, ¼ lb of bacon cut into small thick strips, ½ lb of small mushrooms, 4 large ripe tomatoes, ¼ lb stoned black olives, 1 lb of new potatoes, a small glass of brandy, garlic, olive oil, fresh thyme.

Warm a little olive oil in a deep, narrow casserole, put in the beef, which has been rubbed with salt and pepper. Let it brown gently on both sides; add the bacon, the tomatoes peeled and cut into quarters, 2 or 3 cloves of garlic, seasoning, the thyme, and the olives. Pour over the brandy. Cover the pan and cook in a very slow oven for 2 hours. When the meat is all but cooked, add the mushrooms, and the potatoes which have been cooked in olive oil or butter until nearly tender. Cook another 10 to 15 minutes. There is no need to add any liquid to this stew; the tomatoes make sufficient. Take care not to add too much salt to start with.

✧ FARSO MAGRO ✧

(A Sicilian Dish)

2 lb of lean beef, rump steak for preference, in one piece, 1 lb of minced beef, 6 eggs, 1 lb of green peas, 3 oz of tongue, 3 oz of ham, an onion, a clove of garlic, 2 tablespoons of breadcrumbs, 3 tablespoons of grated Parmesan, celery leaves, a carrot, olive oil, salt, pepper, nutmeg, parsley, 2 teaspoons of concentrated tomato purée, a small glass of red wine.

Chop the parsley and the garlic together and mix them in a bowl with the minced meat. Add the breadcrumbs, which should have been softened in a little water and then pressed dry, the grated cheese, salt, pepper and nutmeg, and two beaten eggs.

Hard boil the remaining 4 eggs; cut them, with the ham and the tongue, into strips.

Flatten out the piece of rump steak on a board, cover it with the prepared stuffing; on top of this arrange the sliced tongue, ham and hard-boiled eggs; roll up the meat like a sausage and tie it round with string, but not too tightly. See that the ends are closed so that the stuffing does not escape.

In a pan which will just about hold the rolled meat, warm the olive oil; put in the chopped onion, carrot and celery leaves; on top of the vegetables put the meat; let it brown all over; add the red wine and let it bubble a little. Stir in the tomato purée, then add about ½ a teacupful of water. Cover the pan and cook gently for an hour; if the pan is not too big the liquid will not dry up, but if it does add a little stock or water. When the meat is all but cooked add the shelled peas and cook another 20 minutes, or until they are tender. Remove the string and serve the *farso* surrounded by the sauce and the peas.

To serve cold (and it is really at its best this way) omit the peas, do not untie the meat until it is cold and remove the fat from the top of the sauce.

◇ *SIKH KEBAB* ◇

1½ lb lean meat without bone, either beef, mutton or veal, 1½ tablespoons of curry powder, 1 tablespoon of curry paste, lemon juice, a cupful of curds or yoghourt.

Mix the curry powder and the curry paste together, moisten with lemon juice, and mix it with the curds or yoghourt.

Score the meat deeply across in several places, and steep it in the curry mixture for an hour; then cut it up into inch squares, and leave it another hour or so. Now thread the meat on skewers, and grill for about 10 minutes, basting once or twice with a little dripping. If you have green ginger, which is fresh ginger root, a few thin slices on each skewer, between the pieces of meat, give a delicious flavour.

This form of curry is usually eaten not with rice but with chappattee, flat bread made on a griddle. The skewers can also be served on a bed of shredded lettuce, dressed with oil and lemon, and a chutney or a cucumber sambal (p 49) makes a nice accompaniment.

◇ *BEEF SALAD* ◇

The beef which has been boiled for a consommé or stock is better made into a salad rather than reheated in a hash or rissoles; cut it into thinnish slices, arrange in a shallow dish, and pour over it a vinaigrette sauce made with plenty of olive oil, a little lemon juice, chopped *fines herbes* (parsley, tarragon, chives, or whatever fresh herbs are available), a few capers, a little garlic, salt and pepper, and, if you like, a little mustard.

Leave the meat to marinate in the sauce for an hour or two, then add 3 or 4 boiled, skinned and sliced potatoes, well seasoned with the same vinaigrette sauce; garnish with slices of hard-boiled eggs, a very few radishes, or sliced cucumbers.

Made on a large scale, this salad is an admirable, and relatively cheap, cold supper or buffet party dish.

PAUPIETTES OF BEEF
✧ *BRAISED WITH GAME STOCK* ✧

1½ lb of good-quality lean beef, preferably rump steak, a casserole grouse, a glass of port, a 4–oz tin of liver pâté, or home-made chicken-liver pâté (see page 42) or minced pork, parsley, herbs, garlic.

Cook a casserole grouse as described on page 149. Chop the breast of the bird and mix it with the liver pâté or minced meat, the chopped garlic and fresh herbs. Cut the beef into four slices, trim off the fat and skin, beat the meat slices out flat, season with salt and pepper, and cover each with a thin layer of the prepared game and liver mixture. Roll them up and tie them. Heat an ounce of butter in a thick pan, brown the paupiettes all over, pour over the port. Let it bubble, then add just enough of the grouse stock to come half-way up the meat. Cover the pan and simmer very gently for 1 to 1½ hours. Take out the paupiettes, remove the string and transfer to the serving dish. Reduce the sauce if necessary, pour over the paupiettes, garnish with parsley.

COLD BAKED SALT
✧ *SILVERSIDE OF BEEF* ✧

5 to 6 lb of salt silverside of beef; onions; carrots; garlic; bayleaves; peppercorns. Optional: a tumbler of red wine or cider.

Salt silverside is a true English speciality often overlooked when it comes to home entertaining. A pity, for it can be delicious, and when served cold is economical, and presents the minimum of cooking and serving problems.

Give your butcher due warning that you will be needing a handsome piece of salt beef, otherwise he may not have any which has been long enough in the pickle.

Before cooking it, soak it in cold water for a couple of hours.

Put the beef in a deep ovenproof pot in which there is not too much room to spare. Surround it with a couple of large carrots and onions sliced, a crushed clove of garlic, 2 bayleaves, half a dozen peppercorns and, if you are using it, the wine or cider (all these extra flavourings not only improve the taste of the meat but help to produce a stock which, next day, will make the basis of a beautiful beetroot and onion soup), and fill up the pot with water. Cover the pot closely.

Place in a very moderate oven and leave untouched for 3 to 4 hours. Test to see if the meat is tender. Don't let it overcook, or it will crumble when carved. Take the joint from the liquid, wrap it in greaseproof paper, put it in a deep bowl, on top of it put a tea plate or a small board, and a 2-lb weight. Leave until next day.

With the beef have tomato and cucumber salads, and a mild fruit chutney.

✧ BAKED BRISKET OF BEEF ✧

Brisket can be baked in exactly the same way as the silverside above. It is a cheaper cut than silverside, but if cooked in a reasonably large piece, not less than 5 or 6 lb, it is, I think, even better. In small joints, however, there is seldom the correct proportion of lean to fat, so then it is no economy.

When you get towards the end of these beef joints and they can no longer be properly carved, the rest can be cut in small pieces and with a vinaigrette dressing containing chopped shallots, plenty of parsley, and perhaps a few capers and little bits of cucumber, will make an excellent beef salad.

⋄ COLD ROAST PORK ⋄

A joint of pork always seems to me better cold than hot. It is usually a fat meat, so when cold is moist, but firm and easy to carve. (The crackling is the great attraction about hot roast pork to most English people, but if you are going to serve the meat cold, the rind must be cut off, and if you like, roasted with the meat and served at the same time. It is just as delicious cold. In France pork is always bought from the butcher with the rind already cut off, and the rind, called *couenne*, is sold separately for adding to soups and *daubes*.)

To get a really perfectly cooked piece of cold pork get the butcher to bone a piece of leg or loin, and cut off the rind. Make a few incisions in the meat and in these put a little garlic mixed with chopped fresh herbs (fennel, or lemon thyme, or a very little rosemary mixed with parsley) and ground black pepper and salt. Put the meat in a baking tin, cover it with the rind, put the bone in the tin, add water to come half-way up the meat and cook in a slow oven (about Regulo 4), allowing at least 35 minutes to the pound. When it is cooked pour off all the liquid into a bowl, and when it is cold take off the fat. It should have set to a light jelly to serve with the cold pork. If it has not, reduce it by fast boiling for a few minutes, and let it cool again. If the rind is not crisp enough let it go on cooking in a gentle oven. It is delicious to serve in little pieces with drinks.

A good accompaniment to cold pork, instead of the usual potato salad, is honeydew or sugar melon, cut into cubes, and served very crisp and cold, but with no sauce or seasoning other than lemon juice.

⋄ TERRINE OF VEAL AND PORK ⋄

1 lb of veal, 1 lb of pork, 6 oz bacon, 2 cloves of garlic, thyme, a bayleaf, mace, salt, ground black pepper, a glass (about 4 oz) of white wine, 1 pint of aspic jelly prepared from calf's or pig's feet.

Chop the meat fairly coarsely with the bacon and garlic. Season with herbs and spices, stir in the white wine. Put into a terrine, add melted aspic to come just level with the meat. Put a bayleaf on top, cover the terrine, and cook in a bain-marie in a moderate oven for two hours. When cold cover with the rest of the aspic. If to be kept, seal with melted dripping when the aspic has set.

Ingredients can be varied – for instance, ham can be used instead of bacon, more or less garlic can be used, and port or red wine instead of white; spices and herbs can be varied according to taste.

⬥ PIG'S HEAD ⬥
IN JELLY

Half a pig's head, about ¾ lb of pork meat (loin chops, or a piece of leg), 2 or 3 carrots, white wine, pepper, salt, a teaspoonful of coriander seeds, a small piece of orange peel, parsley or tarragon, thyme.

Have the pig's head cleaned and the rind cut off. Rub it lightly with salt. Put the pork meat at the bottom of a deep pan, strew it with a little salt, ground pepper, the pounded coriander seeds, a sprig of thyme, the orange peel and 2 or 3 cloves of garlic. Put the pig's head in the pan with its rind on the top, and the carrots round it. Pour over a small glass of white wine and 1½ pints of water. Cook in a slow oven for about 3 hours until the meat is falling from the bones. When cool strain off the stock into a basin, and remove every scrap of bone from the head. Cut all the meat into fairly large rough pieces, and arrange them in a deep bowl with the sliced carrots, taking care that there are absolutely no chips of bone, and no hard pieces of gristle or skin. See that the pieces of tongue are well distributed amongst the rest of the meat. When the stock in the basin has set take off the fat, heat it up, clarify it if you like, leave it to cool again, and just before it sets stir into it about two tablespoons of finely chopped tarragon or parsley mixed with one or two chopped cloves of garlic. Pour this over the meat and leave to set. This is not intended to be an elegant dish, it is coarse country food, but with plenty of flavour, and rather more interesting than the ordinary brawn. Serve a good green salad with it, or boiled new potatoes.

MANET, EDOUARD, (1832-1883), *The Ham*.

✧ *HAM OR GAMMON* ✧

A good ham or gammon is so delicious cold, served quite plain or with a potato or green salad, or with a mild fruit chutney or a Cumberland sauce, that it seems unnecessary to do anything further about it. Twice-cooked ham is always disappointing, and even for ham and eggs the ham is best, to my way of thinking, cold; it dries up and tastes salty when grilled or fried. The end of a ham, however, can be made into a very successful mousse or mixed with veal and pork for a terrine; there are soups, sauces, vegetable and meat dishes described in this book which require small quantities of ham in their composition, and they will be found listed under ham in the index, as well as under the actual names of the dishes.

⋄ BAKED WILTSHIRE ⋄
GAMMON

This simplest of all methods of cooking a handsome piece of Wiltshire-cured corner or middle gammon, weighing about 6 lb, will produce one of the best English specialities in its most perfect form.

Steep the gammon in cold water for a minimum of 18 hours. Wrap the joint in two or three sheets of aluminium foil so that it is completely enclosed. Stand this parcel on a rack which is placed in a baking tin containing a little water, so that the steam rising from it during the baking helps to keep the gammon moist.

Reckoning half an hour to the pound, cook the gammon in the centre of a moderate oven, gas No. 3 or 330°F. All you have to do is to turn the parcel over at half-time. When the time is up, take the gammon, still standing on its rack, from the oven and let it stand 45 minutes before unwrapping it, gently peeling off the rind, and replacing it with fine golden breadcrumbs. Leave until the next day. Carve into elegant thin slices, each with its edging of delicate white fat, and serve with a plain green salad.

⋄ TERRINE OF HAM, PORK ⋄
AND VEAL

1 lb each of ham (cooked), pork and veal (raw), white wine, brandy, garlic, bayleaves, ¼ lb bacon, mace, pepper, salt, juniper berries, thyme, marjoram.

Mince the pork and the veal, cut the ham into small squares. Mix all together, add a clove of garlic chopped with 5 or 6 juniper berries, a little fresh thyme, marjoram, coarsely ground black pepper, about half a teaspoon of mace, and a very little salt, as the ham will probably be salty. Put the whole mixture into a bowl and pour over a small glass of white wine and 2 tablespoons of brandy. Leave for an hour or two. Cover the bottom of a fairly shallow terrine with little strips of bacon about 2 inches long. Put in the meat mixture, cover with more little strips of bacon and put a bayleaf or two in the centre. Put the terrine in a baking dish filled with water and bake in a slow oven for 2½–3 hours. Leave to cool.

Serve with toast and a salad.

❖ CERVELLES DE VEAU À ❖ LA PROVENÇALE

Blanch and strain the whole calf's brains. When cool put them to marinate for an hour in olive oil highly seasoned with salt and pepper and a clove of garlic. Turn them over two or three times so that they are well impregnated with the oil. Drain them from the oil, cook them in white wine, leave to cool. Cut them in even slices, arrange them in a ring. Fill the centre with mayonnaise, and garnish with a ring of stoned olives. To be served as a cold luncheon dish.

Recipe from *Le Cuisinier Européen* Jules Breteuil, *circa* 1880.

❖ KIDNEYS AND MUSHROOMS ❖

½ lb kidneys (even ox kidney is good cooked in this way), ¼ lb mushrooms, port or marsala, garlic, parsley, butter, flour.

Soak the kidneys in warm salted water for 2 or 3 hours. Cut into slices about ¼ inch thick, salt and pepper them and roll them in flour. Sauté them in butter. Pour over them a small glass (about 2 oz) of port or marsala, let it bubble a few seconds and add enough water to come just about level with the kidneys. Stew very gently for an hour. Now add the mushrooms, which should if possible be the medium-sized flat kind; wash them and leave them whole. At the same time add a chopped clove of garlic. Simmer for another half-hour. Before serving add a little cut parsley. This is an excellent way of dealing with tough kidneys, and the appearance of the dish, black and dark red, is beautiful.

A purée of potatoes, into which some fresh herbs (lemon thyme is especially good) have been mixed, goes well with it. Enough for two.

❖ PAUPIETTES OF LIVER ❖

½ lb of calf's liver, ½ lb of bacon, 4 tomatoes or a coffee-cupful of freshly made tomato sauce, a small glass of port or marsala, a coffee-cupful of chicken or meat stock, 1 oz of butter, flour, fresh thyme or marjoram, lemon juice.

Buy the liver in one piece, and cut it into very thin slices, a little smaller than the rashers of bacon. On each rasher of bacon lay a slice of liver, season with a very little salt, ground black peper, and lemon juice; add 3 or 4 leaves of marjoram or thyme. Roll up the paupiettes with the bacon on the outside, secure with little skewers. Heat the butter, sauté the paupiettes in it, sprinkle sparingly with flour; stir, and add the marsala; let it bubble, then add the tomatoes, skinned and chopped small, or the tomato sauce, then the stock. Cover the pan and cook gently for about 10 minutes. Remove the skewers, and serve.

✧ FOIE DE VEAU FINES HERBES ✧

Season the slices of calf's liver with salt, pepper and lemon juice. Dust with flour. Brown on each side in butter. Pour over a little stock, or two tablespoons of marsala, cover the pan, and lower the heat. Simmer 4 or 5 minutes. Sprinkle with 2 tablespoons of fresh herbs (lemon thyme, marjoram, parsley, fennel, whatever is available) chopped with a little piece of garlic and a little strip of lemon peel. Squeeze a little lemon juice over and serve.

Calf's liver can also be cooked in any of the ways described for escalopes of veal.

✧ OX TONGUE WITH ✧ PURÉE OF PEAS

A brined ox tongue, 2 carrots, an onion, a leek, 3 lb of green peas, 2 oz of butter, herbs.

Soak the tongue for 24 hours in cold water. Blanch for 20 minutes in boiling water. Strain. Put it back to cook with the onion and carrots and herbs and salt and pepper, just covered with water. Simmer very gently for 2 hours.

In the meantime cook the shelled peas and the cleaned and chopped leek in water, sieve them. Heat up the resulting purée with the butter. Put in the middle of a heated dish, and round the purée the tongue skinned and cut in slices, and if necessary reheated a few moments in the cooking liquid, with a little sauce Bercy (page 192) poured over them. Serve more sauce separately.

POULTRY
AND GAME

RENOIR, PIERRE AUGUSTE, *The End of the Lunch*, 1879.

POULTRY AND
GAME

The quality of poultry for the table has greatly improved during the past year or two; the revolt against battery birds is having its effect. An increasing number of respectable poulterers are now able to supply free-range birds at fair prices. It is important therefore to know what kind of bird you need for the dish you intend to cook. A roasting chicken has not necessarily a better flavour and texture than a boiling chicken, but it is much more tender, so that it is not suitable for slow cooking; it will be ready before the vegetables, herbs and wine which go into a stew have contributed sufficient flavours to the dish.

Apart from being roasted or baked, a tender bird can be cut into pieces for frying, grilling, for a fricassée or for braising in butter with quickly cooked vegetables such as tomatoes, mushrooms or green peas.

A boiling fowl is always best cooked whole, so that its juices and flavour are preserved. It can always be carved when ready and kept hot in its sauce in a bain-marie. In spite of lengthy simmering the flesh of a boiling chicken does not disintegrate and there is usually plenty of breast meat, so it is suitable for cold dishes.

Whereas a young roasting chicken is mild and delicate food which repays cooking with good butter, cream and wine with a light-handed addition of herbs (tarragon and fresh basil are particularly good for chicken), an older and tougher bird serves for more aromatic stews flavoured with bacon, garlic and coarse red wine, or as a background for sauces compounded of oriental spices, oil, almonds, walnuts. A boiling fowl also makes a very excellent mousse and the possibilities of cold chicken salads are endless.

Duck makes beautiful cold summer dishes; in fact, being a fat bird, it is always better cold; you get more flavour from it and better value; it will produce lovely jellied sauces, particularly when a calf's foot has been stewed with it; it can be cooked with red, white, or dessert wines, brandy, curaçao, kirsch, and various fruits, oranges, cherries, peaches, figs (not all at once), can be incorporated in some way to make a dish of great character; for those who don't care for the combination of fruit and meat, broad beans, baby turnips, mushrooms, the classic green peas go with duck. Mint, tarragon and other fresh green herbs can go into the sauce, or into the accompanying salad. Frozen duckling are not to be recommended. They are flabby and lacking in savour.

Rabbits and pigeons are not exactly elegant party food, but all the same make good and savoury countrified dishes, and first-class terrines and pâtés.

The only other summer game, technically, is the grouse and venison. Wild duck and teal from the deep freeze may make an occasional variation for summer meals; unlike the domestic duck they appear to suffer very little from the freezing process, and for pies or terrines or sandwiches do very well indeed.

◇ GRILLED CHICKEN ◇

A grilled chicken is perhaps one of the nicest foods at any time; everybody likes it, it needs very little preparation, is quickly cooked, and although expensive, there is nothing to be spent on extras, so it could be much less rare than it is. It is true that the grill on many household cookers is large enough for only one chicken cut in half, but even this inadequate arrangement produces a very delicious meal for two people.

To make a good grilled chicken, you need a really first-rate-quality spring chicken (not a *petit poussin*; I do not understand why these flabby, insipid little birds are considered such a luxury) weighing about 1½ lb when plucked and cleaned and ready to cook. Split them down the back, and then right through, into two halves. Rub them over with lemon juice, season with ground black pepper, stew over them a few fresh herbs such as thyme, lemon thyme or marjoram (no sage or rosemary), paint them with olive oil, and leave them for an hour.

Heat the grill, put the bird on the wire grid, skin side uppermost, and pour over it a little melted butter. Let the skin brown, which will take about 5 minutes; turn it over, baste the inside with a little more melted butter, and grill another 5 minutes. Now move the chicken from the wire grid on to the grilling tray, so that it is farther away from the heat. Turn it over again, and strew a little coarse salt on it , and baste again; leave it about 4 minutes, turn it over again and salt the inside, and again baste it (there should be a certain amount of liquid in the pan by now). In 4 minutes it should be ready, golden, crackling and tender, although the exact timing must be determined by the heat of the grill, which varies in every cooker.

Have ready a long dish liberally spread with a bed of watercress, lettuce, mustard and cress, corn salad, whatever green stuff happens to be in season. Put the grilled chicken on this, a half lemon at each end of the dish, and serve at once on very hot plates. Any sauce or vegetable is unnecessary and would distract attention from the chicken; anyhow there is no room for anything else on the plate, but serve afterwards a salad – not a green salad, as there has been enough with the chicken, but raw mushrooms, or tomatoes, or in the season, a little dish of fresh green peas, or artichoke hearts; or simply a very good and not too heavy cheese – Pont l'Évêque is the ideal, particularly if you are drinking claret or burgundy with the chicken; if white wine, then Gruyère or a fresh cream cheese.

✧ SPICED GRILLED CHICKEN ✧

For 2 small spring chickens weighing about 1 lb each when cleaned, the spices required are 2 teaspoonfuls of coriander seeds, 12 cardamoms, 1 oz of green ginger, * ½ teaspoon of ground cloves, salt, black pepper, with a little butter and olive oil.

For the sauce, 2 onions, ½ teaspoon of turmeric, ½ teaspoon of pounded green ginger, a pot of yoghourt, 2 oz of cream, a handful of currants, a little butter and oil.

To serve with the chicken: lemons, mustard and cress, chutney.

Put the coriander seeds to roast for 2 or 3 minutes in a warm oven. Pound the cardamoms and remove the husks as they split; add the coriander seeds and the peeled and sliced green ginger, the cloves, a little salt, and a few black peppercorns. Pound all these spices together, then work them into a paste with a little olive oil and butter.

Have the chickens each split in half down the centre. Lift up the skins, and with the point of a knife score the flesh very slightly. Rub the prepared spice mixture into the flesh, draw the skin of the bird carefully back into place, and rub also the cut side of the chickens with the spices. These preparations should be made two hours before the chickens are to be cooked. Put a little piece of butter on each half of the chicken and grill them as described in the preceding recipe. Serve on a long dish, on a bed of mustard and cress, with halves of lemon, the prepared sauce, and a mild chutney.

*For a method of storing green ginger root see page 239.

To make the sauce, melt a little olive oil and butter in a frying pan; fry the onions slowly until they turn golden; stir in the turmeric and the green ginger, salt and pepper. Cook another 5 minutes, then add the yoghourt, and stir until thick, then add the cream and the currants. The sauce can be prepared in advance and heated up in a double saucepan.

This recipe is a variation on the Indian kubab chicken, and if preferred, the chickens can be fried in butter, or pot-roasted, the sauce being added towards the end of the cooking.

✧ *LA POULE AU POT* ✧

One of the simplest and best of all chicken recipes when you have a boiling fowl to cook. A large deep saucepan or earthenware pot is essential, so that there is plenty of room for a variety of vegetables and a good covering of water, or the broth will boil away and its goodness be lost.

The chicken, a large boiler, is first stuffed with a mixture of the pounded liver of the bird, a good handful of breadcrumbs and a little chopped bacon, garlic and parsley, into which you stir an egg or two. Brown the chicken all over in good dripping or butter, add carrots, a couple of turnips, an onion, a sliced leek, a piece of celery, and salt and pepper. Pour in boiling water to cover the bird and the vegetables, and when the water comes to the boil again remove any scum which has risen to the top. Cover the pan and simmer very slowly for about three hours. Thirty minutes or so before serving, the vegetables which have been cooking in the pot and which will probably be rather sodden, can be removed, and fresh ones added.

Serve with the sauce *vinaigrette aux œufs* described on page 191. The broth can either be served as a first course, or kept for another meal. In this case a little rice can be boiled in it to give it body.

✧ *CHICKEN SALAD* ✧

A cold roast or boiled chicken with all the flesh taken from the bones and cut into nice fillets, ¼ lb of mushrooms, cooked as for champignons *à la grecque* (page 40) or sliced raw mushrooms, 1 lb of cooked new potatoes, 2 cos lettuce hearts, a few tails of Dublin Bay prawns, or ordinary prawns, cooked and shelled, the yolk of a hard-boiled egg, about ¼ pint of mayonnaise flavoured with grated horseradish (see page 188).

Put the pieces of chicken with the sliced potatoes and the mushrooms into a bowl and mix them with half the mayonnaise. Cover them with the rest of the mayonnaise. On top put the lettuce hearts, cut into quarters, the prawns, and the egg yolk put straight through a sieve on to the salad, so that it rests lightly and decoratively on the top.

This obviously is not a cheap dish, but using a 3-lb chicken the amounts given should be enough for seven or eight people. For four people use half a chicken, ½ lb of potatoes and the rest of the ingredients in the quantity given.

❖ POULET CÉLESTINE ❖

A 2–2½-lb roasting chicken, 1½ oz butter, a liqueur glass of brandy, 4 oz of white wine, 3 oz of cream, 2 slices of ham, ½ lb of tomatoes, ¼ lb of mushrooms.

Season the chicken inside with salt and pepper; melt the butter; add the slices of ham; on top of this put the chicken, breast side downwards; when it is golden on both sides add the brandy, and set it alight; when the flames have gone out add the wine; leave to bubble a couple of minutes, then put in the peeled tomatoes, and the whole mushrooms, then the heated cream. Season the sauce, cover the pan and cook gently for 30–40 minutes (25 if cut-up chicken is used). By the time the chicken is cooked the tomatoes should have melted into the sauce but if it is too thin remove the chicken to the serving dish and reduce the sauce by fast boiling for a minute or two. Serve with the mushrooms all round and the sauce poured over the chicken.

A chicken of this size is always supposed to feed four people, but personally I find it enough only for two with a little left over, or possibly three not very hungry people.

❖ POULET À L'ESTRAGON ❖

A simple version of chicken cooked with tarragon, one of the nicest of chicken dishes, and essentially a summer one, as it can be successfully made only with fresh tarragon.

Work a tablespoon of chopped tarragon leaves with 2 oz of butter, season with salt and pepper, and stuff a 3-lb roasting chicken with this mixture.

Cook the chicken in butter in a thick, covered casserole. The bird should be laid on its side, not breast upwards, and should be turned over half-way through the cooking, and basted now and again with the tarragon-flavoured butter which comes out of it.

When it is tender remove to a serving dish and stir into the juices in the pan a walnut of butter worked with a teaspoon of flour. When this has amalgamated, add ¼ pint of cream and 2 tablespoons of chopped tarragon. Bring to the boil and when it has thickened pour it over the chicken.

◇ *POULETS AU FENOUIL* ◇

Prepare two small chickens as for roasting. Line a small deep pan as for braised veal (i.e. sliced carrots and onions and a little bacon all melted in butter). Put in the chickens, add the usual seasonings, with a little bunch of fennel. Cover the pan. Cook over a moderate fire without liquid. Take out the chickens when they are cooked, press the juices and vegetables through a fine sieve. Blanch some small, tender hearts of fennel, add them to the sauce together with a good piece of butter worked with flour. Let the sauce thicken, taste for seasoning, and serve poured over your chickens.

Recipe from *Les Dons de Comus*, 1758

◇ *POULET EN GELÉE* ◇

A chicken of about 4 lb, a calf's foot or 2 pig's feet, 2 or 3 onions, 4 cloves of garlic, a leek, a carrot, 2 bayleaves, salt, pepper, a lemon and a half bottle of medium dry white wine.

First of all clean the calf's foot and blanch it in boiling water for 10 minutes, clearing it of the scum which will come to the top.

Rub the chicken all over with the cut lemon, then with salt and pepper. Wrap the bird in a piece of muslin. Put it in a capacious pot with the vegetables, the bayleaves, a few whole peppercorns, and the calf's foot. Cover with about 3 pints of water. Bring it to the boil and after it has simmered for an hour add the white wine.

Cook for another hour, or a little longer if the chicken is a tough one. Remove the bird from the pan and leave it to cool. Cook the rest of the contents of the pan for another hour, then strain the liquid into a bowl. Next day take off all the fat, heat the jelly a little, see that the seasoning is right and pour it through a fine muslin on to the chicken, which can either be left whole or cut up ready for serving. Leave to set. A mild dish which will in no way obtrude upon any wine which is to be served with it.

To make the dish more elegant, the jelly can be clarified in the following manner: when the fat has been removed, put the jelly into a saucepan with the very slightly beaten white of an egg. Bring gradually to the boil. Let it boil a minute, and when the egg has formed a kind of crust on the top of the liquid, turn off the flame. Let it settle. When the liquid has cooled, pour it though a double muslin over the chicken. All the little particles which have come from the chicken and vegetables during the cooking adhere to the white of egg, and the jelly emerges clear and soft.

◇ POULE EN DAUBE ◇

A good cold dish, the slow cooking of which will break down the oldest and toughest of hens. At the bottom of a deep oval fireproof casserole, put two or three rashers of bacon; on these lay the chicken, season with salt and pepper, rub over with lemon juice, and lay another rasher of bacon over the breast. Round the bird put three or four carrots, two onions, two cloves of garlic, a bouquet of thyme and bayleaf and a calf's foot cut in four pieces. (Failing the calf's foot, a pig's foot will do.) Pour a tumbler of white wine over the bird and just cover it with water. Put it to cook, covered with greaseproof paper and the lid of a casserole, in a very slow oven, for about four hours. When it is quite tender, remove it carefully to a serving dish, with the carrots round it. Strain the stock over it, and next day when it has set remove the fat.

◇ SPICED CHICKEN ◇
COOKED IN MILK

A small boiling chicken, a pint of milk to every pound which the chicken weighs when ready for cooking, an ounce of green ginger,* a teaspoonful of coriander seeds, a teaspoonful of cardamoms, ¼ teaspoonful of ground cloves, salt, pepper, lemon, 2 eggs, a few pistachio nuts or roasted almonds.

*See page 239 for a method of storing green ginger root.

BENDALL, MILDRED (1891-1977), *A Milk Pan and Lemons.*

Roast the coriander seeds for 2 or 3 minutes in the oven; peel the green ginger; pound both in a mortar with the cardomoms and the ground cloves; remove the husks of the cardomoms. Add salt and ground black pepper. Prick the chicken all over with a fork, rub it with lemon then press some of the spices into the chicken, and put some more in the inside. Leave for an hour or two. Bring the milk to the boil with the remainder of the spices. Pour it over the chicken and cook very slowly for about 2½ hours, for the first hour on top of the stove, with the pan covered, for the remainder of the time in the oven, without the lid. When the chicken is quite tender, take it out and leave to cool. When cold, cut all the flesh from the chicken in nice neat pieces; measure about 1 pint of the sauce, heat it up. Add to two whole beaten eggs, through a sieve, and heat it in a double boiler till thick and pour it over the chicken. Serve cold, garnished with a few halves of pistachio nuts or roasted almonds and quarters of lemon. Serve with it the spiced rice salad described on page 46.

⟡ *ITALIAN FRICASSÉE* ⟡
OF CHICKEN

The breasts and livers of 2 tender chickens, an onion, parsley, 1 oz of pine kernels, 1 lb of new green peas, 2 cupfuls of chicken stock, a lemon, the yolks of 2 eggs, 1 oz of butter.

Melt the butter and soften the chopped onion in it without letting it brown. Add chopped parsley. Put in the chicken breasts (4 fillets to each bird) and let them fry golden on each side. Add the pounded pine nuts. Pour the hot stock over, put in the uncooked peas, and cook gently for 10–15 minutes, until the peas are tender. Add the sliced livers and cook them for two or three minutes. Remove the fillets to a serving dish, and stir a little of the liquor into the eggs beaten with the juice of the lemon. Return the mixture to the rest of the stock, stir till it thickens, It must not boil, and the operation must be carried out quickly.

Serve if you like with rice.

⟡ *PARSLEY PIE* ⟡

A Devonshire and Cornish dish. From the *Cookery Book* of Lady Clark of Tillypronie (Constable & Co., 1909).

'Prepare 2 chickens for the pie jointed as for a fricassée. Lay in the bottom of a pie dish a layer about an inch deep of very young parsley (nipped off the stalks and squeezed in a cloth, as the juice is very bitter). Season the joints of chicken, mince a little blanched Portugal onion and 2 shallots, and strew over the chicken with a seasoning of pepper, salt, a breakfast lump of white sugar powdered, and a *very little* mace and nutmeg also, if you like spices. Lay the joints on the bed of parsley; cover with another layer of parsley, and add more chicken and more parsley in alternate layers until the pie dish is full.

'Pour in a very little good veal stock, and cover all with an ordinary pie crust made so: ½ lb flour, 4 oz butter, 1 egg, a little salt, and enough water to make into good stiff paste; work it well.

'In Cornwall they cover the bottom of the pie dish with a few slices of veal and bacon (to flavour it only, *not to eat*) and the yolks of hard-boiled eggs cut in half, with bacon or ham or tongue cut in dice, are laid in with each layer of chicken and improve the pie much. When the pie is baked, make a small hole in the centre of the crust and pour in ½ pint of double cream, *boiling hot*.

'The spices and shallots are often omitted, and only half an onion used.'

⋄ FOIES DE VOLAILLE ⋄
SAUTÉS

½ lb of chicken livers, 3 oz of ham, butter, flour, port, a cupful of chicken or light meat stock, parsley, salt, pepper.

Cut the carefully cleaned livers in half. Season, dust with flour. In the melted butter sauté the ham cut into strips. Add the livers. After two minutes, pour in a small glass of port (or madeira or marsala). Let it bubble a few seconds, add the stock. Cook gently for 5 minutes, stirring frequently. Stir in 2 tablespoons of cut parsley, and serve either with fried onions or on a dish of white rice.

⋄ TURKEY STUFFED WITH ⋄
HERBS AND ROASTED
IN BUTTER

A young turkey weighing about 7 to 9 lb, roasted in butter with a fresh herb stuffing, makes a delightful change both from the more usual roast chicken and from the 25-lb monsters which are such a tyranny to cook at Christmas time. Turkey breeders have been experimenting for some time in England with the supplying of small birds all year round, and they are becoming more plentiful on the market.

For the stuffing of a 7-lb turkey the ingredients are 4 oz each of breadcrumbs and butter, the grated rind of a lemon, 3 or 4 tablespoons of chopped fresh parsley, a teaspoon each of thyme or lemon thyme, and marjoram, 2 eggs, salt, pepper, a squeeze of lemon juice. To make the breadcrumbs put slices of white bread in the oven until they are dry, but not browned, then pound them. Mix all the ingredients together. What makes this stuffing so good is the use of fresh herbs as opposed to packet herbs, and the absence of sage. When the bird is stuffed rub it all over with butter and put it on its side in the roasting pan, covered with liberally buttered greaseproof paper. Put in a preheated fairly hot oven (Regulo 4 or 5) and cook it for about 15 minutes to the pound, and 15 minutes over. After the first hour turn the bird over and baste with more butter. For the last 20 minutes or so remove the greaseproof paper and turn the bird breast upwards so that it browns. This way of cooking a small turkey gives it a very delicate taste, and it will be moist and tender.

The only sauce necessary is the juice and butter in the pan poured off into a small pan and brought to bubbling point, with the addition of a very small glass of white wine.

⋄ LE CANETON AUX ⋄
PETITS POIS

A *caneton aux petits pois* and a duckling with green peas are not so alike as they sound. The two dishes demonstrate one of the fundamental differences between the cooking of France and England. The English dish consists of a roast duckling served with boiled and buttered green peas, and there the matter ends.

In the French version, the peas are added to the duck while it is cooking, with little pieces of smoked bacon and small onions, good stock is added, all is simmered together sufficiently long for the peas to absorb the stock and some of the fat from the duck.

You will need 4 lb of small new peas. Blanch them in boiling water. Brown some small whole onions in butter. Put them together with the drained peas in the pan with the duckling which has been two-thirds roasted (allow 15 minutes to the pound) and from which you pour off the fat. Add ¼ lb of smoked bacon cut into thick strips, and about half a cupful of very good stock (made from the giblets of the duck if you have no meat stock) and leave to cook very gently for about 20 minutes more, or until both duckling and peas are tender.

❖ SALMI OF DUCK ❖

A duck, ½ pint of jellied stock, 2 shallots, garlic, a small wineglass each of port and brandy, salt, pepper, bayleaf.

Roast the duck and, when it is all but cooked, carve the breast into fillets. Separate the legs and wings and leave them in the roasting pan to cook gently a little longer while the sauce is prepared in the following manner.

Crush the carcass in a mortar and put the juice which comes out of it into a pan with the giblets of the bird, a clove of garlic, 2 chopped shallots, ground black pepper, a bayleaf and the port. Reduce the liquid by half. Add the stock, cook 10 minutes. Strain, see that the seasoning is right and heat the fillets in this sauce, which should emerge in the final stages quite syrupy and shiny. Now warm the brandy, set light to it and pour it flaming into the sauce. Put the legs and wings of the bird in a serving dish and in the centre the fillets with the sauce.

❖ DUCK WITH ❖
CHERRIES

A 4–5-lb duck, ½ lb morello cherries, red wine, carrots, onions, garlic, fresh marjoram or basil, seasoning, veal bones, bayleaf, sugar.

Put the seasoned duck into a braising pan with 3 or 4 carrots, a small onion, a clove of garlic, a bayleaf, a sprig of fresh marjoram or basil, the giblets of the bird and 2 small veal bones. Pour a wineglass of red wine over the duck, and two of water. Add a little salt, sugar, and pepper. Cover the pan and cook in a slow oven (Regulo 3–4) for 2 hours. When the duck is tender take it out, put the pan with the rest of its contents over a fast flame and reduce the sauce by about half. Strain into a bowl, leave to cool, take off the fat. Reheat the sauce, which should have jellied, and pour it hot over the stoned cherries.

Serve the duck surrounded with squares of the jellied sauce in which the cherries are embedded.

If preferred, the duck can be carved for serving and the sauce either poured over or served separately in a bowl.

FRENCH, 19th C., *Still life with a Rabbit, Two Eggs and a Glass of Wine*.

⋄ DUCK IN ORANGE JUICE ⋄

A 4-lb duck, ½ pint of orange juice, ½ lb of tomatoes, an onion, 2 cloves of garlic, a sprig each of marjoram and parsley, a bayleaf, 1 oz of ground almonds, 1 oz of raisins, 2 tablespoons of vinegar, half a teacupful of water, salt and pepper.

Put the seasoned duck into the casserole or deep pan with all the ingredients, and the giblets of the bird. Cover the pan and cook gently either on top of the stove or in a slow oven (Regulo 2–3) for 2¾–3 hours. Take out the duck, strain the sauce; if to be served hot, carve the duck and put back to heat in the sauce, from which you have poured off as much fat as possible. If to be eaten cold, pour the sauce into a bowl and remove the fat when it is cold.

A very good dish, adapted from a Mexican recipe.

⋄ LAPIN À LA FERMIÈRE ⋄

A wild rabbit weighing about 1¼–1½ lb and cut in pieces, 1½ lb young broad beans, a leek, ½ lb green peas, 2 potatoes, butter, a vinaigrette sauce.

Melt the butter in a large pan, brown the seasoned pieces of rabbit gently on each side. Add the shelled peas (unless you have *mange-tout* peas which do not have to be shelled), the leek and potatoes cut in pieces, and the broad beans in their pods, the black ends near the stalks having been cut off (if the beans are too old for the pods to be cooked, twice the quantity at least will be needed). Just cover the vegetables with water, season with salt and pepper and 3 lumps of sugar and cook at a moderate pace for 1½–2 hours.

Take out the pieces of rabbit, and while they are still hot pour over them a vinaigrette sauce made with olive oil, lemon, a little garlic, and chopped herbs, which should if possible include fresh thyme or lemon thyme.

Sieve the vegetables (you need a food mill for this). There should be a thick and fairly firm purée (the liquid in which they have been cooked should of course be kept for soup).

Arrange the purée in the middle of a large shallow dish with the pieces of rabbit all round. Serve cold. If you like, serve more vinaigrette sauce separately, or a mayonnaise if you prefer. The dish can be garnished with a few quarters of hard-boiled eggs.

If you prefer to serve the dish hot, simply pour a little oil, pepper and salt over the pieces of rabbit when they are taken from the pan, and while you are heating up the purée, fry the rabbit gently or heat it under the grill. The reheating process will not harm it.

✧ COLD PIGEON FILLETS ✧
WITH CHERRIES

2 pigeons, ½ lb cherries, ½ pint of aspic jelly (page 194), kirsch, seasoning, parsley, thyme, bayleaf.

Put salt and pepper inside the pigeons and place them in a roasting tin with water half-way up. Add a bouquet of parsley, thyme and bayleaf, cover the pan and cook in a very gentle oven for about 1½ hours. (Pigeons can be very tough, and need careful slow cooking.) Meanwhile, stone the cherries (morellos if possible) and put them in a bowl to macerate with a small glass of kirsch poured over them. When the pigeons are tender take them from the oven and leave them to cool. Cut each side of the breast of the pigeons into two fillets. Put them in a shallow dish. Arrange the cherries round them. Cover with the melted aspic and leave to set.

If there is no aspic jelly to hand, do not spoil the dish by using gelatine, but cook a calf's or pig's foot with the pigeons, in a little more water. Cook it an extra half-hour or so after the pigeons have been taken out, then strain it and remove the fat when cold.

✧ GROUSE ✧

As grouse shooting starts on 12 August, grouse can be counted as summer food. Young grouse are at their best wrapped in a piece of bacon and very carefully roasted, served either hot or cold, but in either case *without* game chips, which are usually sodden and always dull, and no wonder, as they usually come out of a packet.

Old grouse, sold in the shops as 'casserole grouse', are usually so dry and have so powerful a flavour that they are all but uneatable, however carefully and patiently simmered. They can, however, make quite an acceptable dish if first marinated and then stewed in wine, and stock from grouse can be used

THORBURN, ARCHIBALD, *A Grouse*, 1893.

in several very delicious ways, notably for stewing mushrooms; a little added to a dish of eggs *sur le plat* also makes a lovely dish, and the beef stuffed with chopped grouse and stewed in the stock (recipe on page 123) is quite excellent. These are really dishes for people who have their own game to be used up, as few people will care to buy a casserole grouse simply in order to use the stock, although as far as the mushroom dish is concerned it is really worth the trouble and expense.

Lady Clark's recipe for a grouse pudding (page 151) is also worth a trial; the idea of using old game birds to flavour beef is a fairly common one in old English cookery.

✧ *STEWED GROUSE* ✧

Make a red wine marinade in the following way: heat a coffee-cupful of olive oil in a small pan; when warmed put in a sliced carrot, an onion, a clove of garlic, a few crushed juniper berries, a sprig of fresh thyme and a bayleaf. Add a large glass of red wine and a little ground black pepper. Simmer altogether for 15 minutes and when cold pour over the bird or birds. Marinate for not less than 4 hours. Take out the bird, put it in a pan with 2 oz of chopped bacon and pour over the strained marinade. Add a fresh carrot and onion and herbs and stew very slowly with the lid on for 2 hours. If the juice is going to be needed for stock, add water after the marinade has been poured in.

❖ GROUSE PUDDING ❖

'A pudding made with quite *old unboned* grouse, juicy rump steak and good stock. The pudding to boil rather slowly or it will get dry. The birds are *not meant to be eaten*, merely put in to flavour the stock.'
From the *Cookery Book* of Lady Clark of Tillypronie (Constable 1909)

❖ POTTED VENISON ❖

2 lb of venison, 8–10 oz of fat bacon, garlic, juniper berries, coriander seeds, black pepper, very little salt, red wine, clarified butter or dripping.

Cut the venison and the bacon into slices. Put into a deep earthenware pot, add half a dozen each of crushed juniper berries and coriander seeds, a fair amount of ground black pepper and a very little salt. Just cover the meat with coarse red wine, put a lid on the pot and cook in the lowest possible oven for at least 3 hours. When cold, drain off all liquid, chop the venison and bacon fairly finely, press into small pots, and seal with clarified butter or dripping.

Admirable for sandwiches.

❖ CLARIFIED ❖
BUTTER

To clarify butter (New Zealand is a good one to use for the purpose), all you have to do is melt it in a pan over a low heat, let it cook a minute or two, and then leave it to get half-cold so that the sediment settles. Filter it through a fine cloth, wrung out in hot water, into a small pot or jar. Store it, covered, in the refrigerator until you are ready to use it.

Clarified butter will keep almost indefinitely in the refrigerator. For frying bread and many other things such as escalopes of veal, and fish to be served in the *meunière* fashion, clarified butter is so infinitely more satisfactory than fresh butter that, ideally, one should always have a small supply to hand.

VEGETABLES

GRANT, DUNCAN, *The Kitchen*, 1902.

VEGETABLES

The tender young vegetables of early summer, broad beans, green peas, new potatoes, new turnips, young carrots, are nearly always best quite plainly cooked and eaten with plenty of fresh butter. A little later, when they are more plentiful, cheaper, but less tender, they can be cooked in a variety of enterprising ways, with cream and sauces and stock, with ham and bacon, made into purées, soufflés, soups and salads, and flavoured with fresh herbs.

As well as the classic vegetable dishes such as *petits pois à la française*, glazed carrots and *navets glacés*, I have given in the following chapter a few recipes which may provide new ideas for English kitchens. Most of these are for vegetables to be served as a separate course. The time and trouble necessary to the preparation of fresh vegetables, as well as their delicious fresh flavour, deserve full recognition.

For a summer luncheon what could be better than a cold pâté or terrine, followed by a dish of hot green peas cooked in butter, or peas and carrots mixed, or well-buttered french beans and new potatoes? Small new beetroots, hot, with butter and chives, are good with a grilled pork chop, while baby turnips make one of the nicest accompaniments to braised lamb or mutton. English tomatoes, plentiful from May onwards, are at their best raw, as salads to go with grilled or roast meat and chicken; Florentine fennel, now imported in fairly large quantites, makes the most refreshing of salads. Mediterranean pimentos, aubergines and courgettes (the Italian zucchini) begin to get reasonable in price by early September, and for people who like Southern food and garlicky smells this is the time for oil-flavoured Provençal *ratatouilles*, and rich Basque *pipérades* of eggs, pimentos, and onions served with grilled gammon or coarse country sausages.

❖ ASPARAGUS ❖

Cut the cleaned asparagus all the same length, tie them together in bundles, and put them upright in a deep pan of boiling water, to which a lump of sugar as well as salt has been added. Cook them so that the heads do not come into contact with the water, but are cooked by the steam. Cooking times vary between 15 minutes for small asparagus to 30 minutes for the large ones. Drain them very carefully or they will break.

They are best served with the classic melted butter, *sauce hollandaise*, *sauce maltaise* or the vinaigrette sauce with eggs described on page 191, which goes well with them whether hot or cold. Oil and lemon is good too but asparagus won't stand up to vinegar. The tips of the small green asparagus make delicious omelettes and go well with eggs cooked in cream (see page 77).

ASPARAGUS WITH ❖ PARMESAN CHEESE ❖

One of the Italian ways of eating asparagus is to cut off the entire part of the stalk which is inedible, after they are cooked; then put them in a fireproof dish, sprinkle them lightly with grated Parmesan, then with melted butter, and put them in the oven just long enough for the cheese to melt.

❖ ASPARAGUS WITH ❖ MAYONNAISE

Use the large fat asparagus for this dish. Cut the stalks fairly short and cook the asparagus in the usual way, and leave them to cool. Serve them with a mayonnaise to which a beaten white of egg has been added (see Mayonnaise Mousseuse, page 188).

❖ BROAD BEANS ❖

Imported broad beans start arriving early in May; English broad beans are not usually on the market until early June.

When new, they are best plain boiled and served with butter. They are also exquisite eaten raw (see page 50) when young and tender. When they begin to get large they can be cooked in sauces with ham or bacon, and in soups. Delicious purées can be made from very young broad beans, using the pods (see the soup recipes, page 57, and rabbit with broad bean purée, page 148). Some people dislike the rather earthy flavour of the skins of broad beans, but to me this taste is an important part of the flavour of these lovely vegetables. The French insist that savory must always flavour broad beans, but for once I disagree with them; this herb seems to make them bitter.

⬦ *FÈVES À LA CRÈME* ⬦

2 lb of very young broad beans, 1½ oz of butter, 2 oz of cream, a teaspoon of flour, salt, sugar, pepper.

Melt the butter, put in the broad beans, and stir until they have absorbed most of the butter. Sprinkle with flour, stir again, and just barely cover the beans with hot water. Add pepper and sugar, but salt only when the beans are practically cooked. Simmer steadily for 15 minutes, then stir in the cream previously boiled in another pan.
    Enough for four.

⬦ *FÈVES À LA POULETTE* ⬦

2 lb of broad beans, the yolks of 2 eggs, parsley, ½ oz butter, 1 teaspoon of flour.

Cook the shelled beans (medium-sized ones are best for this dish) in a little salted water. Strain them, keep a little of the water in which they have cooked. Melt the butter, stir in the flour, add a small cupful of the water from the beans; put in the beans and cook for two or three minutes. Stir in the beaten yolks of the eggs, and let them get hot, but the sauce must not boil. Sprinkle with a little cut parsley.
    Enough for four.

⬦ *BROAD BEANS AND BACON* ⬦

Melt 2 oz of diced bacon (or ham, or cold pork) in a little butter. Add 2 lb of cooked broad beans, 2 or 3 tablespoons of light béchamel sauce, a little cream, a very little chopped parsley. Simmer together for 5 minutes.

⬦ *BROAD BEANS AND* ⬦ *YOGHOURT*

1½ lb of broad beans, 2 tablespoons of rice, a clove of garlic, 1 egg, a small pot of yoghourt.

POTTER, BEATRIX. *Broad Beans in Flower*, 1903.

Boil the beans and the rice separately, strain them and mix them together while hot. Stir the pounded garlic into the yoghourt, season with salt and pepper and add the mixture to the beans and rice. Heat gently, then stir in the beaten egg. As soon as the sauce has thickened slightly, it is ready.

Can be eaten hot or cold. A Middle Eastern dish, called *fistuqia.*

◇ BROAD BEANS WITH ◇
EGG AND LEMON

Cook the beans in boiling salted water. When they are ready drain them, reserving a teacupful of the water in which they have cooked. Add this to the yolks of 2 eggs and the juice of a lemon. Heat over a very gentle flame, whisking all the time until the sauce is frothy and slightly thickened. Pour over the beans. Serve hot or cold.

Cooked artichoke hearts mixed with the beans are a good combination, and for an hors d'œuvre add a few prawns or tails of Dublin Bay prawns.

◇ BROAD BEANS AND PORK ◇

½ lb of belly of pork, 2 lb of broad beans, ½ pint of milk, flour, seasoning.

Cut the pork into small strips; put it into a thick pan over a slow fire, and let it cook very gently, with the lid on the pan, for 15 minutes. Season with salt and pepper, sprinkle with flour, stir, and gradually add the warmed milk. Cook gently for another 20 minutes, while the shelled beans are boiled in the usual way. When they are tender, drain them and put them into the pan with the pork. Let them get thoroughly hot before serving.

◇ PURÉE DE FÈVES ◇

Cook broad beans exactly as for Broad Bean Soup 2 on page 57. Strain off all the water and sieve them. Heat up with a little butter. Delicious with bacon, ham, pork chops and duck. A little of the dripping or sauce in which either of these last two has been cooking can be added to the purée before serving. Some cooks remove the inner skin of the beans before sieving them; not only does this take hours but it is quite unnecessary and also lessens the flavour.

⬦ *BEETROOT WITH* ⬦
HERB BUTTER

Small boiled beetroots, peeled and sliced, heated one minute in a butter worked with chopped chives, a squeeze of lemon juice and a scrap of garlic.

⬦ *BEETROOT WITH* ⬦
CREAM SAUCE

Boil some small young beetroots. Peel them and put them in a pan with a little butter. When they are thoroughly hot pour over them a tablespoonful of vinegar, and then 2 oz (for 1 lb beetroots) of boiling cream.

⬦ *PEAS* ⬦

Shelling peas is certainly a good deal of trouble, but with butter, perhaps a little cream, or ham, or little lettuce heart, they make one of the most perfect summer dishes, not just something to put round the meat, but as a course by themselves.

When obliged to shell the peas some hours before they are cooked, wrap them in a damp cloth. In this way they will not lose their moisture. A pound of peas in the pod yields about 6 oz when shelled, so that if the peas are to be served as a separate course allow about 3 lb for four people.

LES PETITS POIS À
⬦ *L'ANCIENNE MODE* ⬦

'Shell 4 lb of new green peas, and wrap them in a damp cloth until it is time to cook them. Open out the leaves of a good lettuce heart and inside place two sprigs of freshly picked summer savory. Tie the lettuce round with string, put it in a saucepan and all round put the peas, season with salt, add half a glass (¼ pint) water and ¼ lb of very fresh butter. Cook a quarter of an hour, take out the lettuce; immediately before serving pour into the peas three tablespoons of fresh cream beaten together with the yolk of an egg, a little sugar, and a little pepper.'

Edmond Richardin, who gives this recipe in *L'Art du Bien Manger* (Paris, 1912) claims that it came from the monks of the Abbey of Fontevrault, where the remarkable kitchens can still be seen today.

I do not think anyone need worry unduly about the savory, a herb which has rather too strong a taste for delicate green vegetables, but the method of cooking the peas is excellent.

◇ *PETITS POIS À LA FRANÇAISE* ◇

2 lb of small peas, 3 oz butter, 8–12 very small onions, the heart of a lettuce, seasoning.

Put the shelled peas, 2½ oz of butter, the onions (spring onions are best for this dish, the bulb part only) and the lettuce heart into a small thick pan or earthenware pot. Season with salt, and a teaspoonful of sugar. When the butter is bubbling just cover the peas with hot water. Cover the pan and simmer gently until the peas are tender. They will take from 30 to 45 minutes according to the size of the peas. By the time they are cooked, most of the liquid will be absorbed. Stir in another ½ oz of butter, cut the lettuce into four, and serve.

◇ *PEAS WITH HAM* ◇

2 lb of green peas, 2 oz of ham, 2 lumps of sugar, 2 oz of butter.

Melt the butter in a small thick pan, put in the ham cut into small strips, then the peas. Salt very lightly, add the sugar, and pour over just enough hot water to come level with the peas. Cover the pan and cook gently for about 30 minutes. If you like, before serving, thicken the sauce with 2 tablespoons of thick cream.

◇ *PETITS POIS À LA CRÈME* ◇

Put small green peas into a pan in which you have melted some good fresh butter; when it is all absorbed, pour over enough boiling cream to cover the peas; season very lightly with salt and a little sugar, cover the pan, and cook very gently until the peas are tender.

PURÉE OF FRESH PEAS

To a purée made from 2 lb of fresh peas, cooked in salted water and drained, add 1 oz of butter, a little sugar and pepper, a scrap of fresh mint, and 2 or 3 tablespoons of fresh cream. Heat in a double boiler. Delicious with veal, and a good way of using mature peas.

PETITS POIS AUX CAROTTES

2 or 3 lb (according to their age) of green peas, 1 lb of new carrots, the heart of a small lettuce, a small onion, 2 oz of butter, salt, sugar.

Clean the carrots, cut them in strips, and cook them for about 5 minutes in boiling water.

Put the shelled peas, the shredded lettuce, the whole onion with a little salt and sugar in a pan with the carrots and just cover with boiling water. Cook gently; by the time the vegetables are ready the water should be almost all absorbed; stir in the butter, see that the seasoning is right and serve.

CAROTTES À LA NIVERNAISE

1 lb carrots, ½ lb very small onions, stock, sugar, butter.

If the carrots are large cut them into pieces about the size of a cork; if they are very young carrots leave them whole. Blanch them in boiling salted water for 5 minutes. Drain them, put them in a shallow pan with 1½ oz of butter, and barely cover them with stock. Cook slowly but steadily until nearly all the stock is absorbed. By this time the carrots should be tender and the remaining sauce of a syrupy consistency. Season with salt, pepper, and sugar, and mix them with the onions which have been first browned in butter, sprinkled with sugar, and simmered in stock in the same way as the carrots, until the sauce is entirely absorbed and the onions brown and shiny.

BONZI, PIETRO PAOLO (c. 1576-1636), *A Still Life with Fruit, Vegetables, Flowers and Birds.*

✧ GLAZED CARROTS ✧
WITH MINT

Blanch a pound of small new carrots in boiling salted water for 6 or 7 minutes. Strain, and put them in a heavy pan with 2 oz of butter; after 5 minutes' gentle cooking add a tablespoon of sugar; simmer gently. When the carrots are tender, season with salt and ground black pepper and stir in a tablespoon of chopped fresh mint.

CAROTTES
✧ À LA PAYSANNE ✧

A large onion, 1 lb small carrots, butter, sugar, salt, cream.

Melt the thinly sliced onion in butter; when it is just turning golden add the carrots, previously blanched for 5 minutes, and cut in half lengthways. Add a very little stock or water, cook slowly with the pan covered. When the carrots are nearly cooked, add a seasoning of salt and sugar and two or three tablespoons of cream. Simmer until the carrots are quite tender.

⬦ *CARROTS STEWED WITH RICE* ⬦
(A Turkish dish)

Clean 1 lb of young carrots and cut in halves lengthways; cover the bottom of a thick pan with oil; when it has warmed put in the carrots and let them get thoroughly impregnated with the oil; add 2 tablespoons of rice, and stir it round with the carrots; just cover carrots and rice with water, add a little salt. Simmer for about 25 minutes until the carrots and rice are cooked and most of the liquid evaporated; stir in a handful of chopped parsley and mint.

Serve cold, in their liquid, which will be quite thick, with a squeeze of lemon juice.

⬦ *POTATOES* ⬦

It is not until June that English new potatoes become reasonably cheap. The early imported new potatoes never seem to be worth their high price, so in the early part of the summer the old potatoes will have to do. For a change, they are good grilled in the way described on page 166. Also a potato purée, with the addition of fresh new vegetables or herbs (see the Soup chapter), makes a very good spring soup. The smallest new potatoes are at their best cooked slowly in butter, so that they emerge pale golden outside, melting inside. When they are larger, they make a lovely dish cooked in good stock. Perhaps in this country we eat potatoes so often that very little trouble is taken over their preparation. They repay careful treatment as much as any other vegetable. Because they absorb a good deal of whatever fat they are cooked in, it follows that the fat should always be the best possible; olive oil, butter, pure pork fat, the dripping from a duck, bacon fat, all give their different savours to potatoes. When they are roasted with meat they, as well as the meat, will taste all the better for the flavour of herbs and possibly garlic which has cooked with the meat. If new potatoes are to be boiled they are best put into boiling water.

Although boiled potatoes are one of the first dishes anybody learns to cook, they always remain a nuisance, as the timing must be accurate, and varies with the quality of the potatoes, so for occasions where there are other dishes to be attended to, or when the meal may be late, it is advisable to learn one or two other simple methods of cooking potatoes, by which they will not suffer if kept waiting a few minutes. Two such potato dishes are *pommes de terre à la crème* and *pommes de terre fromagées*, for which the recipes are on page 166.

⋄ *POMMES DE TERRE AU JUS* ⋄

Cut medium-sized new potatoes into quarters. Just cover them with well-flavoured meat or chicken stock. Simmer, uncovered, until the potatoes are tender and the stock nearly all absorbed. Add a good lump of butter and when it has melted serve the potatoes.

⋄ *POMMES DE TERRE* ⋄
RISSOLÉES

1 lb of new potatoes, as much as possible all the same size, 2 oz of butter.

Choose a small thick pan in which the potatoes will just fit, all in one layer. Melt the butter in the pan, put in the potatoes, whole, cover the pan. Cook very slowly so that the butter does not burn. Turn the potatoes round several times during the cooking, so that they turn golden all over.

Small potatoes should be cooked in 25 to 40 minutes (according to the size) by which time the butter will all be absorbed by the potatoes. Add salt only when the potatoes are cooked.

⋄ *POMMES DE TERRE* ⋄
SABLÉES

Cook the potatoes as for *pommes de terre rissolées*. When they are tender, add a little more butter and throw in a handful of fresh white breadcrumbs and shake the pan so that the breadcrumbs absorb the butter and turn crisp within two or three minutes.

Particularly good with grilled meat.

✧ POMMES DE TERRE ✧
À LA CRÈME

Boil some small whole new potatoes, keeping them rather underdone. Make a cream sauce as described on page 191 and heat the potatoes in this, seasoning them with a little nutmeg.

✧ POMMES DE TERRE MESSINE ✧

Make a Sauce Messine (page 191) and in it heat sliced boiled new potatoes, in a double saucepan, stirring carefully so that the potatoes do not break.

✧ POMMES DE TERRE ✧
FROMAGÉES

Fill a small shallow baking dish with new potatoes, boiled but kept rather undercooked. Pour melted butter over them, then cover them lightly with a mixture of breadcrumbs and grated Gruyère cheese. Cook in a moderate oven, turning the potatoes round from time to time until they are lightly browned.

✧ GRILLED POTATOES ✧

Boil medium-sized yellow potatoes in their skins. Peel them, cut them in half lengthways, paint with butter and put under the grill until they are golden. Serve with coarse salt, ground black pepper, fresh butter. Delicious.

A useful recipe where cooking space is restricted.

POMMES DE TERRE
✧ À LA MÉRIDIONALE ✧

Have some small new potatoes, as much as possible all of the same size. Heat some olive oil in a thick saucepan, put in the potatoes, season with salt and pepper and cook at a moderate heat with the cover on the pan for about 15 minutes. When the potatoes are cooked lift them out on to the serving

HODGKIN, ELIOT, *Pink and White Turnips*, 1971.

dish and sprinkle them liberally with a mixture of freshly chopped parsley and garlic; if you like pour over them a little of the oil from the pan, very hot, but most people prefer them dry. The potatoes should be a very light golden colour, and only slightly crisp on the outside.

◇ *NAVETS GLACÉS* ◇

Recipe from *Le Cuisinier Européen*, an old French cookery book of about 1880. The author was Jules Breteuil, a professional chef.

'Peel the turnips and trim them all to the same size, roughly in the shape of a pear. Blanch them two or three minutes in boiling water. Drain them, put them in a small thick sauté pan. Cover them with clear bouillon. Sprinkle them with a mixture of salt and pepper, and add 2 or 3 little pieces of whole cinnamon. Cook over a fast flame and remove the cinnamon after 2 or 3 minutes. Let the stock reduce until it is beginning to stick to the bottom of the pan. Take out the turnips and put them on the serving dish. Pour into the pan a little white wine, just enough to detach the remainder of the sauce from the bottom of the pan. Pour this short and thick sauce over the turnips so that they look glazed.

'Serve very hot.'

⋄ NAVETS AU JAMBON ⋄

Cut a fairly thick slice of ham into cubes; brown it lightly in butter; add some young turnips, previously blanched in boiling water and also cut into cubes; season with ground black pepper, and very little salt. Cover the pan and cook slowly until the turnips are tender; before serving sprinkle with parsley and a very little chopped garlic.

⋄ NAVONI ALL' AGLIATA ⋄

(Turnips with garlic sauce)

A Genoese dish. Blanch the peeled turnips in boiling salted water for 5 minutes. Cut them in quarters, and put them to stew gently in a small heavy pan with plenty of olive oil, and season them with salt.

Prepare the *agliata* by pounding two or three cloves of garlic in a mortar, and adding a very little vinegar. When the turnips are cooked, add this mixture to the turnips; stir well so that the garlic sauce is well amalgamated with the oil, add a little parsley, and serve.

⋄ PURÉE OF SORREL 1 ⋄

Wash the sorrel in several waters and pick it over carefully, as for spinach. Cook for about 10 minutes in a little salted water. Drain as dry as possible, and chop finely. Put into a pan with a lump of butter. For a pound of sorrel add a quarter pint of cream and then two beaten eggs. When the purée thickens, it is ready.

On a basis of the sorrel purée may be served poached or hard-boiled eggs, white fish such as fillets of sole or rock salmon, pork chops or grilled gammon or escalopes of veal; and the purée can also be served cold.

✧ PURÉE OF SORREL 2 ✧

A handful of sorrel leaves, 2 or 3 tablespoons of cream or béchamel sauce, butter.

Chop the cleaned sorrel and melt it in a little bubbling butter. Stir it for two or three minutes, season with salt, and add the cream or béchamel; cook a few more minutes until the mixture has thickened a little. Serve in the same way as the preceding purée, as a filling for an omelette, or the basis of a soup.

✧ SPINACH AND EGGS ✧

Clean 1 lb of spinach very carefully and drain it well. Cook it, without water, for about 5 minutes, adding a little salt. Squeeze the water out of it, put it into a fireproof dish in which a good lump of butter has been melted; heat it very gently in the oven. When it is hot, add 2 or 3 tablespoons of boiled cream and 2 sliced hard-boiled eggs and cook for another minute or two.

Serve very hot, as a separate vegetable course. 1 lb of spinach is enough for two people.

FRENCH BEANS WITH
✧ EGG AND LEMON SAUCE ✧

1 lb of french beans, 2 eggs, a lemon, a tablespoon of grated Parmesan cheese, olive oil.

Cook the beans in boiling salted water; drain them, reserving about a cupful of the water in which they have cooked. Keep them hot. Have ready the eggs whisked to a froth with the lemon juice, a tablespoon of olive oil, and the cheese. Add a little of the water from the vegetables and heat this sauce over a low flame, whisking all the time until it has thickened a little. It will only take a minute or two. Pour over the beans and serve at once. Also good cold.

HARICOTS VERTS À L'ITALIENNE

The coarse variety of french beans called scarlet runners are particularly good cooked this way. Boil the beans in salted water, keeping them rather undercooked. Cover the bottom of a small pan with olive oil, and when it is warm put in the strained beans; add, for 1 lb of beans, 2 or 3 chopped tomatoes and a little chopped garlic. Cook gently, shaking the pan from time to time for about 10 minutes, until the tomatoes have melted.

FRENCH BEANS AND NEW POTATOES

Cook equal quantities of small new potatoes and french beans together in boiling salted water, adding the beans 5 minutes after the potatoes. When both are cooked, pile the beans in the middle of a hot dish, put the potatoes round, and pour hot butter over both.

BRAISED LETTUCE WITH TOMATO

A useful recipe for people who grow their own lettuce, and have more than they can use for salads.

For 4 small lettuces the other ingredients are a small onion, a thin slice of ham or bacon, parsley, olive oil and butter, 3 or 4 tomatoes, seasonings and a dozen black olives.

Wash your lettuces but do not separate the leaves; plunge them into boiling salted water and when the water comes back to a full boil take them out and put them in a colander to drain.

In a shallow pan heat a tablespoon each of olive oil and butter; put in the finely chopped onion, ham or bacon and parsley; stir for a minute or two; add the skinned and chopped tomatoes; when they are reduced almost to the consistency of a sauce put in the lettuces; season with salt, pepper, nutmeg, and a lump of sugar. Cover the pan and cook gently on top of the stove for about 30 minutes. Add the stoned black olives and cook for another 10 minutes. A good vegetable dish to serve on its own or with lamb.

For another method of cooking lettuce to serve as a vegetable see the recipe for lettuce and egg gratin, page 77.

Black olives are an acquired taste. Those who have not acquired it or do not have the opportunity to make the attempt, have only to leave the olives out of this dish. It is not advisable to substitute green olives for black. They do not at all suit the lettuce.

✧ *AUBERGINES* ✧

Aubergines, or eggplant, are one of the most useful vegetables as a background for using already cooked meat, particularly mutton, the most difficult of cold joints to utilize to advantage, as it rarely makes an attractive cold dish. The best known of aubergine and meat dishes is *moussaka*, which is to be found in varying forms all over the Balkans and the Middle East, and several of the recipes which follow are also from the Middle East where mutton is the most plentiful meat. Aubergines are also particularly successful when mixed with tomatoes in some form or other, as in the Provençal *ratatouille* (see page 45), and they also make interesting purées and salads, the kind of little dishes which are served either as an hors d'œuvre or with meat, like a chutney. Two of these recipes are in the hors d'œuvre chapter. Aubergines are best cooked in olive oil rather than in butter or dripping; they always have a warm southern look about them, especially when they are cooked with their purple skins on. Most aubergine dishes are as good cold as they are hot, and they can also be heated up without deteriorating in any way, so they are a most versatile vegetable.

✧ *PAPETON D'AUBERGINES* ✧

The story goes that one of the Avignon Popes complained that Provençal cooking was not as good as that of Rome, and his cook invented this recipe in order to prove that he was wrong. It is also recounted that the first *papeton* was presented to the Pope in the form of a mitre.

Peel 6 aubergines, cut them in thick slices, salt them and leave them to drain. Stew them in olive oil in a covered pan, so that they remain moist; drain them and chop or sieve them. Season and add a chopped clove of garlic, a teacupful of milk and three eggs. Turn in to a lightly oiled mould. Cook

25 minutes in a bain-marie. Turn out and serve covered with a thick fresh tomato sauce flavoured with garlic and fresh basil.

Instead of being turned out, the *papeton* can be served in the dish in which it has been cooked, with the sauce poured on top, or offered separately. A much easier system.

AUBERGINES À
◇ LA PROVENÇALE ◇

3 aubergines, 1 lb of tomatoes, garlic, parsley, breadcrumbs, olive oil.

Cut the unpeeled aubergines into thick rounds, salt them and leave to drain. Dry them and fry them gently in olive oil, turning them over two or three times, for about 6 minutes. Remove them to a gratin dish; fry the peeled and chopped tomatoes in olive oil, season them with salt, pepper, 2 chopped cloves of garlic, a handful of chopped parsley. Spread the tomato mixture on top of the aubergines, sprinkle with breadcrumbs and a few drops of olive oil. Cook them in a moderate oven for about three-quarters of an hour.

◇ MOUSSAKÁ ◇

There are a good many different versions of this dish, which is known in Rumania, Yugoslavia, Greece, and all over the Near East. Here is a very simple version.

3 aubergines, ¾ lb minced mutton, 1 onion, 3 large tomatoes, parsley, a clove of garlic, salt, pepper, olive oil, fresh tomato sauce made from 1 lb tomatoes, peeled and cooked to a pulp in a little olive oil and flavoured with garlic and herbs.

Slice the unpeeled aubergines in rounds about ½ inch thick, salt them, leave to drain for an hour, then dry them with a cloth and fry them in olive oil until they are soft. Chop the onion, let it turn golden in the oil in which the aubergines were fried, stir in the meat and the garlic, season with salt and pepper. Simmer 2 or 3 minutes. Arrange the aubergines, the meat, and the sliced peeled tomatoes in alternate layers in a square cake tin about 2 inches deep. Pour over the sauce and cook for 45 minutes to 1 hour in a moderate oven. By this time most of the liquid should have evaporated. Serve in the tin in which it has cooked, with parsley strewn over the top. *Moussaká* can be reheated quite successfully.

✧ *AUBERGINES À LA TURQUE* ✧

2 large aubergines (the round variety are best for this dish), 3 large onions, ½ lb tomatoes, sugar, salt, ground allspice (sometimes called pimento), garlic.

Cut the unpeeled aubergines into thick, round slices. Salt them and leave them to drain on a colander for an hour or two. Fry them in oil so that they are browned on both sides. Take them out of the pan and fry the thinly sliced onions, not crisply, but just golden yellow, then add the skinned and chopped tomatoes, and a clove or two of garlic. Season with salt, a teaspoonful of the allspice, and a little sugar. Cook until you have a thick sauce. Arrange the aubergine slices in an oiled baking tin, put a tablespoonful of the sauce on each slice of aubergine, and bake in a moderate oven for 40–50 minutes. Can be served hot but best cold.

✧ *MARINATED AUBERGINES* ✧

Cut unpeeled aubergines in half lengthways; make gashes in the centre part of the flesh, salt them, and pour over them some olive oil, black pepper, chopped garlic and herbs. Leave them to marinate for an hour or two. They should then be grilled, being basted with the marinade, but under a gas or electric grill they cook too fast and get blackened, so it is best to bake them in an uncovered dish in a moderate oven for about an hour. Cook them, cut side downwards, in the pan for all but the last quarter of an hour; then turn them round and baste them with the juices in the pan, and squeeze a little lemon juice over them. Very good as an accompaniment to roast mutton, or grilled chops.

✧ *KAZAN KABABI* ✧

4 medium-sized aubergines, ½ lb minced mutton, olive oil, salt, garlic, marjoram, mint, or basil, pine nuts or walnuts.

RENOIR, PIERRE AUGUSTE, *Fruits from the Midi*, 1881.

Cut the stalk end from the aubergines and make long slits almost the whole length of them, about an inch apart, but taking care not to cut right through. Rub them with salt and leave for an hour. Season the minced meat with salt, pepper, chopped garlic and marjoram, mint or basil, add 2 tablespoons of chopped pine nuts or walnuts. Push this stuffing into the slits made in the aubergines. Warm a little olive oil in a pan in which the aubergines will just fit. Lay them side by side in the pan, let them heat in the oil, then add hot water to come half-way up. Cover with a plate which fits inside the pan over the aubergines so that they do not move during cooking. Simmer very slowly for 1½ hours until they are quite soft and only a little of the oil is left in the pan.

◇ *MAQLUB OF AUBERGINES* ◇
(A Persian dish)

4 medium-sized aubergines, ¾ lb of minced mutton, cooked or raw, ¼ lb of rice, 1 onion, 2 cloves of garlic, 2 oz almonds, half a teaspoon of ground allspice, ¾ pint of meat stock, thyme or marjoram.

Cut the unpeeled aubergines in slices about a quarter-inch thick, salt them and leave them for an hour. Put the rice in to soak in water for an hour. Mix the spice, a little thyme or marjoram and chopped garlic with the meat. Dry the aubergines and fry them lightly in oil, then fry the sliced onion. Put a layer of the fried aubergines in a round flameproof dish; on top put a layer of the meat. Sprinkle with a few sliced blanched almonds and the fried onion. Repeat until all the aubergines and meat are used up, and on top put the drained rice. Pour over half the meat stock, cover the dish and cook over a low flame for about 20 minutes. Add the rest of the stock and cook for another 30–40 minutes until the rice is almost cooked.

Put a fireproof serving dish upside-down over the pan, turn out the contents and put in the oven for another 10–15 minutes.

The rice will finish cooking and any liquid left will be absorbed. Although this is rather a trouble to make it is one of the best of all aubergine dishes, and the rice, which has absorbed some of the flavour of the meat, is particularly good. A good bowl of yoghourt can be served with it, and a tomato or green salad.

Enough for six people. It can be reheated quite successfully, in a covered pan in a gentle oven.

◇ *COURGETTES* ◇

Courgettes, small marrows, or zucchini, should be prepared for cooking in the same way as aubergines; cut, preferably unpeeled, into rounds or lengthwise, salted, and left to drain for an hour or so. (If they are very small and young the salting is not necessary.) They can be cooked in most of the ways applicable to aubergines, although of course they do not take so long. If liked they can be used instead of aubergines in any of the Provençal or Oriental ways given in this book. They make excellent fritters, and go well in a *ratatouille*, or any of the dishes which contain tomatoes and onions.

The relative cheapness, growing popularity and excellent quality of English-grown courgettes is due to the enterprise of Poupart's the market gardners of Weybridge. Since about 1957 this firm has been cultivating courgettes for the market. Every year the output increases while quality is maintained. We have, in these courgettes, a new English vegetable, the first for some sixty years. Before the deep-freezers and the canners can get their hands on courgettes, let us seize the opportunity of enjoying this exquisite vegetable in its fresh form. I think that as well as adapting Mediterranean courgette dishes we should make every effort to evolve and establish our own recipes for courgettes, ignoring all attempts on the part of greengrocers, professional gardeners and cookery school teachers to make us believe that courgettes should be reduced to the status of all other English vegetables by being boiled and then buried under a blanket of white sauce. There is another school which treats courgettes like asparagus, instructing that they should be, again, boiled or steamed but served with *hollandaise* sauce. This seems to me to be an attempt to frighten people off courgettes by giving them an aura of luxury which is quite alien to them, making the sauce the *raison d'être* of the dish.

Courgettes, sliced or cubed, and cooked gently but directly in butter or olive oil, retain their proper texture and fresh flavour, giving out a most enticing scent while they are cooking; and with a sprinkling of parsley or chives, or a very little Parmesan cheese, provide a cheap summer luxury of fresh ingredients freshly cooked and to be appreciated for their delicate charm.

BEIGNETS DE
◇ COURGETTES ◇

Cut small marrows, unpeeled, into thin strips, lengthwise. Salt them and leave them for an hour or so. Dry them carefully on a cloth, dip them in frying batter (page 96) and drop them one by one into a pan of very hot oil, so that they are completely covered. As soon as they are golden (about 2 minutes), take them out and drain them on absorbent kitchen paper, and serve as soon as they are all cooked.

With some mushrooms or aubergines treated in exactly the same way (the aubergines must be cut very thin, mushrooms rather thick, with the stalk left on) these fritters make a very nice vegetable dish for luncheon.

✧ COURGETTES AU JAMBON ✧

1 lb small marrows, 3–4 oz ham, garlic, olive oil, pepper.

Cut the unpeeled marrows into four, lengthwise, then into small squares. Salt them, and leave to drain for an hour or so.

Cover the bottom of a thick frying pan with olive oil, put in the courgettes (previously drained and dried in a cloth). Let them sauté gently for 5 minutes, add a little chopped garlic, the ham cut into strips, ground black pepper. Cover the pan, and simmer on a low heat for about 15 minutes, until the courgettes are soft but not mushy. Sprinkle with parsley or other fresh herbs before serving. Can be eaten hot or cold, either as a separate course or with escalopes of veal, roast veal, or pork.

✧ COURGETTES WITH ✧ PARSLEY BUTTER

This is a dish which brings out the delicate flavour of the vegetables.

Wash, cut and salt the courgettes as in the previous recipe.

In a heavy sauté or frying pan melt about 1 oz of butter and a teaspoon of olive oil. Put in the courgettes. Cover the pan. Cook very gently for 10 minutes. Turn them over. Put back the lid. Cook another 20 minutes, turning the courgettes over from time to time.

Meanwhile work 1 oz of butter with two teaspoons of finely chopped parsley and a squeeze of lemon juice.

When the courgettes are quite tender, translucent and very pale golden, turn off the heat. Add the parsley butter divided into tiny knobs. Shake the pan. When the butter has melted, and before it oils, the dish is ready. There is enough for two people. Try it quite on its own, for a summer lunch, after something quite simple – an omelette, a veal escalope, a baked egg, a grilled fish.

❖ PIMENTOS STUFFED WITH ❖
RICE AND HERBS

4 medium-sized red pimentos, 1 teacupful of rice, olive oil, lemon juice, fresh parsley and herbs.

Boil and drain the rice; season it, and mix with it 2 or 3 tablespoons of chopped fresh herbs (parsley, marjoram, thyme or lemon thyme, or fennel, or simply parsley and a little of the green part of spring onions, or chives). Squeeze in a little lemon juice.

Cut the pimentos in half lengthways, take out the seeds. Put about 2 tablespoons of the rice mixture into each half and pour over a little olive oil. Pour a thin film of oil into a baking dish, put in the pimentos, cover the dish and cook in a gentle oven for about an hour. From time to time baste the pimentos with the oil in the dish, to prevent a hard crust forming on top of the rice.

❖ PEPERONATA ❖

One of the best Italian dishes of pimentos.

4 large red pimentos, 6 large tomatoes, 1 onion, butter and olive oil, garlic.

Cut the pimentos in half, remove the seeds, and cut them into strips; skin and chop the tomatoes. Melt the sliced onion in a mixture of olive oil and butter. Add the pimentos, and simmer, with the cover on the pan, for 15 minutes. Add the tomatoes, salt, and a clove of garlic. Cover until both tomatoes and pimentos are quite soft, and most of the oil absorbed. The mixture should be fairly dry. Peperonata can be eaten either hot or cold, and it can also be reheated without spoiling. Add a little fresh basil when it is in season.

❖ DOLMÁDES, OR STUFFED ❖
VINE LEAVES

3 dozen vine leaves, 2 teacups of cooked rice, a small onion, a few pine kernels if possible, lemon, stock, olive oil, a little ground allspice.

Fry the chopped onion in olive oil, mix it with the rice and add the pine kernels, salt, pepper, spice and a little olive oil to moisten. If you like, a little chopped mutton can be added, or a chicken liver or two, fried and finely chopped.

Blanch the vine leaves and drain them. Spread them flat on a board, the underside of the leaves uppermost. On each leaf lay about a teaspoonful of the rice mixture, roll the leaf up like a sausage, with the ends tucked in, and squeeze each one in the palm of your hand, so that the *dolmádes* will stay rolled up during the cooking. There is no need to tie them. Arrange them in a pan in which they will just fit, in layers. Pour over them enough stock (or water) to come half-way up, cover them with a plate or saucer which fits inside the pan so that the *dolmádes* do not move during the cooking, and simmer them for about ½ hour. Serve cold with lemon juice squeezed over.

Dolmádes can also be served with yoghourt or with an egg and lemon sauce (about a teacupful of stock with the yolks of 2 eggs and the juice of a lemon whisked over the fire until it is thick and frothy, and poured over the *dolmádes* when cool).

I have often seen it written that *dolmádes* are just as good made with cabbage leaves instead of vine leaves, but it is the taste of the vine leaves and the flavour they give to the stuffing which is so delicious, and which gives them their characteristic Oriental flavour.

✧ MUSHROOMS COOKED IN ✧ GROUSE STOCK

Sauté the cleaned mushrooms in butter, adding salt, pepper and a little chopped garlic. When they are almost ready to serve add 2 tablespoons (for ½ lb mushrooms) of very much reduced stock from a stewed grouse (page 150) and stir until the sauce is thick.

✧ MUSHROOMS COOKED IN ✧ VINE LEAVES

Many people who have a vine growing in their gardens will be glad to know of this excellent dish.

Blanch about a dozen vine leaves in boiling salted water. Drain them and arrange them in a heavy, shallow baking dish which has a well-fitting cover.

Pour a film of olive oil over the vine leaves, and fill the pan with cleaned whole flat mushrooms (the great point about this dish is that the vine leaves make cultivated mushrooms taste like field mushrooms). Add a little salt and pepper, 3 or 4 whole cloves of garlic, a little more olive oil, and cover the mushrooms with 2 or 3 vine leaves. Put the cover on the dish and cook in a slow oven for about 35 minutes to an hour, according to the size of the mushrooms. Remove the top covering of vine leaves before serving.

Tinned plain vine leaves (not to be confused with rice-stuffed vine leaves – examine the tins carefully before you buy them. The ones containing stuffed vine leaves usually have a picture showing the little rolls or parcels, while the plain leaves bear a label showing a branch of the vine) in natural juices or a very mild brine are now imported from Greece. They are to be bought in many delicatessen shops and self-service stores. For the above mushroom dish they do very well. No blanching is necessary. Simply rinse the requisite number under running cold water. The remainder can be stored in the refrigerator for a few days.

SAUCES

HARVEY, HAROLD, *Lunch*, 1918.

SAUCES

Butter, cream, eggs, wine, olive oil, fresh herbs; these are the ingredients which make the sauces, whether intricate or primitive, for summer food. A few fresh herbs and a little butter or olive oil, or an egg and a lemon, or perhaps a cupful of stock and a shilling's worth of cream well seasoned and carefully mixed will make little sauces which will turn the salads, vegetables, fish and meat of every day into fresh and original dishes. Fresh butter mixed with chives or parsley and tarragon melting into the juices of a grilled steak is just as delicious in its way as a grand sauce of truffles and madeira, and more fitting for the summer time. For grilled lamb or mutton chops use mint instead of parsley. Vinaigrette sauces (oil, lemon, herbs) and mayonnaises give plenty of scope to an inventive cook. For example, for a chicken salad add a little grated horseradish to the mayonnaise, or pounded tunny fish and anchovy in the Italian way; blanched and pounded herbs stirred into a mayonnaise make the *sauce verte* which is so good with salmon trout, a beaten white of egg lightens a mayonnaise to serve with salmon.

One condition essential to the success of any sauce, however simple, is the absolute freshness of the ingredients; use the best-quality butter you can afford, unsalted whenever possible, the freshest eggs, and above all the very best olive oil. It is the actual flavour of these ingredients which is important to the sauces, so that although substitutes may give approximately the same consistency and appearance they cannot give the same taste, so why bother with them?

✧ SAUCE BÉARNAISE ✧

The yolks of 3 or 4 eggs, 4–5 oz butter, ½ a wineglass of white wine, 2 tablespoons of tarragon vinegar, 2 shallots, black pepper, salt, lemon juice, a few leaves of fresh tarragon.

Put the white wine, vinegar, chopped shallots, and a little ground black pepper into a small pan, and reduce it by fast boiling to about 2 tablespoons. Strain it and add a few drops of cold water. Put in the top half of a double saucepan or in a bowl which will fit into the top of an ordinary saucepan. This underneath saucepan should be half full of warm water and put on to a gentle flame. To the liquid already in the top pan add half the butter, cut into small pieces. Let it melt quickly, then add the rest, stirring all the time. Now add the beaten yolks of the eggs and stir very carefully until the sauce thickens. Now add salt (the amount depends on whether the butter used is salted or unsalted) and a few drops of lemon juice and a few of cold water. Take the sauce from the fire, and stir in the chopped tarragon, and the sauce is ready. At no time should the water underneath the sauce boil and the sauce is not intended to be served hot, but tepid.

Without tarragon, there is no true Béarnaise, but naturally variations can be made by the addition of other herbs. A combination of mint and chives makes a very good sauce for lamb or mutton.

⬧ *SAUCE HOLLANDAISE* ⬧

For enough *hollandaise* (nobody ever refuses a second helping) for four people the ingredients are

> 4 to 5 oz of the best butter, the yolks of 3 or 4 eggs according to how large they are, 1 tablespoon of wine vinegar or 2 of dry white wine, salt, peppercorns, lemon juice, water.

Put the vinegar (on no account use malt vinegar) or white wine in a small pan with 3 tablespoons of water and 3 or 4 peppercorns. Reduce by fairly fast cooking to half its original quantity, then add a pinch of salt (if you are using salt butter be very cautious about the amount of salt added at this stage), remove the peppercorns, transfer to the top half of a double boiler, or to a bowl which will fit into a saucepan without moving about, add a tablespoon of cold water, and while the water in the bottom half of the double boiler is getting warm add the beaten yolks of the eggs, stirring all the time until the mixture looks creamy. Now start adding the butter, which should be soft, not straight off the ice, and divided into small cubes. Add only a little at a time, and whisk continuously. Keep the water underneath hot but not boiling. When all the butter is melted the sauce should already be quite thick, about the consistency of a mayonnaise; now add about 2 more tablespoons of cold water (this gives lightness to the sauce) and a few drops of lemon juice, and taste to see the seasoning is right.

The sauce should now be rather frothy and is ready to serve; it can be kept warm (it is never at any stage more than tepid) over hot water, but not on the fire; but if it is kept waiting long it will lose its characteristic frothiness and resemble a Béarnaise. It is also possible, with care, to heat the sauce up again, provided it is stirred all the time. If the eggs and butter separate, they can be reamalgamated by the addition of a few drops of hot water, but if the eggs have curdled there is nothing to be done, for they have scrambled, and cannot be unscrambled.

Hollandaise is one of the most delicious of sauces to serve with fish, asparagus, globe artichokes or any food which has a slightly astringent quality to contrast with the rich smoothness of the eggs and butter in the sauce.

✧ *SAUCE MALTAISE* ✧

This is a *sauce hollandaise* to which is added, just before serving, the juice of a blood-orange and a little of the grated peel.

For the quantities given above, a teaspoon of the grated peel and the juice of half an average-size orange is sufficient. It is served with the same dishes as *hollandaise*, particularly asparagus, and is perhaps even more delicious than the classic *hollandaise*.

✧ SAUCE MOUSSELINE ✧

To the quantity of *hollandaise* given above, add 3 tablespoons of thick whipped cream.

✧ BÉCHAMEL SAUCE ✧

Although the preparation of this sauce is extremely simple many amateur cooks are frightened by it. Anyone who has sufficient perserverance to practise making the sauce a couple of times according to the recipe which follows should never again have cause to worry as far as the making of a béchamel is concerned. And mastering the preparation of this sauce opens up a large repertory of very excellent and often cheap recipes.

> To make a half-pint of béchamel the ingredients are ¾ pint of milk, 1½ oz butter, 2 heaped tablespoons of plain flour, seasonings of salt, freshly milled pepper (preferably white peppercorns for white sauces; but the point is a minor one) and grated nutmeg.

Choose a heavy saucepan of 2-pint capacity, and have ready a wooden spoon and a measuring jug. Measure out the milk, bring it to simmering point in your saucepan. Pour it back into the jug, rinse out the pan, and put in the butter. When it is hot, but before it turns colour take the saucepan from the heat and with a wooden spoon stir the flour into the butter. Within a few seconds the two ingredients will have amalgamated into a smooth thick paste. Now, still keeping the pan away from the heat, start adding the hot milk, a little at a time, and stirring constantly; as each small quantity of milk is added, stir until the paste is again smooth. When you have added about half the milk, return the pan to the heat, turned very low and preferably with a mat over the burner, at least until all the milk has been added. Continue adding the milk. At this stage you begin to think you have already made the sauce too thin. Do not worry. Go on adding the milk and stirring, taking care, as always when making a sauce, that your spoon does not just move the surface of the sauce but reaches right to the base and sides of the pan.

When all the milk is added and the sauce is a smooth and thin cream, add seasonings of about a teaspoon of salt, two or three turns from the pepper-mill and a generous scraping of nutmeg. A well-cooked béchamel requires 15 minutes' gentle cooking and stirring and almost imperceptible reduction and thickening, the time to be calculated from the moment when all the milk has been added.

Let us not pretend that a béchamel sauce never goes wrong even if you follow the directions exactly. Minor accidents happen to the best of cooks but remedies are usually very easy. If there appear any tiny lumps of flour in your sauce, sieve it while it is still very liquid and therefore takes only a few seconds to run through the sieve placed over a jug or bowl. Rinse out your saucepan, return your sauce to it, put it back over the mat on the low heat, and when it is again warm it is sufficiently cooked. It is safe to leave it. But before doing so, put a piece of buttered paper right down inside the saucepan over the hot sauce. As the butter melts, it makes a little protective film which prevents a skin forming on the top of the sauce.

To re-heat béchamel, it is best to use the bain-marie system (i.e. with the saucepan standing in, not over, another one containing water) rather than direct heat.

⬧ MAYONNAISE ⬧

The excellence of a mayonnaise depends upon the quality of the olive oil employed to make it. Use genuine olive oil, heavy but not too fruity, as a mayonnaise always accentuates the flavour of the oil. The more yolks of eggs used the less tricky the mayonnaise is to make, and the quicker. Lemon juice is better than vinegar to flavour mayonnaise, but in either case there should be very little, as the flavour of the oil and the eggs, not the acid of the lemon or vinegar, should predominate.

In France, a little mustard is usually stirred into the eggs before adding the oil; in Italy only eggs and olive oil are used, or sometimes lemon juice.

It is very difficult to give quantities, owing to the difference in the weight of different olive oils, and also because mayonnaise is one of those sauces of which people will eat whatever quantity you put before them. For an average amount for four people you need the yolks of 2 eggs, about one-third of a pint of olive oil, the juice of a quarter of a lemon or a teaspoonful of tarragon or white wine vinegar, salt.

Break the yolks of the eggs into a mortar or heavy china bowl; if you have time, do this an hour before making the mayonnaise; the eggs will be easier to work; stir in a very little salt, and a teaspoonful of mustard powder if you like it. Stir the eggs for a minute; they quickly acquire thickness; then start adding the oil, drop by drop, and pouring if possible from a small jug or bottle with a lip. Stir all the time, and in a minute or two the mixture will start to acquire the ointment-like appearance of mayonnaise. Add the oil a little faster now, and finally in a slow but steady stream; when half the oil is used up add a squeeze of lemon juice or a drop and vinegar, and go on adding the oil until all is used up; then add a little more lemon juice or vinegar. If the mayonnaise has curdled break another yolk of egg into a clean basin, and add the curdled mixture a spoonful at a time. Well-made mayonnaise will keep, even in hot weather, for several days. If you make enough for two or three days, and it does separate, start again with another egg yolk, as if it had curdled.

✧ MAYONNAISE FOR ✧ POTATO SALAD

Add a little warm water or milk to a mayonnaise made as above, until it is of creamy consistency, easy to mix with the potatoes.

✧ MAYONNAISE MOUSSEUSE ✧

Add a teacupful of whipped cream to a plain mayonnaise, but only immediately before serving.

Another way of making this mayonnaise is to fold the stiffly beaten white of one egg into the mayonnaise, also just before serving. Good for cold salmon, and for asparagus.

✧ HORSERADISH MAYONNAISE ✧

Add 1 or 2 tablespoons of freshly grated horseradish (according to how hot you like the sauce) to a cupful of home-made mayonnaise; stir in a little chopped parsley.

Serve with fish and salads.

❖ SAUCE RÉMOULADE ❖

The yolks of 2 hard-boiled eggs, 1 raw yolk, ¼ pint of olive oil, teaspoonful of french mustard, salt, pepper, a teaspoonful of vinegar, tarragon, chives, a teaspoonful of capers.

Pound the hard-boiled yolks to a paste, with a few drops of vinegar. Stir in the raw yolk; add the seasonings and oil as for a mayonnaise; stir in the freshly chopped herbs and capers.

The difference between *rémoulade* and mayonnaise is in the consistency as well as in the addition of the herbs. The hard-boiled yolks make a *rémoulade* creamier, not such a solid mass of oil and eggs as a mayonnaise.

❖ SAUCE TARTARE ❖

Tartare sauce can be made either with an ordinary mayonnaise, or with a *rémoulade* as above; the additions are parsley, a little very finely chopped lemon peel and a finely chopped gherkin, with a few capers and if possible a little tarragon. The chopped white of an egg can also be added.

❖ SAUCE VERTE ❖

8 to 10 leaves of spinach, the same number of sprigs of watercress, 3 or 4 branches of tarragon, 3 or 4 sprigs of parsley.

Pick the leaves of the watercress, tarragon and parsley from the stalks. Blanch, with the spinach, in a very little boiling water for 3 minutes. Strain, squeeze quite dry, and pound the herbs in a mortar, then press them through a wire sieve. Stir the resulting purée into a ready prepared mayonnaise. The herb mixture should not only colour but flavour the mayonnaise, and the tarragon is an important element. This quantity will be sufficient for about ½ pint of mayonnaise.

For a hot *sauce verte* add the herb mixture to a *hollandaise* sauce.

❖ SAUCE RAVIGOTE ❖

A big bunch of mixed fresh herbs comprising whatever is available among the following: parsley, chervil, chives, cress, watercress, burnet, thyme, lemon thyme, savory, marjoram, wild marjoram, tarragon. A heaped teaspoon of capers and 2 or 3 anchovy fillets, a yolk of egg, olive oil, vinegar.

Chop the herbs, then pound them in a mortar. Add the chopped anchovies and the capers (to rid them of excess vinegar, put them in a small sieve and rinse them under running cold water), a little salt and pepper. Stir in the yolk. Gradually add 2 or 3 tablespoons of olive oil, as for a mayonnaise, then a little vinegar.

There are a good many versions of this sauce, hot as well as cold. This one comes from *La Cuisine Messine* by Auricoste de Lazarque, whose sauces are always just a little better than other people's.

POTTER, BEATRIX, *Onions*, 1903.

SAUCE
⬦ À LA CRÈME ⬦

Heat 2 oz each of butter and thick fresh cream in a double boiler; stir until thick. Season with salt and ground black pepper. Serve hot. Nice with roast chicken or veal.

⬦ SAUCE MESSINE ⬦

½ pint of fresh cream, 2 oz of unsalted butter, a teaspoon of flour, 2 yolks of eggs, chervil, parsley, tarragon, 2 or 3 shallots, a lemon, a teaspoon of french mustard.

Chop the herbs and the shallots with a little lemon peel. Work the butter with the flour. Mix all the ingredients together in a bowl, then put them in a double saucepan and heat, stirring all the time. Do not allow to boil. Season with salt and pepper. Squeeze in the juice of the lemon immediately before serving.

This sauce, which is perfectly exquisite, is intended to be served with a poached fish.

Auricoste de Lazarque, who gives the recipe in *La Cuisine Messine*, suggests that with this sauce the fish can be dispensed with; it can; it is perfect poured over hard-boiled eggs, or *œufs mollets*, either hot or cold.

⬦ SAUCE VINAIGRETTE ⬦
AUX ŒUFS

First prepare a vinaigrette, much as you would a salad dressing, with oil, lemon, salt, pepper, chopped parsley, chives and a little shallot or onion. Have ready two soft-boiled eggs (three minutes). Scoop out the yolks and stir them into the sauce. The addition of the barely cooked yolks gives a good consistency, as well as a really delicious flavour to the sauce, which is all the better for being made an hour or more before it is to be eaten.

This is one of the most useful sauces in existence; it goes well with fish, vegetables, chicken and salads, takes a few minutes to make, and can be varied with the addition of fresh tarragon, chervil, chopped prawns or fennel.

⋄ SAUCE BERCY ⋄

3 or 4 finely chopped shallots, 2 oz of white wine, 2 tablespoons of meat glaze or natural gravy from a roast, 1 oz fresh butter, lemon juice, fresh parsley.

Put the chopped shallots into a small pan with the wine and reduce it by fairly fast boiling to half its original quantity. Stir in the meat glaze or gravy, season, beat in the butter, add a squeeze of lemon juice and a little chopped parsley.

One of the classic French sauces for steak, fish, eggs and grills. When used for fish, the meat glaze is replaced by concentrated fish stock.

⋄ FENNEL SAUCE ⋄

Recipes for fennel sauce to serve with fish appear in nearly all old English cookery books. The following, from Richard Dolby's *Cook's Dictionary and Housekeeper's Directory* (1832) is one of the more interesting.

'Pick green fennel, mint and parsley, a little of each; wash them clean, and boil them till tender, drain and press them, chop them fine, add melted butter, and serve up the sauce immediately, for if the herbs are mixed any length of time before it is served up to table they will be discoloured. Parsley becomes equally discoloured from the same cause.

'If approved, there may be added the pulp of green gooseberries rubbed through a hair sieve, and a little sifted sugar.'

⋄ BEURRE MAÎTRE D'HÔTEL ⋄

3 oz butter, unsalted if possible, the juice of quarter of a lemon, a heaped tablespoon of very finely chopped and very fresh parsley, salt, pepper.

Beat the parsley into the butter with a wooden spoon, seasoning lightly with salt and freshly ground pepper; then add the lemon juice, taking care that the whole is well amalgamated. When the butter is to be served with a steak or vegetables or grilled fish, it is not heated but put on a very hot dish and the meat, or whatever it may be, is placed on top of it.

The amounts given will make enough *maître d'hôtel* butter for four helpings of steak.

✧ *MINT BUTTER* ✧

2 oz of butter, a heaped tablespoon of fresh mint leaves, salt, pepper, lemon juice.

Pound the mint in a mortar, add the butter and pound to a smooth ointment, season with salt (very little if salt butter is being used), ground black pepper, a squeeze of lemon juice.

Good with lamb cutlets, grilled sole, and, in very small quantities, with carrots, potatoes, green peas.

✧ *TOMATO SAUCE* ✧

The nicest way to make a tomato sauce when tomatoes are cheap and good is to cook it only very slightly, so that the flavour is preserved. Cookery schools and professional chefs teach that fresh tomato sauce should be thickened with flour. To me this is a cardinal mistake. Flour spoils the taste and the consistency of tomato sauce, depriving it of all its spontaneous charm and much of its essential character.

Put 1 lb of skinned and chopped tomatoes into a little heated butter or olive oil, add seasoning and if you like a little chopped garlic, and some fresh parsley, basil or marjoram. Cook until the tomatoes have melted, not more than 5 minutes.

Especially good for grilled fish or fried eggs.

A little port or marsala can be added to the sauce, in which case it should be cooked a little longer.

For a very good tomato sauce in purée form see the recipe in the chapter on Preserves, page 235.

✧ *WALNUT SAUCE* ✧

Pour boiling water over 2 oz of shelled walnuts; leave a minute or two and then rub off the skins. Soak a thick slice of white bread, without the crust, in water, and then squeeze dry. Pound the walnuts in a mortar with a clove of garlic, a little pepper and salt. Add the bread, a little vinegar, and enough olive oil to form a thick sauce. Press through a sieve, add a little chopped parsley. The sauce should be of the consistency of a thick mayonnaise. Very good with a poached fish, either hot or cold.

⋄ *AVOCADO SAUCE* ⋄

Scoop all the flesh from an avocado pear. Mash or pound it to a purée. Add salt, pepper, lemon or fresh lime juice, and enough olive oil to make the mixture about the consistency of a mayonnaise. Serve with a dry meat such as spiced beef or cold tongue or with a coarse white fish. One avocado makes a surprising amount of sauce – enough for four people. Make it only a short time before it is to be served, or it turns black.

⋄ *MINT CHUTNEY* ⋄

A fresh chutney, served in India with curries, but very good also with roast lamb instead of mint sauce, and with grilled fish. Although uncooked, this sauce or chutney will keep for several days in a covered jar or plastic container in the refrigerator.

Pound together a large handful of fresh mint leaves, a small onion, 2 oz of sugar and a peeled and cored cooking apple. When all the ingredients have turned to a thick paste, season with salt and a little cayenne pepper.

In India a green mango is used instead of the apple.

⋄ *ASPIC JELLY* ⋄

1½ lb shin of beef, 2 pig's or calf's feet, 2 carrots, 2 medium-sized onions, 2 tomatoes, 2 bayleaves, a sprig of thyme, parsley, black pepper, salt, 3 or 4 bacon rinds, a clove of garlic, a small piece of lemon peel, a small glass of sherry.

Cut the beef into three large pieces, split the pig's feet and wash them. Pack them into a deep pan with the carrots and the onions, unpeeled (the onion skins give a good golden colour to the jelly), add the crushed clove of garlic, bacon rinds, lemon peel, the tomatoes cut in halves, the seasonings (only a little salt). Pour over the sherry, and simmer gently for 2 or 3 minutes; then add 2 pints of cold water. Bring gently to the boil, cover the pan, and keep barely on the boil for 4 hours. Strain the stock into a basin, leave to set. Next day remove every scrap of fat with a spoon repeatedly dipped in hot water. If

VAN HULSDONCK, JACOB (1582-1647), *Breakfast*.

the jelly is not clear, put it into a pan, bring it to the boil, beat in two lightly whipped whites of egg and leave barely simmering for 10 minutes. Leave to cool a little and strain through fine muslin. These quantities will make 1¼–1½ pints of good, strong aspic.

Having removed the meat from the pan to make into a salad (see page 122), put some fresh vegetables in and cover the contents of the pan (the pig's feet, etc.) with about 2 pints of water. Two hours' slow cooking will yield another 1¾ pints of jellied stock, not such a good colour or so meaty tasting as the first, but very adequate as a foundation for soups and certain sauces, or for mixing with chicken creams or mousses to make them firm.

To store aspic in a limited space in a refrigerator pour it while still firm into large glass jars, and cover them. If to be kept for any length of time, boil it up every 2 days.

SWEETS

BONNARD, PIERRE, *La Tarte aux Cerises*, 1908.

SWEETS

The sweet course presents no problem in the summer. There is nothing more delicious than fruit and cream, quite plain when strawberries and raspberries come into season, later, when they get cheaper, made into fools, purées, pies; gooseberry fool and gooseberry tart and summer pudding made with raspberries and redcurrants are among the best things of the English table. Water ices made simply from fruit juice and sugar and frozen in the ice tray of a refrigerator make a delicious and refreshing end to a meal. Very simple cream ices, made only with cream and fruit purée, can be varied a good deal. A gooseberry ice cream, for instance, is excellent and unusual. In the early summer, before the berry season starts, lemons are comparatively cheap, and make delicious creams and ices; so do the early imported Spanish apricots which are not ripe enough for dessert. Cream cheeses can be flavoured with liqueurs or candied fruit or simply with sugar. For July and August, when fruit is plentiful and very varied, there are open fruit pies in the French manner, made with sweetened pastry (page 201) and filled with apricots, peaches, greengages, cherries, plums.

I do not myself think it necessary to keep a large stock of liqueurs for flavouring fruit compotes and salads, or to bring them blazing to the table at every meal. Indeed the habit of flambéing everything from prawns to figs has become so prevalent that one can now scarcely dine out in London without for a considerable part of the meal being hemmed in with sheets of flame. An alarming experience in some of those Soho restaurants no larger than a passage. . .

As far as fruit is concerned only the smallest amounts of liqueurs should be mixed with them. Kirsch certainly helps cherries, and for a change a little port is good with strawberries, but if it is overdone the fruit will be sodden. Miss Eliza Acton's recipe for lemon brandy, quoted on page 239, makes an excellent flavouring for fruit salads. As an all-round liqueur which goes well with almost any fruit, Grand Marnier is perhaps the most useful to keep at hand.

❖ APRICOTS BAKED WITH ❖
VANILLA SUGAR

Put fresh apricots in a fireproof dish, with a very little water. Cover them with vanilla sugar (caster sugar kept in a jar with a stick of vanilla). Cook in a very slow oven for about an hour, until the apricots look wrinkled and soft, and coated with sugar.

Serve with fresh unsalted cream cheese (home-made, or Isigny, or Chambourcy). Particularly good for the hard unripe apricots which start arriving from Spain in early June.

❖ APRICOT MOUSSE OR ❖
ICED SOUFFLÉ

An iced soufflé or mousse neither cloying nor rubbery, neither pasty nor rock hard, but creamy, light and with just enough gelatine to make it set and hold its shape, is quite a rarity. It is not difficult, but you have to be generous with the cream and sparing with the gelatine. And personally, I find the old-fashioned leaf gelatine more satisfactory than the powdered variety. It is never gluey in either taste or consistency. It can be bought at many large stores, and about six or eight leaves go to the ounce.

This method for an iced soufflé or mousse, once mastered, can be applied in principle to all kinds of fruit and also to savoury things such as ham, tongue, chicken and fish.

½ lb of fresh apricots, 2 oz sugar, ¼ pint water, 3 leaves of gelatine, ½ pint of thick cream, the whites of 4 eggs.

Stew the apricots with the sugar and water until quite soft. Drain off the juice and reserve it. Stone and sieve the fruit, or pulp it in the blender. Cut the gelatine leaves into small pieces, put them into the top half of a double saucepan with the reserved juice, and steam over hot water until melted. Strain into the fruit pulp. Fold in the lightly whipped cream, put in the refrigerator until chilled and just beginning to set.

At this stage whip the whites of the eggs until they stand in peaks and fold into the fruit and cream. Turn the mixture into a pint-sized soufflé dish and pile it high up over the top of the dish so that it looks as if it were about to topple over (but it won't). Return to the refrigerator to set. An alternative method is to put it in little glass custard cups, one for each person. These quantities will fill six to eight cups or jelly glasses.

⋄ TARTE AUX APRICOTS ⋄

Halve and stone 1 lb of apricots, and cook them only a very few minutes in a little sugar and water. Make a pastry as described in the following recipe, then proceed as for the *tarte aux peches* (page 208).

⋄ SWEET PASTRY FOR ⋄ OPEN FRUIT PIES

For a small open fruit pie or tart the quantities are

4 oz of flour, 2 oz of butter, 2 oz of sugar, the yolk of one egg, a very little water.

Rub the butter into the flour, add the sugar, the beaten yolk, and enough water to make a moderately soft dough. Knead very lightly, roll out quickly and lay in a lightly buttered flan tin.

The fruit is packed into the pastry, the edges dusted with sugar, and the pie baked for 25–30 minutes, in the top of a hot oven (Regulo 7 to 8) for the first 10 minutes. Then turn the heat down to Regulo 4 or 5 until the pastry is cooked.

For a large open tart or to fill two 6–inch tins, increase the quantities to 7 oz of flour, 3½ each of butter and sugar, 2 egg yolks, and about ½ teacupful of water. Vanilla sugar (caster sugar stored in a jar with a vanilla pod) is an improvement on ordinary sugar for some fruit pies, particularly those made with apricots, peaches or plums. The grated peel of a small lemon can also be added to the dough for the pastry with very good effect.

⋄ WALNUT SANDWICHES ⋄

These sandwiches are very good with ices, instead of the usual biscuits or wafers.

Cream together 1½ oz butter and 2 tablespoons of shelled and chopped walnuts. Sandwich between very thin slices of lightly buttered brown bread. Remove the crusts.

⋄ *STRAWBERRIES AND CREAM* ⋄

When strawberries are good there seems to me to be no necessity to dress them up in any way, but there are different theories even as to how strawberries and cream should be presented. Some like strawberries with their cream; for this you fill a bowl with thick cream and add a few whole strawberries which have already been sugared. Others prefer their strawberries, unhulled, and the cream and sugar separate, so that they can dip each berry into sugar then into cream before tasting it. The ordinary way is to hull the strawberries, sugar them, and serve the cream separately. Some like lemon on their strawberries, others orange juice, or port. I have even seen people put pepper on them.

My own preference is for strawberries accompanied by the little cream cheeses which the French call *cœur à la crème* and the Italians *mascarpone*, but of course this needs fresh cream as well, and plenty of sugar to strew over it.

Wild strawberries are, to my way of thinking, infinitely more delicious than any cultivated strawberry, and they don't need any adornment except sugar, although the Italians often put red wine with them, and sometimes orange juice. They make the best ice cream in the world. Anybody who has the chance of trying can use the recipe for strawberry and cream sorbet on page 218.

⋄ *ICED STRAWBERRY FOOL* ⋄

1 lb of strawberries, 3 oz sugar, ¼ pint double cream.

Sieve the hulled strawberries. Stir in the sugar. Add this purée gradually to the whipped cream, so that it is quite smooth. Turn into a shallow crystal or silver dish, and put in the refrigerator for several hours, if possible underneath the ice-trays, so that the fool gets as cold as possible without actually freezing. It is important to cover the bowl, or everything else in the refrigerator will smell of strawberries.

STOSKOPFF, SÉBASTIEN (1597-1657), *A Bowl of Strawberries.*

✧ *STRAWBERRY SOUFFLÉ* ✧

½ lb strawberries, 3 eggs, 1 oz of dried breadcrumbs, 3 oz sugar.

Sieve the strawberries. Cream together the yolks of the eggs and the sugar, add to the strawberry pulp, then add the breadcrumbs. Fold in the stiffly beaten whites of the eggs. Turn into a sugared soufflé dish and steam, uncovered, on top of the stove for about 45 minutes. For the last ten minutes move the dish into a slow oven so that the soufflé turns a pale biscuit colour on the top.

This does not turn out like an ordinary soufflé, but has a very soft spongey consistency and can be eaten either hot or cold.

❖ *ICED STRAWBERRY MOUSSE* ❖
OR SOUFFLÉ

To make a fresh strawberry mousse or iced soufflé use the same proportions of fruit, sugar, water, egg whites, cream and gelatine as given for the apricot mousse on page 200 but instead of cooking the fruit press it through a fine stainless steel, nylon or hair sieve (wire discolours the fruit), make a syrup with the sugar and water, melt the gelatine in this and then proceed as for the apricot recipe.

❖ *SUMMER PUDDING* ❖

Although nearly everybody knows of this wonderful pudding, authentic recipes for it are rare.

For four people stew 1 lb of raspberries and ¼ lb of redcurrants with about ¼ lb of sugar. No water. Cook them only 2 or 3 minutes, and leave to cool. Line a round fairly deep dish (a soufflé dish does very well) with slices of one-day-old white bread with the crust removed. The bread should be of the thickness usual for sandwiches. The dish must be completely lined, bottom and sides, with no space through which the juice can escape. Fill up with the fruit, but reserve some of the juice. Cover the fruit with a complete layer of bread. On top put a plate which fits exactly inside the dish, and on the plate put a 2 or 3 lb weight. Leave overnight in a very cold larder or refrigerator. When ready to serve turn the pudding out on to a dish (not a completely flat one, or the juice will overflow) and pour over it the reserved juice. Some people put strawberries into summer pudding. To me that's a waste of strawberries. They don't go well with raspberries and redcurrants.

Thick fresh cream is usually served with summer pudding, but it is almost more delicious without.

❖ *RASPBERRY SHORTBREAD* ❖

6 oz flour, 3½ oz moist brown sugar, 2 oz butter, ½ teaspoon ground ginger, 1 teaspoon baking powder, 1 lb raspberries, a little white sugar.

Put the raspberries in a fairly large shallow pie dish, strew them with white sugar. Cut the butter into very small pieces and crumble it with the flour until it is thoroughly blended. Add the sugar, ginger and baking powder. Spread this mixture lightly over the raspberries, and smooth it out evenly, but do not press down. Bake in the centre of a medium oven (Regulo 4 or 5) for 25 minutes. Can be served hot or cold and is excellent.

RASPBERRY AND
⋄ REDCURRANT MOUSSE ⋄

½ lb each of redcurrants and raspberries, 4 to 6 oz sugar, 2 whites of egg.

To the sieved raspberry and redcurrant juice add the sugar and then the stiffly whipped whites of egg. Put into a saucepan over a low flame and whisk continually for about 3 minutes, until the mixture starts to thicken and rise like a soufflé. Pour into wine glasses and serve hot with cream, or into a tall dish in which there is just room for the mousse, and leave to cool. When cold some of the juice will separate and sink to the bottom but can be whipped up again before serving.

A nice sweet for children.

⋄ GOOSEBERRY FOOL ⋄

Although this is a traditional English sweet it is not often well made, and owing to the lack of cream for so many years a good many people have never made it.

Put 1 lb of hard green gooseberries in a pan with ¼ lb sugar (there is no need to top and tail them). Steam them until they are quite soft. Sieve them, and when the purée is cold stir in ¼ pint of thick cream. Add more sugar if the fool is too acid. Serve very cold.

⋄ TARTE AUX CERISES ⋄

Line a tart tin with sweet pastry as described on page 201. Fill with 1 lb of stoned cherries, arranged closely together, as they shrink so much during the cooking. Sprinkle with sugar. Beat together a teacupful of cream and the yolk of an egg. Pour over the cherries and bake, taking care that the cream remains somewhat liquid.

✧ *CHERRY SOUFFLÉ OMELETTE* ✧

2 eggs and an extra white, 2 dessertspoons sugar, the grated peel of half a lemon, morello cherry jam.

Spread the bottom of a small oval soufflé dish with a thin layer of bitter cherry jam (or simply stoned, stewed morello cherries). Grate the lemon peel into the beaten yolks of egg, add the sugar. Fold in the beaten whites of the eggs. Pour immediately into the prepared dish so that it is nine-tenths full; strew sugar over the top, make a deep incision along the top with a palette knife, put immediately into a hot oven (gas 6 or 7) and cook for 9 to 10 minutes.
Enough for two.

✧ *BLACKCURRANT PURÉE* ✧

Blackcurrants seem to me best hot, with plenty of very cold cream, but of course they are very good cold too, particularly instead of raspberries in Summer Pudding. To make a hot purée, stew 1 lb of blackcurrants with ¼ lb of sugar (no water). Sieve them, return the purée to the pan, add a squeeze of lemon juice, and heat up again.
If left to go cold this purée sets almost to a jelly, and is very good; ¼ pint of thick cream can be added to it to make a fool, although I think myself it is best with the cream served separately.

✧ *SUGARED NECTARINES* ✧

In the late summer and early autumn we can buy nectarines and peaches imported from southern Europe. In the winter, usually just after Christmas, the South African fruit starts arriving in the country. A variety of nectarine known as *Marina*, grown in Cape Province, is particularly good for slicing into a fruit salad.
Do not peel nectarines. Simply slice them, with a silver or stainless knife, into sections, and straight into a bowl or glass. To achieve the best visual effect, it is necessary to understand the proper way to slice raw nectarines and peaches. It is the easiest and most obvious way; and for that reason perhaps the method occurs to few people. All that is required is that you start

CUNDELL, NORA, *Still Life with Peaches and a Potted Plant*, 1940.

by making an incision down the natural division of the fruit, from stalk to flower end. Slice out one section. Then continue slicing, turning the fruit as you cut, all round the fruit, until all you have left in your hand is the stone. In this manner none of the fruit is wasted, all sections are approximately of equal size, and in the case of nectarines, each has its due proportion of flesh and skin, so that when all your fruit is sliced you have a bowl full of most inviting contrast of colour and texture – bright smooth skin, pale, melting flesh.

Over the nectarines strew a little fine white sugar, then a squeeze of lemon juice – say half a lemon to four nectarines. Nothing else is necessary, or desirable.

⬦ *TARTE AUX PÊCHES* ⬦

Make a pastry as described on page 201. To fill a 6-inch pie tin, 8 medium-sized peaches are needed.

Plunge them into boiling water and leave them a minute or two. Remove the skins. Stew them in water just to cover with about 3 oz of sugar until they are soft enough to cut in half, and for the stones to be removed. Arrange the half peaches in circles on the prepared pastry. While the pie is cooking thicken the syrup from the peaches by fast boiling. When the pie is taken from the oven pour the cooked syrup over the top, then dust with vanilla sugar. Serve cold.

⬦ *PEACHES IN WINE* ⬦

Pour boiling water over some good fresh peaches (a large one per head), preferably the yellow-fleshed variety. Leave them a couple of minutes and peel off the skins.

Slice the peaches, as in the nectarine recipe described on page 206, straight into wine goblets. Strew the fruit with a little sugar. Fill up the glasses with ordinary red table wine, to cover the peaches.

Although seldom described in cookery books, this method of serving peaches is quite common in France. The peaches should be prepared only on the day they are to be eaten, and if possible only just before the meal. They become sodden if left too long soaking in the wine.

✧ MELON STUFFED WITH ✧ RASPBERRIES

¾ lb to 1 lb of raspberries, a medium-sized melon, sugar, kirsch or Grand Marnier.

Strew the raspberries with sugar, pour over them a very small glass of kirsch or Grand Marnier, and leave them for several hours. Cut a slice off the top of the melon, throw away the seeds. Scoop out some of the flesh, cut it into cubes, mix it with the raspberries, and then fill the melon with the mixture.

Wild strawberries are really the ideal filling for a stuffed melon, but raspberries are next best. If using strawberries, then flavour with port instead, but very little, or the fruit will become too sodden. When the small, sweet Cavaillon melons, no larger than a grapefruit, are available, one for each person makes an attractive sweet.

Do not put melons into the refrigerator. Their scent penetrates everything else in it, especially butter.

✧ HOT FRUIT SALAD ✧

This fashion of serving summer fruit has, to me, all the flavour and scent of a warm summer fruit garden. The proportions are important and the gooseberries must be red ones, not green.

1 lb of red gooseberries, ½ lb of raspberries, ¼ lb of redcurrants, sugar.

Stew the gooseberries, redcurrants and sugar together for 5 minutes (no water). Add the raspberries for 2 minutes only. Serve very hot, with fresh cream.

✧ PLUMS ✧

Cold stewed plums must be one of the dullest dishes on earth. Accompanied by custard it is one of the most depressing. English plum tart runs it pretty close.

Hot stewed plums, provided they are a good variety, have been cooked with very little water, and are served with plenty of cream, are much more

VALLAYER-COSTER, ANNE, (1744-1818), *A Basket of Plums, a Tumbler of White Wine and Two Cakes.*

acceptable than cold plums. But plums don't seem to be what they were. Like all other fruit nowadays they are presumably grown for looks and high yield, not for flavour. The little yellow bullace plums still to be found in old gardens have a much better flavour than any of the shining purple, red, or golden monsters to be bought in shops. The red-skinned Victorias make a good open plum tart, but damsons are best of all for cooking, and greengages (not greengage-plums) for dessert. The little yellow plums which the French call *mirabelles* make lovely jam and open pies, and purple Pershores are also a good variety for jams and pies. So are Monarchs, Czars, and Presidents (what happened to the Moguls and the *Impératrices?*). Among the best cooking plums are the imported Switzers, the Yugoslav version of the *quetsch.*

The recipe for apricots baked with vanilla sugar (page 200) can be very successfully applied to Victorias or other large and juicy plums.

❖ PLUMS BAKED IN WINE ❖

1 lb Victoria, Czar or other good cooking plums, 3 tablespoons of sugar, 2 tablespoons each of port wine and water.

The plums should be, preferably, slightly under-ripe. Wipe them with a soft cloth. With a fruit knife make a slit in each plum, following the natural division of the fruit.

In a baking dish (I use a deepish ovenproof china bowl but almost any baking dish will do provided it is not too large for the quantity of fruit, which should, if possible, be piled up rather than spread out in one layer) put the fruit, strewn with sugar, which can be brown, white or vanilla-flavoured; alternatively, a vanilla pod can be cooked with the fruit. Add the wine and water. Bake near the top of a slow oven, gas No. 2, 210°F, for 35 to 40 minutes. The timing depends upon the variety and relative ripeness of the plums. They should be tender but still retain their shape. They are delicious hot or cold.

❖ PLUM OR APRICOT ❖ CROÛTONS

Butter some slices of day-old sandwich bread: place them on a buttered baking sheet. On each slice put 3 ripe plum or apricot halves, stones discarded, and the spaces filled with sugar. Press the fruit well down on the bread. Bake near the top of a very moderate oven, gas No. 3, 330°F, for about 40 minutes, and serve hot.

A delicious sweet for children, for the bread is crisp, the fruit soft and sticky, the sugar almost caramelized.

❖ CREAM CHEESE ❖

Fresh cream cheeses make charming spring and summer desserts, and can be flavoured in many different ways. The following few recipes are simply to provide ideas. Many variations can be made, but these sweets are perhaps best when they are least complicated.

✧ CREAM CHEESE ✧
WITH WINE

Put a pound of fresh cream cheese through the food mill (it is always advisable to do this for cream cheese sweets as it makes a smoother mixture). Add ¼ lb of caster sugar, and gradually a large glass of white wine and the juice of a lemon. Serve with it plain biscuits.

✧ CREAM CHEESE WITH ✧
ANGELICA

To 1 lb of cream cheese add 3 oz of sugar, the beaten whites of 2 eggs and as much chopped angelica as you like.

Put into a muslin and leave to drain in a cool place for a few hours. Turn out on to a dish and serve with fresh cream.

A cool and fresh-looking dessert for the weeks before the fresh fruit comes in.

✧ GERANIUM CREAM ✧

½ pint of fresh cream, 6 small fresh cream cheeses, either Isigny or Chambourcy, sugar, 2 sweet-scented geranium leaves.

Put the cream into a double saucepan, add 4 tablespoons of sugar and 2 whole sweet-scented geranium leaves. Steam gently, and let the cream get thoroughly hot without boiling. Leave to cool, with the geranium leaves still in the cream. Mix gradually with the cream cheese, until a thick smooth cream results. Leave, in a refrigerator, covered, for 12 hours. Remove the geranium leaves only just before serving.

The cream can be served either by itself or as an accompaniment to fresh blackberries thickly strewn with sugar. The flavour of the geranium leaves is exquisite.

❖ CREAM CHEESE WITH ❖ APRICOT BRANDY

Mix ½ lb cream cheese with 2 oz sugar, 2 tablespoons apricot brandy, 2 chopped glacé apricots, or 4 fresh apricots when in season.

❖ CRÉMETS D'ANGERS ❖

Whip ½ pint of thick cream until it is absolutely stiff. Fold in the beaten whites of 3 eggs; turn into a clean muslin and place in little heart-shaped baskets or pierced moulds and leave to drain in a cool place for about 12 hours. Turn out on to a dish and cover with fresh cream. Serve with sugar. The best of all accompaniments for strawberries, raspberries and apricots.

❖ CHOCOLATE CHINCHILLA ❖

A good recipe for using whites of eggs.

Mix together 2 oz of unsweetened cocoa powder and 3 oz of caster sugar. Add 1 heaped tablespoon of ground cinnamon, or 3 of powdered coffee, or very finely ground almonds.

Whip the whites of 6 or 7 eggs to a stiff snow. Tip the cocoa and sugar mixture on to the egg whites. Fold the two together, gently but thoroughly. Turn into a buttered mould or soufflé dish of 1½ to 2 pints capacity. The dish should be full almost to the brim. Stand it in a baking tin with water to come half-way up the dish.

Cook the Chinchilla – which is really a kind of soufflé without egg yolks – in the centre of a moderate gas oven, gas No. 3, 330°F, for about 45 minutes. It will rise in a spectacular manner. Serve it quickly with fresh, cold, pouring cream to which has been added a little sherry, rum or brandy.

Chocolate Chinchilla can also be eaten cold. If this is to be its fate, then cook it 5 to 10 minutes longer and be sure that, once cooked, it is left to cool in a warm place and not subjected to draughts or a violent change of temperature.

When cold it will have shrunk and become compact enough to turn out easily. It will have a good texture and a very rich dark colour.

The most satisfactory mould for puddings with a high content of whisked egg white is a deepish one with a central funnel, such as a kugelhopf mould.

⬦ *To store egg whites* ⬦

Store egg whites in a *covered* bowl, jar or plastic container in the refrigerator or larder but don't keep them too long, especially in warm weather. Before they become *visibly* unhealthy egg whites can develop germs which are liable to cause food poisoning.

⬦ SAND CAKE ⬦

Sand cake came originally from Austria, where it is called *Sandtorte*. It makes a most excellent cake for luncheon, or to serve with a fruit salad or creamy sweet, or an ice.

This recipe is based on the one given in the 1906 edition of Mrs Beeton. It is worth recording that the cost in those days worked out at 1s 3d.

> 7 oz cornflour, 1 oz plain flour, 8 oz butter, 6 oz caster sugar, 1 oz shelled almonds, ground or pounded, but not skinned, the whites of 3 eggs, the yolks of 2 eggs, 1 teaspoon of finely grated lemon rind, the juice of half a lemon.

Clarify the butter. This should be done either the day before or in the morning for the afternoon. The butter is heated slowly until it is melted, then poured into a basin through a fine strainer so that all the froth at the top is cleared off – it can also be taken off with a spoon. Leave it to set slightly. When ready to make the cake, add the sugar to the clarified butter and beat until creamy and white. When the proper consistency has been obtained, beat in the yolks of eggs, the ground almonds, the lemon rind and juice, and lastly the flour and cornflour.

Whip the whites of eggs to a very stiff froth, add them as lightly as possible to the rest of the ingredients, and pour the mixture at once into a buttered cake tin. I prefer a square one for a sand cake. Bake in a moderate oven for an hour or a little longer. (I always put the cake into the oven, well heated, at Regulo 6, and after ten minutes turn it down to 5 for the remainder of the cooking time, but this must depend on individual experience.) Test with a skewer, which should come out dry when the cake is done.

When it has cooled a little turn out upside-down on to a wire cake rack. Keep until next day before cutting.

NICHOLSON, WILLIAM, *Cake for Tea*, 1919.

ICE CREAMS
AND SORBETS

In 1955 when this book was first published few people made ices at home, and those who did mostly used one of the trusty old hand-cranked freezers, a metal container set within a wooden pail packed with crushed ice and coarse freezing salt. In those days obliging fishmongers would still deliver a block of ice, and coarse salt was obtainable in bulk from city depots responsible for maintaining supplies for the salting of streets during spells of icy weather. Once you had prepared your sorbet or ice cream mixture, filled the inner container of the freezer pain, crushed the requisite amount of ice – about 10 lb, for a single freezer pail – and measured out about a third of its weight in coarse salt, you still had twenty minutes or more of energetic and fairly noisy hand-cranking to get through before your sorbet or ice cream was frozen. If it didn't freeze it meant that there was too much sugar in your mixture and if it appeared to be freezing to a solid mass of ice then there wasn't enough. Professional confectioners had long since abolished the guesswork in composing their cream and water ice mixes by using a gauge or saccharometer which tested the density of the sugar syrup on which all their ices were based, regardless of whether they were making up straightforward sorbets or rich cream mixtures.

Personally, I didn't use a saccharometer. My ices were rarely made for more than four to six people, and on that scale the density of a basic syrup is easy enough to determine. It is merely a question of boiling sugar and water, say ¼ lb sugar to ¼ pint of water, until you have obtained a syrup just thick enough to have a consistency but not so thick that it hangs from the spoon.

Using that quantity of syrup you can sweeten a purée made from 2 lb of sieved strawberries, raspberries, gooseberries, blackberries or mulberries, in fact all the berry fruits, as also blackcurrants and redcurrants which should be used uncooked, and which make the best of summer sorbets. Stone fruit such as apricots and greengages, which make delicious cream ices, are best cooked gently in a little water but without sugar. When the fruit is soft, take out the stones, strain the juice off into a measuring jug, then weigh the fruit. To make the syrup, allow ¼ lb of sugar and ¼ pint of the fruit juice to every

216

pound of the fruit. If necessary make up the amount with extra water. Boil the sugar and fruit juice to a syrup as already explained.

As for the freezing of my ices, in the 1950s that was carried out in my refrigerator trays, a rather laborious and inconvenient method which I was able to abandon when I acquired, in turn, one of those electrically-operated sorbetières which fitted into the freezing compartment of my large refrigerator, and later into a freezer. Eventually the sorbetière was discarded when, in the 80s, the new Italian ice cream makers, fitted with their own built-in freezer units, appeared on the scene. There are now, in 1988, several versions of the most recent generation of Italian gelato-makers, none of them cheap, but all simple to operate. Most of them are fast-acting, taking no more than twenty-five minutes to freeze a litre of ready-prepared and chilled mixture into sorbets and cream ices with textures as perfect as any from a professional *glacier*. Even Gunters, the great Berkeley Square confectioners of blessed memory, could hardly have done better than some of the fruit sorbets and rich cream ices turned out by the machine I acquired back in 1980. The sorbet-maker in question was I believe the first of its kind made for domestic use to appear in this country. Loaned to me by the importers, the new toy weighed 60 lb, and took up a lot of kitchen space. All the same, it very soon became indispensible, so I bought it and had a sturdy little table made especially for it, so that it stands at exactly the right height. Unless a machine of this kind is readily accessible and easy to use it's just another encumbrance.

✧ APRICOT ICE CREAM ✧

1 lb fresh apricots, 3 oz sugar, ¼ pint of double cream, water.

Halve and stone the apricots. Steam them until soft and sieve them. When cold add a syrup made from the sugar and ¼ pint of water simmered for 10 minutes. Immediately before freezing add the whipped cream. Freeze.

To make a firmer ice, the ice cream can be cooked to a thin custard with the beaten yolks of 2 eggs. When cool, mix the apricot purée with its syrup into the cream caramel. Add also a few of the apricot kernels, skinned and crushed.

❖ *STRAWBERRY SORBET* ❖

This is an Italian granita.

Quantities are 2 lb of strawberries, the juice of half a lemon and of half an orange, ½ lb white sugar, ½ pint of water. Hull the strawberries, purée them in the blender, press them through a stainless steel wire, or nylon sieve. (Tinned wire or tinned steel discolours the fruit.) Add the strained orange and lemon juice.

Boil the sugar and water for about seven minutes to make a thin syrup (to make a sorbet of greater density boil the syrup for 10 minutes or unitil it is beginning to thicken) and leave it to cool before adding it to the strawberry pulp.

Chill the mixture before freezing it.

As the name implies, this type of water ice should be slightly grainy, no more than just barely frozen. The quantities given should provide enough helpings for six to eight people.

❖ *STRAWBERRY AND CREAM* ❖
SORBET

According to Escoffier, a fruit juice with added whipped cream is still a sorbet. It is the basic egg-thickened custard mixture which turns an ice into an ice cream. Whatever its name, this type of ice is very light and delicious. Make the mixture as for *granita*, boiling the syrup rather longer to increase its density. For 2 lb of strawberries allow ¼ pint of double cream. Whip it very lightly, fold it swiftly into the chilled fruit and syrup mixture, freeze immediately.

❖ *RASPBERRY ICE CREAM* ❖

1 pint of raspberry juice (i.e. about 2 lb of fruit, include about ¼ lb of redcurrants they will intensify the flavour), the juice of half a lemon, ½ lb of sugar, ¼ pint of water, ¼ pint of cream.

Make a syrup of the sugar and water by boiling them together for 5 minutes.

When cold add it to the raspberry pulp. Squeeze in the lemon juice. Add ¼ pint of whipped cream. Freeze.

Enough for six or seven.

❖ *RASPBERRY WATER ICE* ❖

1 lb of raspberries, ¼ lb redcurrants, 3 to 4 oz sugar, water, the juice of half a lemon.

Sieve the raspberries and redcurrants. Make a syrup by boiling the sugar with ¼ pint of water for a few minutes. When cool, add to the raspberry purée. Stir in the lemon juice. Freeze.

❖ *GOOSEBERRY ICE CREAM* ❖

Prepare the gooseberries and cream exactly as for gooseberry fool on page 205. Freeze. A very good and unusual ice.

HUNT, WILLIAM HENRY (1790-1864), *Fruit Piece.*

❖ BLACKBERRY WATER ICE ❖

1 lb of blackberries, ¼ lb of sugar, ¼ pint of water, if possible 2 or 3 sweet-scented geranium leaves.

Make a syrup by boiling the sugar and water together for 5 or 6 minutes, with the 2 sweet scented geranium leaves. When cool add the syrup to the sieved blackberries, and freeze with a fresh sweet scented geranium leaf on the top. A tablespoon or two of rose water makes a fair substitute for the sweet-scented geranium leaves.

This sorbet has been extraordinarily popular. Perhaps it was the sweet-scented geranium leaves which caught the imagination of the readers.

❖ LEMON ICE CREAM ❖

2 lemons, 3 oz white sugar, ¼ pint double cream.

Put the thinly peeled rind of the lemons with the white sugar in 4 oz of water, and simmer gently for 20 minutes. Leave the syrup to cool, strain and add to it the juice of the lemons. When quite cold, add it gradually to the whipped cream, stirring gently until the whole mixture is smooth. Freeze.

❖ MULBERRY WATER ICE ❖

Sir Harry Luke, author of *The Tenth Muse** one of the most civilized and original of modern cookery books, claims that the mulberry, his favourite berry fruit, makes the best of all water ices.

Made according to the same method as the strawberry *granita* (page 218) , but omitting the orange juice, a mulberry ice is indeed both delicious and beautiful.

*Putnam 1954. Second edition, revised, 1962.

JAMS, JELLIES AND OTHER PRESERVES

GILBERT, VICTOR (b.1847), *The Brioche.*

JAMS, JELLIES AND OTHER PRESERVES

A generation which has grown up since the end of the last war, remembering little or nothing of the shortages and rationing, is in revolt against factory-produced food and the standardization of everything we eat. A growing number of these young people are discovering, without prompting from their elders, how delicious home-made jams and jellies can be, or how satisfactory is the sight of a larder shelf laden with pots of clear red jellies, thick apricot jam like jars of clouded amber, crimson and purple damson and plum and blackberry, translucent greengage preserves and solid cornelian-coloured quince cheese. This is food with an ancient history, delicacies which once were a comfort for wintry breakfasts and at tea-time, to be eaten with thick white bread toasted in front of the fire, with the curtains drawn and the winds blowing outside. Miss Dorothy Hartley, in her fascinating book *Food in England* (Macdonald & Co., 1954) has described how north country housewives, in order to show off the number of different jams in their larders, would make huge jam tarts, criss-crossed with pastry, each section filled with a different jam. Sometimes there would be as many as twelve.

Then there are the fruit relishes and chutneys and jellies made in the late summer and autumn to be eaten with game, roast mutton, cold beef and ham; they are worth all the time and trouble that has been spent on them. These things are not cheaper (except for those who grow their own fruit) than bought preserves, but they are much nicer, and it is gratifying simply to fetch a new jar of redcurrant jelly or raspberry jam from the larder instead of having to go out and buy it from the grocer.

All preserves should be made with the finest ingredients; the fruit should be ripe but not over-ripe, and absolutely dry. Fruit that is all sodden will not set properly and will not keep. When the jam-making season starts lay in a stock of preserving sugar, which is similar to cube sugar, and of the best quality; the jam will have less tendency to stick and burn and the scum will be easier to remove as it rises, giving a fine clear jam.

As well as the usual large preserving pan an asset for jelly making is a 7 lb, or larger, stone jar in which the fruit is packed and left in a very slow oven until the juice flows; a tall narrow earthen casserole serves the same purpose. A large, fine hair or nylon sieve, or a supply of double muslin for straining juice for jellies, clean long-handled wooden spoons, and absolutely spotless, dry jars are necessities for jam and jelly making.

There are so many different kinds of jam jar covers now on the market that there need be no bother with cutting out paper and tying with string, but a round of paper dipped in brandy and fitted inside the jar on top of the jam helps to preserve the jam. For pickles and chutneys, brown sugar makes a richer syrup than white, in both taste and colour, and wine vinegar or Orléans vinegar is much milder than the savage English malt vinegar; although I have often been told that pickles made with malt vinegar keep better than those made with wine vinegar I have not found this to be the case. English home-made jams and jellies are usually delicious, but pickles and chutneys are often far too acid, and I nearly always halve the quantity of vinegar given in any English recipe, however reliable I know the author to be in other respects. Meg Dods, whose *Cook's and Housewife's Manual* (1817) is in most ways worthy of all praise, gives one of the most gruesome recipes for pickles I have ever seen (a handful each of salt and horseradish, 3 bottles of vinegar, ½ oz of cayenne and a cupful of mustard seed to pickle 6 lemons). Indeed the English appetite for strong sauces and pickles apparently knows no bounds, and I have heard it suggested that if a tax were put on vinegar it would shortly enable the Chancellor to make a substantial reduction in the duty on wine.

For my jam and jelly receipts I have drawn considerably on the work of Miss Eliza Acton (as so many, including Mrs Beeton, have done before me). Her book, *Modern Cookery*, published about fifteen years before that of Mrs Beeton, is the expression of English country-house cooking in the mid-nineteenth century when it must have been very good indeed. It is clear from her directions that she cooked, or supervised the cooking of, every dish many times. It is 120 years since her book was published, but she writes with such certain knowledge and calm authority that there is scarcely a recipe in her book which could not be followed today with perfect confidence.

Other Victorian works which give splendid recipes for preserves are two manuals of the eighties, Cassell's *Dictionary of Cooking* and Spon's *Household Manual*. Two later books of great interest to those who have their own country produce are the *Cookery Book* of Lady Clark of Tillypronie, published in 1909, and *Pot Luck*, a misleading title for a lovely collection of country recipes edited by May Byron and published in 1914, the end of an era when the uninhibited use of the best ingredients, and pride in a well-stocked larder, were taken for granted.

❖ *APRICOT CHEESE* ❖

Halve the apricots, stone them, and steam them until soft. Sieve them. Add a pound of sugar to every pint of pulp. Cook, stirring frequently, until the purée starts to candy at the edges. Store in jars.

An excellent and very useful preserve, better than jam for omelettes and puddings, delicious with unsalted cream cheese, or mixed with whipped cream to make a fool for the winter. The flavour is even better if a few of the stones are cracked and the kernels added to the apricots when sieved. Or a few blanched split almonds can be used instead of the apricot kernels.

❖ *APRICOT CHUTNEY* ❖

2 lb ripe apricots, 10 oz brown sugar, 1 onion, ¼ lb sultanas, 1 teaspoon of grated green ginger root or ½ teaspoon of ground ginger, a tablespoon of salt, ½ pint Orléans vinegar, 1 teaspoon of coriander seeds, 2 or 3 cloves of garlic.

Halve the apricots and stone them. Slice the onion and the garlic. Put all the ingredients into a large pan and boil until the apricots are quite soft. Take them out and put into jars. Boil the rest of the liquid rapidly until it turns to a thickish syrup, and pour into jars. Seal down.

A mild chutney which goes well with cold boiled gammon or tongue.

❖ *STRAWBERRY JELLY* ❖

'Take the small scarlet strawberries, put them in an earthen jar, and stand the jar in a pan of boiling water. Let them steam 3 or 4 hours, the water being always boiling. When they are quite soft pour the strawberries into a sieve, or a cloth, and strain out the juice. Allow 1 lb of fine white sugar to each pint of juice. Boil it till it stiffens, which it will do in 30 or 40 minutes. The jelly must be made at once, that is to say as soon as the strawberries are strained, as it will not jelly after it has once cooled'.

From the *Cookery Book* of Lady Clark of Tillypronie (Constable, 1909)

❖ *RASPBERRY JAM, UNBOILED* ❖

Equal weights of raspberries and fine white sugar.

Put raspberries and sugar each in a large dish which will go in the oven.

Let them get very hot, but not boiling. (This takes 20–30 minutes in a medium oven.)

Turn sugar and fruit into a large bowl and mix them thoroughly together, using a wooden spoon. Turn at once into jars and seal down, putting a round of paper dipped in brandy inside each jar.

This is by far the best raspberry jam I have ever tasted. It preserves almost intact the fresh flavour of the fruit, and will keep for a year. Sometimes a mould forms on top of the jam, but the jam itself is unaffected. In the year following the beautiful summer of 1959 the raspberry jam I made by this method had the most intense flavour of any I have ever tasted.

This jam and the redcurrant jelly which follows are delicious eaten with fresh cream cheese and sugar.

SUPERLATIVE
◇ *REDCURRANT JELLY* ◇

(Norman Receipt)

'Strip carefully from the stems some quite ripe currants of the finest quality and mix with them an equal weight of good sugar reduced to powder; boil these together quickly for exactly eight minutes, keep them stirred all the time, and clean off the scum – which will be very abundant – as it rises; then turn the preserve into a very clean sieve, and put into small jars the jelly which runs through it, and which will be delicious in flavour, and of the brightest colour. It should be carried immediately, when this is practicable, to an extremely cool but not a damp place, and left there until perfectly cold. The currants which remain in the sieve make an excellent jam, particularly if only part of the jelly be taken from them. In Normandy, where the fruit is of richer quality than in England, this preserve is boiled only two minutes, and is both firm and beautifully transparent.'

This recipe is from Miss Eliza Acton who adds: 'This receipt we are told by some of our correspondents is not generally quite successful in this country, as the jelly, though it keeps well and is of the finest possible flavour, is scarcely firm enough for table. We have ourselves found this to be the case in cold damp seasons, but the preserve even then was valuable for many purposes, and always agreeable eating.'

Miss Acton would perhaps have been shocked at the idea, but I find this jelly just as successful if the fruit is put into the pan with the sugar after being washed, but without being stripped from the stalks. The stalks in no way injure either the flavour or colour of the jelly, which, as Miss Acton says, does not set very firmly, but is delicious. It is ideal for serving with mutton, venison and hare, and for making Cumberland and other sauces to go with game.

Made in a good dry season, the redcurrant jelly will keep for as long as three years.

GAUGUIN, PAUL, *Still Life with Cherries*, 1886.

✧ BLACKCURRANT JELLY ✧

¾ lb sugar to each pound of fruit. Put the blackcurrants, stalks and all, into a large pan with the sugar. Bring to the boil, take off the scum as it rises, and boil fast for 10 minutes. Pour on to a fine sieve placed over a bowl and let the juice run through. Press the fruit lightly with a wooden spoon.

Pour the jelly while still warm into small glass jars and seal. Excellent for making winter desserts.

✧ MORELLO CHERRY PRESERVE ✧

Put 6 oz of sugar to every pound of stoned morello cherries. Break a few of the stones and add the kernels to the fruit. Boil, without the addition of water, until the juice is thick.

A very good preserve for sweet omelettes, soufflés, and sauces for puddings. But it is one for quick consumption rather than for storage.

✧ SWEET-SOUR CHERRIES ✧

For 2 lb of morello cherries 1½ pints of white wine vinegar, ¾ lb sugar, 12 cloves.

Leave about ½ inch of the stalks on the cherries. Put them, unstoned, into wide-necked bottling jars. Boil the vinegar, sugar and cloves together for about 10 minutes. While still hot pour over the cherries and seal the bottles. They will be ready in about a month. Good with boiled tongue, and to use for sauces for duck, venison, teal, wild duck and pigeons.

In some country places in southern France I have come across these cherries served as an hors d'œuvre, like olives. Incidentally, they shrivel with age. This does not detract from their flavour.

✧ CHERRY BRANDY ✧

Allow 1 lb of morello cherries to one bottle of brandy, and 3 oz of white candy sugar to each pound of fruit.

Leave about ½ inch of stalk on the cherries, wipe them with a soft cloth, prick them with a needle and half fill fruit bottling jars with them. Add the sugar and fill the bottles with brandy. Seal the bottles. Pour off in 6 months. Use a standard 3-star brandy. Do not, as Cassell's *Dictionary of Cookery* remarks, 'make the mistake of supposing that the fruit and sugar will make bad spirit pass for good.'

◆ GREEN GOOSEBERRY ◆ JELLY

Choose the yellowish-green variety of gooseberry, very ripe. They must be well washed, but there is no need to top and tail them. Put them into a pan with about ¼ pint of water to every pound of fruit.

Simmer gently until the fruit is broken and all the juice flowing out. Pour into a hair sieve placed over a large bowl, or into a muslin, and let the juice drip through. The fruit can be gently pressed but not too much. To each pint of juice measure ¾ lb of sugar. Bring the juice to the boil, add the sugar, and boil in the usual way, until the jelly sets when a drop is poured on to a plate.

◆ GOOSEBERRY AND ◆ MINT JELLY

Make green gooseberry jelly as above. During the final boiling add, for every pint of juice used, 4 tablespoons of very finely chopped fresh mint and a tablespoon of wine vinegar.

Delicious instead of mint sauce.

◆ GOOSEBERRY JELLY ◆ FLAVOURED WITH ELDERFLOWERS

'Make gooseberry jelly the ordinary way, and when it is ready to take off the fire, have ready a bunch of elder flowers tied up in a piece of muslin, which turn round and round in the jelly until it has the desired flavour; it is really like a most delicious grape.'

A Lincolnshire recipe given by May Byron in *Pot Luck*, 1914

❖ *GROSEILLÉE* ❖

'Cut the tops and stalks from a gallon or more of well-flavoured ripe gooseberries, throw them into a large preserving pan, boil them for 10 minutes, and stir them often with a wooden spoon; then pass both the juice and pulp through a fine sieve, and to every three pounds weight of these add half a pint of raspberry juice and boil the whole briskly for three-quarters of an hour; draw the pan aside, stir in for the above portion of fruit, two pounds of sugar, and when it is dissolved renew the boiling for 15 minutes longer.

'When more convenient a portion of raspberries can be boiled with the gooseberries at first.'

Eliza Acton, *Modern Cookery*, 1855 edition, (first published 1845)

HAMMER, WILLIAM, *A Still Life of Figs, Walnuts, an Orange and a Lemon*, 1855.

GREENGAGE AND RED
⬦ GOOSEBERRY PRESERVE ⬦

'Boil for three-quarters of an hour in 2 pints of clear red gooseberry juice 1 lb of very ripe greengages, weighed after they have been stoned and pared; then stir to them one pound and a half of good sugar, and boil them quickly again for twenty minutes. If the quantity of preserve be much increased, the time of boiling it must be so likewise; this is always better done before the sugar is added.'
Eliza Acton's recipe from *Modern Cookery*, 1855 edition

⬦ PRESERVED PEACHES ⬦

Take an equal weight of fruit and sugar; lay the fruit in a large dish, and sprinkle half the sugar over, in fine powder; give them a gentle shaking; the next day make a thin syrup with the remainder of the sugar; and instead of water, if you have it, allow one pint of redcurrant juice to every pound of peaches; simmer them in this till sufficiently clear.

   N.B. Pick them when not dead ripe.
From *Pot Luck*, edited by May Byron, 1914

⬦ FIG JELLY ⬦

Fresh figs are so rare in this country that it is madness to do anything but just eat them and be thankful. Imported figs are an absurd price and are rarely good. People who like figs like them very much and need a large quantity, not one or two wrapped up in cotton wool. However, the small green figs which will not ripen make an excellent preserve.

   The following recipe comes from May Byron's *Pot Luck*, and is very successful.

   'Take one pound of small cooking figs, remove the stems, and pour over them some very hot, but not boiling water. Leave them for a minute or two, then drain off the water. Then cut each fig in pieces, and to each pound of figs put one pound of sugar, a little grated lemon peel, and the juice of one lemon. Put them into a pan and let them cook very slowly, until the syrup thickens and the figs become clear; stir carefully, and if it gets too thick add a little water. When cold, pour off into jars and cover tightly.'

⬥ *GRAPE PRESERVE* ⬥

'A delicious preserve from unripe grapes can be made in the following way: They should be carefully picked and all that are at all injured should be rejected.

'To 1 lb of grapes add ½ lb of sugar; no water but what hangs about them after they have been washed. Put the grapes into a preserving pan, then a layer of sugar, then a layer of grapes. Boil on a moderate fire, stirring it all the time to prevent its burning, and as the grape stones rise take them out with a spoon, so that by the time the fruit is sufficiently boiled the stones will have all boiled up and been taken out.'
Recipe from Spon's *Household Manual*, *circa* 1886

⬥ *PICKLED PLUMS* ⬥

5 lb rather under-ripe plums, 5 lb sugar, 1½ pints wine vinegar, a stick of cinnamon, cloves.

Prepare a syrup by boiling the sugar and vinegar together for a few minutes; add the cinnamon and 2 tablespoons of whole cloves. After a few minutes boiling put in the plums which should have been jabbed here and there with a small skewer. Bring to the boil again, remove the scum, and take out the plums at once. Put them in a large bowl. Boil the syrup for another 3 or 4 minutes, pour over the plums. Leave in a cold place for 24 hours, and then repeat the boiling process; i.e. strain off the syrup, bring it to the boil, put in the plums, boil them half a minute, remove them, continue to boil the syrup a minute or two, pour over the plums. Next day the pickle can be put into bottles or jars and sealed. Leave for six weeks before opening.

⬥ *DAMSON CHEESE* ⬥

To make the best-flavoured damson cheese, the fruit should be placed whole in a stone jar and baked in a very slow oven until it is quite soft. Turn it out into a pan and boil it fairly quickly until it has dried somewhat. By this time the stones should have come to the top and will be easy to remove. Put the fruit through a food mill (mouli légumes), add a pound of sugar for every 4 lb of fruit you have used, and simmer for about ½ hour, until the paste begins to candy round the edges of the pan. Pour into jars. The addition of some of the kernels to the cheese improves the flavour; to do this, boil the stones again when you have removed them from the fruit, then crack them. Add the kernels when you have put the pulp and sugar into the pan. Some people put a little stick of cinnamon into the fruit when it is baking, which gives a rich spicy flavour.

An alternative to putting damson cheese into jars is to pour it into shallow bowls, dry it out in a just warm oven, or the plate drawer of an electric oven, and serve in the winter turned out on to dishes so that it can be cut into slices for dessert.

❖ TO PICKLE DAMSONS ❖

'3 quarts fresh damsons, rub dry with cloth, prick them. Dissolve 1 lb lump sugar in 1 pint best distilled vinegar; when boiling pour over damsons in deep jar, and cover close. Next day pour off the liquor, reboil and pour over again; the same on the third day. Let stand one day longer, and then scald altogether, pour into jars and keep from the air.'

The amount of sugar and vinegar seems very small in proportion to the fruit, but in fact a good deal of juice comes from the damsons and the quantities are exactly right. A quart of damsons is approximately 2 lb.

❖ ROWANBERRY JELLY ❖

Rowanberries, the fruit of the mountain ash, are to be had for the picking in many parts of England, Scotland and Wales and are common in suburban gardens. The beautiful red berries have a most attractive sour-sweet flavour and make a lovely jelly for eating with game, particularly hare. Sometimes the rowanberries are mixed with apples to make the jelly, as rowanberries do not jelly very easily, but with the right amount of boiling (approximately 20 minutes, using the following recipe) they will.

Here is the recipe given by Lady Clark of Tillypronie.

'For game, venison, or roe deer.
    'Gather the rowanberries when *quite ripe, quite sound, quite dry*. Pick them from the stalks and put them in a deep pan. Cover them completely with water and boil until they seem soft, which will be in 5 to 15 minutes. Mash

them slightly and strain through a flannel bag, giving the bag a squeeze so as to have part of the pulp. Boil this either directly after straining or next day.

'Allow 1 lb of sugar to 1 pint of juice and skim very carefully. Before putting the jelly into pots, see that it *will* jelly; sometimes it will not become firm under ¾ of an hour boiling; sometimes it gets firm much quicker. When ready pot it. It mellows and improves when 1 or even 2 years old. Miss Lamont, of Pitmurchie, gave this recipe to Mrs Innes, of Learney.'

◇ *THICK BLACKBERRY JELLY* ◇

Stew some blackberries in a very little water until they are quite soft. Put them through a sieve so that you get all the pulp, but no pips. To each pint of pulp put a pound of sugar and boil till the mixture jellies.

If possible, add 1 or 2 sweet-scented geranium leaves to the blackberries while they are stewing; these will give them a delicious flavour.

STANNARD, ELOISE HARRIET, *Greengages, Redcurrants, Black Grapes and Marigolds*, 1898.

✧ MULBERRY JAM ✧

Put equal quantities of mulberries and preserving sugar together in a large bowl and leave overnight. Next day put them in a pan, without water, and bring slowly to the boil; continue boiling for 15 to 20 minutes, until the juice sets when a little is dropped on to a plate.

✧ MULBERRY JELLY ✧

Put the fruit into a stone jar, cover it and put in a very low oven until the juice flows.

Strain through a muslin or fine hair sieve, and allow 1 lb of sugar to each pint of juice. Boil gently for 15 to 25 minutes, according to whether you have a small or large quantity of fruit.

A few blanched split almonds, added while the jelly is boiling, are an improvement.

✧ TOMATO SAUCE ✧
TO STORE

Italian tomato paste in tins is so cheap to buy and so good that it is hardly worth while making it at home, but people who grow their own tomatoes may be interested in this Italian recipe.

A dozen onions, 4 carrots, a head of celery, 1 lb of butter, ⅕ pint of olive oil, 16–18lb of tomatoes, salt.

Put the oil and butter in a preserving pan, and when it is warmed put in the sliced onions, carrots and celery; when they have turned yellow add the tomatoes cut into quarters and a tablespoon of salt to every 3 lb. Cook until the whole is reduced to a thick mass and almost sticking to the pan. Sieve. Pour the purée either into bottles or preserving jars. If bottles, they must be corked and the corks tied down with string; preserving jars should be screwed down. Leave a couple of inches space at the top of the bottles, or an inch for the jars. Put the bottles or jars into a large pan of water (they should not touch each other and can be wrapped in several sheets of newspaper which will prevent their doing so) and steam for about 3 hours. Leave them to cool in the water, and store in a cool dry place.

The same recipe, in smaller quantities, makes an excellent sauce for pasta, or any dish for which a fresh tomato purée is wanted. For these dishes, use it when it has been sieved, adding fresh herbs, garlic, a little port or marsala, and possibly a little sugar.

⋄ VINE LEAVES ⋄

So many English gardens have a vine growing on a wall that it may be interesting to note how vine leaves can be used in cookery. They have a pungent lemony flavour, and the stuffed vine leaves of Greece, Turkey and the Balkans are fairly well known. In France all sorts of small game birds, quails, ortolans, becfigues, and partridges are wrapped in vine leaves and braised; one of the best mushroom dishes is the Italian one of funghi stewed in oil on a bed of vine leaves (see page 179), for vine leaves possess the property of both preserving and enhancing the flavour of whatever is cooked with them. Spon's *Household Manual*, published in the eighties, says that vine leaves placed on top of pickles will preserve the vinegar sharp and clear and impart a nice flavour. In old English cookery layers of vine leaves were placed between greengages which were to be preserved in syrup, in order to give the greengages a good colour. Tinned vine leaves from Greece and Turkey can be bought in Soho shops. They used to be very salt but are now much improved in this respect. Fresh vine leaves can be preserved in oil in the following manner.

⋄ VINE LEAVES PRESERVED ⋄
IN OIL

Pick a large bunch of vine leaves. Blanch them one minute in boiling salted water. Leave them to drain until they are quite dry. Pack them flat into wide shallow jars and cover with olive oil to the depth of a good half-inch above the top layer. Seal the jars. They can be used during the winter for making excellent dishes out of ordinary cultivated mushrooms, or for wrapping round partridges or other small birds to be cooked in the oven, but are too soft to be used for *dolmádes*.

MOILLON, LOUISE (1609/10-96), *A Basket of Mulberries.*

✧ *CANDIED ANGELICA* ✧

Fresh angelica has a most powerful and sweet scent, which it does not, however, communicate to other foods, although it will cling to your hands for hours after you have handled it. It also has very little taste in its fresh state and is rather stringy, but when candied is I think one of the most exquisite of all sweet-meats. It grows successfully in English gardens, and here is an old recipe for candying it, from Henderson's *Housekeepers' Instructor or Universal Family Cook*, 1809.

'Cut your angelica in lengths when young, cover it close, and boil till it is tender. Then peel it, put it in again, and let it simmer and boil till it is green. Then take it up, dry it with a cloth, and to every pound of stalks put a pound of sugar. Put your stalks into an earthen pan, beat your sugar, strew it over them, and let them stand two days. Then boil it till it is clean and green and put it in a colander to drain. Beat another pound of sugar to powder, and strew it over the angelica; then lay it on plates, and let it stand in a slack oven till it is thoroughly dry.'

✧ BASIL VINEGAR OR WINE ✧

'Fill a wide-mouthed bottle with fresh green leaves of basil, and cover them with vinegar or wine, and let them steep for 10 days; if you wish a very strong essence, strain the liquor, put it on some fresh leaves, and let it steep fourteen days longer.'
From Richard Dolby's *Cook's Dictionary and Housekeeper's Directory* 1832.

If the basil is steeped in dry white wine, the resulting concoction makes a good flavouring for winter soups, sauces and meat stews.

Meg Dods (*The Cook's and Housewife's Manual*, 1829) says of basil vinegar, 'the French add cloves and lemon rind: we admire this addition'.

✧ LEMON BRANDY ✧

(For flavouring sweet dishes)

'Fill any sized wide-necked bottle tightly with the very thin rinds of fresh lemons, and cover them with good brandy; let them remain for a fortnight or three weeks only, then strain off the spirit and keep it well corked for use; a few apricot kernels blanched and imposed with the lemon-rind will give it an agreeable flavour.'
Eliza Acton, *Modern Cookery*, 1861 edition, first published 1845.

✧ To Store Green Ginger Root ✧

Fresh green ginger root, supplied by Indian and Chinese greengrocers and provision stores, will keep for a few days in a cool dry place, but for long-term storage can be wrapped in foil and stored in the freezer. Scrape or grate the amount you need, rewrap the rest and return it to the freezer. An alternative method of keeping green ginger is the one advocated by Grace Zia Chu, author of *The Pleasures of Chinese Cooking* (Faber, London 1964). Mrs Chu's system is, or was, to scrape the roots, cut them into convenient pieces, put them in a small glass jar, cover them completely with dry sherry, cover with a cap or stopper and store in the refrigerator. This method is a useful one to know, particularly if you have only an occasional use for green ginger. As a by-product, the ginger-flavoured sherry gives an interesting flavour to a consommé, and to sweet creams and jellies. Use it in very small quantities, by the teaspoonful.

BUFFET FOOD

BLIN DE FONTENAY, JEAN-BAPTISTE, *Buffet under a Trellis*, ca. 1700.

BUFFET FOOD

A very understandable mistake often made at buffet luncheons and suppers is the over-complication of the food and the diversity of dishes offered. Several fine dishes of attractively prepared food look hospitable and tempting, but it is bewildering to be faced with too many choices, especially if some are hot and some cold. The taste of the food is lost when you find four or five different things all messed up on your plate at the same time; so have as the most important dish something rather simple which everyone will like, and provide variety with two or three salads, so long as they are easy ones to eat.

An excellent centrepiece for a party of this kind, particularly for those who haven't time for cooking but do not want to resort to a professional caterer, would be one of the smoked turkeys which an enterprising firm have recently perfected (it is the first time that smoked turkeys, well-known in America, have been put on the market in this country). Smoked turkey is not of course cheap, but all you have to do is unwrap the bird and put it on a dish; with its dark golden skin it makes a handsome appearance, carves easily into thin slices, there is no waste, and the brown and white meat are equally delicious. The salads to go with it should be rather mild, as any strong flavour will conflict with that of the turkey; the classic potato salad with a mayonnaise made with lemon juice instead of vinegar, raw sliced mushrooms with an oil and lemon dressing, cucumbers with a cream dressing, or cubes of crisp cold melon go well with smoked turkey.

If something soft and creamy, such as a chicken or ham mousse, is to be the main dish, have as a contrast crisp raw salad vegetables, cucumber, radishes, or fennel cooled in bowls of salted iced water and perhaps some hard-boiled eggs stuffed with a green or red mayonnaise; these are easy to eat and always popular.

For a less conventional supper party a *roulade* of beef or veal with a colourful stuffing of eggs and parsley and ham,† or a loin of cold roast pork well spiked with garlic and herbs‡ make fine dishes. The main thing is for the hostess not to wear herself out for days beforehand, fussing about with aspic, making patterns with mayonnaise and sticking little things on sticks. If time is

†See the recipe for Farso Magro, page 121.
‡See page 125.

243

limited, buy good-quality ham, plenty of it, and make it interesting by serving something unusual with it, such as pickled peaches, plums or cherries,§ or Cumberland sauce, or avocado sauce.‖

Start with a hot soup which can be served in cups (a walnut soup, or a white fish soup) accompanied by hot biscuits. As dessert, an iced, thick fruit fool whch can be served in bowls is better than a fruit salad which has to be chased all over a plate balanced on your knees.

The presentation of party dishes, and of course all food, is an important point. Cold food should certainly have a lavish and colourful appearance, but to varnish it with gummy gelatine or smother it with whirls of mayonnaise seems to me a misconception of what makes for an appetizing appearance. The effect needed is not of food tormented into irrelevant shapes but of fresh ingredients freshly cooked and not overhandled. The most elementary hors d'œuvre such as a plate of red radishes with a few of their green leaves, a dish of green and black olives and another of hard-boiled eggs (not overcooked), with butter and bread on the table, is ten times more tempting than the same ingredients got up in a pattern all on one dish and garnished with strips of this and dabs of that. You are, after all, preparing a meal, not decorating the village hall.

As for hot food, if it has not acquired an appetizing look during the cooking, a few blobs of cream or a border of mashed potatoes will do little to improve matters. There are of course ways of making good food look especially beautiful. The colour, size and shape of the serving dish is obviously important; food should never be crammed into too small a dish; serve rice and pilaffs on large shallow platters, not pressed into a deep glass casserole; for the serving of fish and of grilled chicken, which should be spread out rather than piled up, a long narrow dish is best.

See that the dishes are appropriate to the food. Peasant and country stews of beans or lentils, deep brown *daubes* of meat and game, onion and oil-flavoured ragoûts of pimentos or purple-skinned aubergines lose some of their particular charm (and also get cold) if transferred from the earthen pots in which they have cooked to a smart silver entrée dish, and all the delicious brown bits on the bottom and sides of the dish are lost. Dark glowing blue china, the dark brown glaze of slip ware pottery and plain white always make

§See chapter on Preserves

‖See page 194

good backgrounds for food; it would be an admirable thing if contemporary porcelain and pottery designers would pay a little more attention to these matters; does it ever occur to them that faded greens or greys, pale blues, washy yellows and garish reds do nothing to enhance the food which is to be served upon and eaten off their plates and dishes?

❖ BŒUF À LA MODE ❖

Bœuf à la mode can be eaten hot, but is at its best cold, when the stock has turned to a clear soft jelly, and the meat, which can be cut with a spoon when hot, is a little firmer and will carve into good slices. It is a dish typical of the best French household cooking, combining the flavours of meat, vegetables, wine and garlic, and as it must be simmered for a long time it is not worth making with a small quantity of meat. It makes a most admirable cold dish for a summer luncheon or supper party. In detail the recipes for *bœuf à la mode* vary from region to region, but the essentials of the dish are always the same – beef, carrots, calf's feet, garlic, wine, herbs.

> The following recipe makes an excellent *bœuf à la mode*: 4 lb of lean round of beef in one piece, 4 rashers of bacon, 4 to 6 cloves of garlic, 2 onions, 2 lb of carrots, thyme, 2 bayleaves, 2 calf's feet, ½ pint of white or red wine, a small wineglass of brandy, meat stock or water, dripping, herbs, salt and pepper, and a large, deep dish in which to serve the meat.

Lard the meat from side to side with strips of bacon and the garlic cut into spikes. Rub a little salt and ground black pepper all over the meat.

Brown the sliced onions in dripping, then put in the meat and let it sizzle, turning it over so that it is well browned all over. Now pour over the warmed brandy and set light to it. When it has stopped burning, pour in the wine. Let this bubble for two or three minutes. Add 2 carrots, the herbs, and the split calf's feet. (Pig's feet will do instead.) Cover with stock or water, and put the lid on the pan. Leave it to simmer as gently as possible for 4 to 5 hours, either on top of the stove or in the oven. An hour before it is cooked the rest of the carrots can be added, or they can be boiled separately and put into the serving dish when the meat is cooked. This last is the better method to my mind, as they are apt to give rather too strong a flavour of carrots to the jelly.

When the beef is tender, take it out, put it in the serving dish. Arrange the carrots round it. Test the stock for seasoning, and pour it through a strainer on to the meat. Next day, when the jelly has set, remove the fat from the top with the aid of a spoon dipped continually in hot water. The few remaining particles can be removed with a cloth dipped in warm water.

The jelly should be firm and clear, the meat soft, and when cut will reveal the pink circles of bacon and the white chips of garlic. Remember that although the meat may seem overcooked when hot, it will be firmer when cold.

COLD CHICKEN
⋄ WITH CREAM SAUCE ⋄
AND RICE

This makes a mild, soothing, summer dish; it takes time to prepare but the result is rewarding.

> Ingredients are a large boiling chicken weighing about 5½ to 6 lb (weight before drawing and dressing), 2 carrots, a piece of celery, an onion, a bunch of parsley, salt, 6 oz of Patna or Italian rice; nutmeg and lemon juice.
>
> For the sauce, 2 oz of butter, 2 full tablespoons of flour, ¼ pint each of milk and cream, 1 to 1¼ pints of the liquid in which the chicken was cooked, a little dried or fresh tarragon.

Put the chicken, with the giblets and feet, in a big pan (preferably one which will go in the oven) with the onion and carrots, the celery and parsley tied together, a tablespoon of salt, and water just to cover. (If you have some to spare, it is an improvement to add a glass of white wine or cider.) Bring gently to simmering point on top of the stove, skim, cover the pot closely and transfer it to a low oven, gas No. 3, 330°F, and cook for just about 3 hours.

Remove the chicken to a dish and let it cool. Discard the vegetables. Strain the stock into a bowl.

To make the sauce, melt the butter in a heavy saucepan, off the fire, stir in the flour and when it is smooth add first the heated milk then, gradually, a pint of the chicken stock. Stir until smooth, simmer very gently, with a mat under the saucepan, for about 30 minutes, stirring frequently. Add the cream. Continue simmering and stirring another 5 minutes or so. If the sauce is too thick add a little more stock, and if it is still too runny let it cook and reduce a little longer. Strain the sauce through a fine sieve into a jug, taste for seasoning, stir in about a teaspoon of chopped tarragon, cover the sauce with a piece of buttered paper and leave until next day.

Boil the rice, drain it, and while it is still warm season it with salt, pepper, nutmeg, lemon juice. Spread it out on a long dish.

Remove the skin from the chicken, take all the meat from the bones, cut it into rather thin longish pieces.

Mix the chicken with the sauce, but keep aside one cupful of the latter. Arrange the chicken and sauce mixture on top of the rice. Some of the sauce will seep through into the rice and make it sufficiently moist.

Just before serving cover the chicken with the reserved sauce and sprinkle with a little chopped parsley or tarragon.

CLAESZ, PIETER, *Still Life*, c.1630.

❖ *CHICKEN MOUSSE* ❖

A boiling chicken weighing 3½–4 lb, a calf's foot or 2 pig's feet, a carrot, an onion, garlic, lemon peel, parsley, ½ pint thick cream, the whites of 2 eggs, 2 tablespoons of brandy, bayleaf, thyme.

Simmer the chicken for 2 hours or so with the calf's or pig's feet, the carrot, onion, garlic, a piece of lemon peel, a little salt, ground black pepper, a bayleaf, thyme, and the giblets of the bird (except the liver), all just covered with water. Take out the chicken when it is cooked and leave the rest to simmer another 1½–2 hours.

Skin the chicken, remove all the flesh from the bones. Chop the flesh, then pound it in a mortar with a clove of garlic, a little extra salt and pepper, and a sprig or two of parsley. Cook the liver of the chicken a minute or two in butter, add the brandy, set light to it. When the flames have gone out add both liver and juice to the chicken, pounding until it is amalgamated with the chicken meat. Stir in ¼ pint of the strained stock, then the whipped cream.

Leave for an hour or so and then stir in the stiffly beaten egg whites.

Next day, when the stock has turned to jelly, remove the fat, cut the jelly into squares and put it round the mousse, which looks best piled up in a fairly shallow dish in which there is just room for the jelly around it.

With it serve a thick mayonnaise into which have been incorporated some strips of raw celery or fennel.

❖ *PORK AND VEAL LOAF* ❖

1 lb each of minced uncooked fat pork and lean veal; 4 oz bacon; ½ teaspoon whole peppecorns; 3 tablespoons sherry or light port. For the cooking: a 2-pint-capacity loaf-shaped terrine or tin, not less than 2½ inches deep.

For the pork choose belly weighed without rind and bone, and for the veal the small trimmings from the leg cuts which the butchers sell as pie veal. Some butchers sell ready minced veal and pork, but sausage meat will not do. Remove rinds from bacon, put aside two or three rashers, cut the rest into tiny cubes, mix with the two minced meats in a capacious china bowl. Crush the peppercorns together with the salt and stir them into the meat. Add the sherry or port and mix very thoroughly. If possible leave, uncovered, for a couple of hours, so that the seasonings and wine have a chance to blend with the meat.

Now turn the whole mixture into your terrine. Because the meat in this type of dish shrinks quite a bit during the cooking it is essential that, initially, the terrine be packed absolutely full to the brim, the loaf slightly domed in the centre.

Cut the bacon rashers which you have kept aside into fine strips; arrange them in a quadrille pattern across the top of the meat.

Place the terrine, covered in a baking tin half filled with water, on the bottom shelf of a preheated but very moderate oven, gas No. 3, 330°F, and cook for one hour. Remove the lid, and leave for another 30 minutes. Remove the loaf from the oven, leave to cool and set. Store in the refrigerator.

Made in large quantities this is an especially useful dish at holiday-time, when children come home from school, when extra guests may turn up, and for picnics, and buffet suppers. Serve it either as a first course, with toast or French bread, or as a main course with a salad and perhaps jacket potatoes.

The seasonings can of course be varied. A crushed clove or two of garlic can be added, two teaspoons of brandy or whisky substituted for an equal proportion of the sherry, a teaspoon of mixed powdered spices or crushed juniper berries added.

If to be made for a large party calculate quantities according to the capacity of your tin or terrine by allowing a minimum 1½ lb of meat to every pint of water which it holds, and an extra 4 to 6 oz will do no harm. Cooking times vary little with the capacity of the utensil – it is primarily the depth of the mixture which counts rather than its weight.

The French firm of Le Creuset make narrow oblong utensils, with lids, especially for pâtés and kindred dishes. In vitreous-enamelled cast iron, white-lined, these come in three sizes and are marvellously useful for the cooking, storage and serving of pâtés and meat loaves such as that here described. In three sizes, Le Creuset terrines are to be bought from many shops specialising in utensils for the serious amateur cook.

⬦ SMOKED TONGUE ⬦

A smoked tongue should be soaked in cold water for at least 12 hours, and simmered with carrots, onions, peppercorns and bayleaves, with water just to cover for 3–3½ hours according to size. If to be eaten cold let it cool a little in the stock, then take it out, peel off the outer skin, and remove the gristly part.

A hot boiled tongue can be eaten with boiled vegetables, and whether hot or cold needs to be accompanied by some kind of sweet-sour sauce or mild chutney.

When it is necessary to provide a variety of cold foods for a number of people, cook a boiling chicken, a piece of gammon and possibly a piece of shin beef in the pan with the tongue, and serve them all cold with the vinaigrette and egg sauce described on page 191 as well as a salad and pickled fruit. One of the best pickles for this type of cold meat is the Italian *mostarda di Cremona*. The stock from the boiled meats makes excellent soup.

❖ WHITE WINE CUP ❖

The directions for wine cups are usually of so complicated a nature, calling for so many different liqueurs and spirits and such a variety of fruit, that most people are bewildered by them. In fact the simpler these drinks are the better. Sodden fruit floating about in a glass is not universally welcomed, and there is no necessity for a profusion of flavourings. Two to avoid are mint and pineapple; they swamp everything else.

Here is a very easy white wine cup, which I have found very successful. The wine I always use is a Muscadet from the Loire, which has a delightful fresh flavour, but there are many other suitable and cheap dry white wines.

Put a piece of cucumber peel, a piece of orange peel, a sprig of borage and 2 lumps of sugar into a jug; pour over it about 1½ fluid oz (a small glass) of brandy. Leave to macerate 20 minutes. Add a bottle of dry white wine, 2 cubes of ice, and a wineglass of soda water.

❖ ICED COFFEE ❖

Make some fairly strong black coffee in the following way: put 12 oz of finely ground coffee and 6 oz of sugar into an earthenware jug, pour over it 4 pints of boiling water. Put the jug in a saucepan of hot water and leave it over a very low flame for ½ hour. Leave to cool, and strain through a fine muslin.

Freeze until semi-solid. When it is to be served, turn out into glasses or

GILMAN, HAROLD (1876-1919), *Mrs Mounter at the Breakfast Table* (Detail).

cups and stir about 2 tablespoons of cream into each one (about ½ pint altogether for the above quantity of coffee which is sufficient for ten to twelve glasses).

⋄ CAFÉ LIÉGOIS ⋄

Make the coffee as for iced coffee, add ½ pint of whipped cream and freeze in an ice cream maker, turning the machine off well before the coffee freezes solid.

Serve in glasses, with a tablespoon of whipped cream on top of each.

IMPROVISED COOKING FOR HOLIDAYS AND WEEK-ENDS

NICHOLSON, WINIFRED, *Jake and Kate on the Isle of Wight*, 1931/32.

IMPROVISED COOKING FOR HOLIDAYS AND WEEK-ENDS

The kitchens of holiday houses, whether cramped and larderless, or vast, bare, with a day's march between sink and stove, usually have a stony bleakness in common. However adequate the beds or satisfactory the view, the kitchen equipment will probably consist of a tin frying pan, a chipped enamel saucepan, one Pyrex casserole without a lid, and a rusty knife with a loose handle.

Some extra organization before setting off, a basket packed with a small supply of kitchen comforts, does much to alleviate the irritation of coping with a capricious and unfamiliar stove and the vagaries of the food supply in the country or at the seaside. A good kitchen knife and a bread knife are essential pieces of equipment (cutting sandwiches with a blunt instrument may be part of holiday routine, but is very exasperating). A food mill for making purées and mashed potatoes saves hours of time, a sieve for sauces is never to be found except in one's own kitchen; some muslin squares for draining cream cheese made from the milk which inevitably goes sour, a large thermos jar in which to store the ice which has to be begged from the local pub or fishmonger, your own potato peeler, a pepper mill – these things may be a nuisance to pack, but they will prove worth the trouble. Assuming that there will be either no oven or that if there is you will only find out how it works on the last day of your stay, it is advisable to take a heavy pan for pot roasting or slow simmering, and an asbestos mat over which it may be left on a low flame while unattended.

As well as being simple, holiday food ought to provide a change from all-the-year-round dishes; it is nice to do away with the routine roast, but without having to rely on tins. One hopes to find garden vegetables, and perhaps butter, eggs and cream; possibly there will be wild rabbits, and river fish, there might even be fish from the sea (the best lobsters and crabs I have ever eaten were bought from fishermen during seaside holidays, carried home with their angry claws tied up in a handkerchief, and dropped thankfully into a pot or bucket filled with boiling water, and eaten with butter and salt).

Village shops, however, will not provide imported cheeses or sausages; so it is worth while taking a small supply of Parmesan or Gruyère cheese, some tins of Frankfurter sausages, wine for cooking (cheap wine is generally only to be found in large towns). Olive oil is another essential supply, or you will have to buy it at considerable expense in medicine bottles from the local chemist. Some good pasta or rice will provide substantial dishes for hungry walkers and swimmers, and since people on holiday usually demand large breakfasts see that there is a good pan for fried eggs and bacon and potatoes. Cheap pans which blacken and burn make for hard work and bad temper.

Marketing and preparing for three or four meals at a time is an obvious necessity at holiday time, and the following few recipes may provide ideas for people who like to provide their family and friends with nice food even though it has to be improvised, but who obviously don't want to spend all day grappling with an inadequate stove, cold washing-up water, and dented saucepans in which the food sticks in the middle while it remains quite uncooked round the edges.

⋄ RABBIT IN WHITE WINE ⋄

Three dishes can be made from one large rabbit or two smaller ones with very little work.

Keeping the hind legs separate, cut the rest of the rabbit into 6 or 8 pieces. Season them well with salt, pepper, lemon juice and plenty of thyme. Into a casserole, with a little dripping put a quarter pound of bacon cut into squares; let it melt a little; add the pieces of rabbit and let them brown on each side. In another saucepan bring half a tumbler of white wine to the boil, set light to it, and when it has finished burning pour it over the rabbit. This process reduces the wine and will give body and flavour to the sauce. (If you happen to be in the cider country use draught cider instead of white wine; in which case simply heat it up before pouring it over the rabbit.) Add hot water to come just level with the pieces of rabbit, cover the pan and let it simmer about an hour. Have ready in a bowl the liver of the rabbit pounded with a clove of garlic, a handful of chopped parsley and one of breadcrumbs. At the last minute add this mixture to the sauce, stirring over the lowest possible flame for a minute or two. The sauce will thicken, but if it boils again the liver will separate into tiny particles, which will not affect the taste of the dish but will take away from its appearance. Should mushrooms be available add half a pound of them, sliced, to the dish ten minutes before finishing the sauce. Tomatoes, fried, grilled or à la Provençale (stuffed with parsley and garlic), go well with rabbit; and so do sauté potatoes.

❖ RABBIT PÂTÉ ❖

Put the two legs of the rabbit which you have kept aside into a pan with a tumbler of white wine or cider. Cook them for 20 minutes and when it has cooled take the meat from the bones (the orthodox way of preparing pâté is to take the meat off the bones before it is cooked, a method which makes a good deal of hard work). Cut a few of the best pieces into small fillets and put the rest through a mincer, or chop it finely. Add 4 or 5 rashers of bacon, also chopped, and the contents of a small tin of liver or pork pâté; season the mixture rather highly with ground black pepper, a little grated lemon peel, thyme, garlic and a scraping of nutmeg; arrange the minced mixture and the little fillets in layers in any small receptacle which can be used for steaming – a pudding basin will do if there is no earthenware terrine, or one of those aluminium tins with a close covering lid which are sold in camping equipment shops; moisten the pâté with some of the liquid in which the legs of the rabbit were originally cooked, preferably reduced by 10 minutes' fast boiling. Cover the pâté with greaseproof paper and steam for half an hour. (Pâtés are usually steamed in the oven, but the top of the stove is quite satisfactory.) When it has cooled pour over it a layer of melted dripping, which will seal it, so that it can be kept for several days; it will be excellent with toast, taken as it is on a picnic, or made into sandwiches.

❖ RABBIT AND LEMON SOUP ❖

Out of the bones of the rabbit and the usual soup vegetables, herbs and seasonings make a stock; it will not be very strong, but it doesn't matter. Add any of the sauce which happens to be left over from the original rabbit dish. Strain the stock and in it boil 2 tablespoons of rice; have ready in a bowl 2 eggs beaten up with the juice of a lemon. Pour some of the soup over this, stirring hard, then return the mixture to the pan, letting it reheat a minute or two without boiling. This soup, although it has not such a fine flavour, is similar to the Greek *Avgolémono* which is made with chicken stock.

BŒUF
⬩ EN DAUBE ⬩

This is another way of making three dishes with one batch of ingredients. 3½ to 4 lb of stewing beef in one piece, 1 lb of carrots, garlic, onions and a calf's or pig's foot, thyme, bayleaves and red or white wine are the necessities. Make a few holes in the beef with a small knife and in these put some half cloves of garlic. Rub the beef all over with salt, pepper and fresh thyme. Brown the meat on both sides in a little dripping; pour over a tumbler of wine and when it bubbles set light to it. Keep it boiling until the flames die down. Remove the meat and wine to a capacious casserole; add a sliced onion, the split calf's foot and the carrots, plus a couple of bayleaves and another branch of thyme. Cover the meat with hot water, set the pan on a very low flame and cook it until the meat is absolutely tender; it may take anything from four to six hours, according to the toughness or otherwise of the meat. This part of the cooking can be done regardless of the time you are going to dine; the daube can be strained, left to cool, the fat skimmed off, and reheated gently, or it can be served as soon as it is cooked. In any case put the hot beef on to a serving dish with the carrots and only a small portion of the gravy. With it serve either a bowl of well-buttered *pasta* or mashed potatoes, to soak up the juice of the meat. For the next day's meal put what is left of the beef into a bowl; over it pour the liquid which you have reserved, which will set to a jelly. With a small spoon dipped in a bowl of hot water skim off the fat, and your dish is ready to serve. Potatoes, baked or boiled in their jackets, a fresh garden lettuce, a salad of finely sliced raw cabbage, a rice and tomato salad, almost anything except brussels sprouts will go with it.

In the meantime, with the calf's or pig's foot which you have kept aside make a second lot of stock; add some more onions, carrots and herbs and 2 pints of hot water; simmer it for about an hour, and strain it. With this any number of soups can be devised but one of the most successful is an improvised onion soup.

◇ *ONION SOUP* ◇

For four people slice six large onions very thinly; on this depends the success of the soup. In your casserole melt two tablespoons of beef dripping; cook the onions in this, stirring fairly often so that they turn gently brown without getting crisp, and finally form an almost amalgamated mass; season with salt and pepper, and pour over the heated stock, adding water if there is not quite enough. Cook for another 10 to 15 minutes; always supposing there is no oven or grill with which to *gratiner* the soup, prepare a thick slice of toast for each person, lightly buttered and spread with grated cheese. Place each one in a soup plate and ladle the onion soup over it.

COOKE, EDWARD WILLIAM, (1811-1880), *Lobster Pots.*

✧ SHELLFISH ✧
RISOTTO

Not quite the orthodox risotto but excellent, and simple. For four people you will need a small lobster or two crawfish (langouste) tails, or 2 dozen prawns, which should have been cooked in a court-bouillon of white wine, water, an onion, and herbs. Leave them to cool in the liquid, and then take them out of their shells. If lobster or crawfish cut them into dice; if prawns cut each in half.

In a fireproof shallow casserole or braising pan melt 2 oz of butter. In this fry a sliced onion until it is golden. Put in the rice (two teacupsful) and stir round until the butter is all absorbed; pour over boiling water to cover the rice; you will have to stir it from time to time, but not continuously. When the first lot of water is absorbed add more until the rice is all but cooked; now add about a breakfast cup of the stock in which the fish was cooked; three minutes before serving stir in the shell fish, two tablespoons of grated Parmesan and a good lump of butter. Serve more cheese separately.

The risotto will take approximately 40 minutes to cook, and for the last 10 minutes it must be stirred constantly.

✧ CHAFING DISH ✧
LOBSTER

Olive oil, spring onions, tomatoes, sherry, marsala or white wine or vermouth, lemon, salt and pepper, a cooked lobster.

Warm 3 tablespoons of olive oil in a chafing dish or sauté pan. Put in the bulbous part of 6 to 8 spring onions, whole. Let them melt a minute, add two quartered tomatoes (skinned if possible), salt and pepper, let them cook 2 minutes; pour over a small glass of the sherry, marsala, white wine or vermouth (white wine or vermouth are best). Let it bubble. Add the lobster meat cut into squares and let it heat through gently.

Squeeze a little lemon juice over, and sprinkle with a little of the green part of the spring onions.

⋄ PRAWNS ON THE GRASS ⋄

1 lb of spinach, 2 hard-boiled eggs, 4 oz of peeled prawns, 3 to 4 oz cream, salt, pepper, nutmeg, butter.

Cook the cleaned spinach, drain, squeeze dry in your hands and chop it, not too finely. Melt a little butter (about 1 oz) in a chafing dish or sauté pan, heat the spinach, season it with salt, pepper and nutmeg. Put the prawns and the sliced eggs on top and pour the cream over. Cover the pan and simmer gently for 3 to 4 minutes.

⋄ MOULES AU GRATIN ⋄

Mussels are not generally obtainable in England during the summer months, but for those people who may find themselves in perhaps a holiday house in France or the Mediterranean, where mussels are eaten all the year round, I include this one recipe, which is one of the best of mussel dishes.

Open the mussels over the fire in a heavy pan, in their own liquid. When they have cooled shell them, and put two mussels into the half-shells. Arrange them in a fireproof dish, and pour melted butter or olive oil over them, then a light sprinkling of breadcrumbs mixed with an equal quantity of Parmesan cheese, a little chopped parsley and garlic, and pepper. Pour over a little of the strained juice from the mussels and put into a moderate oven sufficiently long for them to get hot. Serve quickly, with lemon.

When mussels are to be opened over the fire, shelled, and then reheated in a sauce, take great care not to over-cook them in the first place or they will be shrivelled and tough.

⋄ COLD OMELETTE ⋄

Make a plain omelette with three or four eggs; instead of folding it slide it out flat on to a plate. When it is cold garnish it with a purée made from cold chicken and ham or with the rabbit pâté already described, in fact with any cold meat mixture as long as it is not too liquid. Roll the omelette as you would a pancake.

For other omelette dishes see pages 79–80.

POTTER, BEATRIX (1866-1942), *Chanterelle mushroom.*

✧ *MUSHROOMS* ✧

I have no advice to offer as to the safety or otherwise of eating unfamiliar fungi. My own knowledge of the subject is limited to personal experiment, from which I have so far emerged unscathed; I have only two or three recipes to give for those people who are sure enough of their knowledge or judgement to cook and eat those fungi which they find in the woods or fields. There are only three deadly fungi, and one of these, the Amanita Printania, superficially resembles the common field mushroom. This may account for the fact that in Italy, where all kinds of fungi which would terrify English people are constantly eaten, the ordinary field mushroom is very rarely picked.

On the west coast of Scotland I have, to the horror and disgust of the inhabitants, cooked and eaten several different fungi. The best of these were the apricot-coloured, trumpet-shaped cantharellus. They need plenty of washing and if they are large they should be cut into strips (the small ones are the best). They should be stewed gently in oil for 15 or 20 minutes (longer if they are large ones), with the addition at the last minute of a little garlic, parsley and breadcrumbs (to absorb the oil), salt and pepper. Strips of ham or bacon can be added, and they can be used as a filling for omelettes, or piled on top of scrambled eggs; in France and Italy they are fairly commonly eaten, either as a separate dish or an accompaniment to chicken, or in a risotto.

⬧ BOLETUS ⬧

Boletus edulis, the *cèpes* of France, are quite common in English woods and forests. They are delicious when absolutely fresh, but very quickly go sodden and rotten. The stalks are tough and should be chopped finely; *Boletus* are best stewed in oil, for about 40 minutes, with the addition of chopped shallots, garlic and parsley. There is also an excellent way of stuffing and baking them; prepare a finely chopped mixture of ham or bacon, garlic, breadcrumbs, a very little Parmesan cheese and the chopped stalks. Put a tablespoon of the stuffing in each *cèpe*, fill them up with oil and bake them in a slow oven, in a covered dish, for about an hour. From time to time add a little more oil.

⬧ FIELD MUSHROOMS ⬧

To grill field mushrooms wash them, remove the stalks and marinade them for an hour in olive oil flavoured with salt and pepper and a little fresh thyme. Put them under the grill with a little of the oil, and cook them fairly fast, turning them over and over so they do not dry up. The large flat field mushrooms are also delicious fried, preferably I think in bacon or pork fat, rather than butter. Don't let the fat get too hot before putting in the mushrooms, and when they appear to have absorbed it all, turn the heat down, and in a minute or two the mushrooms start to yield their juice. Continue cooking them gently, sprinkling them with salt and pepper. They should be cooked skin side down and need not be turned over. Eat them with fried bread.

⋄ MUSHROOMS COOKED ⋄
IN CREAM

To make a really good dish of mushrooms in cream very fresh little button mushrooms from the field are needed.

Clean them (say ½ lb) with a damp cloth and do not peel them. Bring a coffee-cupful of water to the boil and squeeze in a little lemon juice and a pinch of salt. Put in the mushrooms and let them cook about 2 minutes. Strain them.

The sauce is prepared by stirring 2 or 3 teaspoons of flour into ¼ pint of cream. Bring to the boil and when the sauce has thickened put in the strained mushrooms and cook another 5 minutes, adding ground black pepper and more salt if necessary.

⋄ POTATOES AND MUSHROOMS ⋄

When you have picked only a few mushrooms, not enough to make a whole dish of them, try this mixture of mushrooms and potatoes.

1 lb of potatoes, ½ lb of mushrooms, 1 oz of butter, a clove of garlic, a small onion, olive oil, the juice of half a lemon, parsley.

Cut the peeled potatoes into thin slices. Heat the oil and butter in an earthenware pan and sauté the chopped onion. Add the garlic, then the potatoes. Simmer for 10 minutes then put in the cleaned and sliced mushrooms, and barely cover with water. Season with salt and pepper, cover the pan, and cook on a moderate flame until the potatoes are tender. Add a little chopped parsley and the lemon juice, and serve in the pan in which it has been cooked.

Two or three fillets of anchovies can be added at the same time as the mushrooms.

⋄ PIGEONS STEWED ⋄
WITH LETTUCES

Pigeons are often tough little birds, but in the country there are often a great many to be disposed of. A pigeon gives an excellent flavour if cooked with the meat and vegetables for a broth; with three pigeons a very nice little terrine or pâté, enough for about 8 people, can be made. Baby pigeons are very good split in half and grilled. Older birds make a good country dish cooked in the following way with lettuces.

For each pigeon you need two cos lettuces, a cupful of meat or chicken stock, a rasher of bacon and some parsley, shallots, herbs and the usual seasonings. First blanch the pigeons in boiling water for 5 minutes and cut them in half. Then blanch the lettuces. Cut the lettuces down the middle, without separating the two halves; spread them with a mixture of chopped shallots, parsley, herbs, salt and pepper. Put half a pigeon in the middle, tie them up, and place them in a pan lined with the bacon rashers; pour the stock over them and simmer gently for about an hour and a half; put them in the serving dish, thicken the sauce with a yolk of egg, squeeze in a little lemon juice and pour over the pigeons.

⋄ ROASTED CHEESE ⋄

This is not a particularly summery dish, but is so quick and easy to make, and provides such a good meal in a hurry, and for people who live alone, that it is worth knowing. The best cheeses to use for it are Cheddar, Gruyère, Emmenthal, or Bel Paese.

Cut 6 or 7 slices from a French loaf, each about ¼ inch thick. Cut the same number of slices of cheese, a little thinner. Cover each slice of bread with a slice of cheese and arrange them in a long fireproof dish (or baking tin if you are making a quantity) and put them in the top of a very hot oven (Regulo 8). In 8 to 10 minutes the dish will be ready, the cheese melting and the bread just getting crisp. Before eating the croûtons sprinkle them plentifully with freshly ground black pepper, or if you like, with a tomato sauce made as follows:

For the amount given, melt two chopped ripe tomatoes in butter, add salt, pepper, a scrap of garlic, and a little chopped parsley, or any other herb you like. Cook for about 3 minutes only. Pour over the cheese as soon as the dish is taken out of the oven.

✧ *BAKED CHEESE SANDWICHES* ✧

Butter thin slices of brown bread (best if two or even three days old), make them into sandwiches with a filling of thickish slices of Cheddar or Double Gloucester cheese, seasoned with freshly milled black pepper and a little mustard.

Arrange the sandwiches in a baking dish. Sprinkle each with a few drops of vinegar (this is important) press the bread well down, bake the sandwiches for 15 to 20 minutes in the centre of a medium hot oven, gas No. 4 or 5, 350 to 375°F.

When the sandwiches are ready, the bread should be crisp and the cheese filling just barely melting.

A highly useful little dish for children, for people who live alone, for those cooking under difficult conditions – and for anybody who knows nothing at all about cooking but would like a change from food out of tins and packets.

✧ *HERB CHEESE* ✧

Into ½ lb of home-made milk cheese stir about half a teacupful of chopped fresh lemon thyme and sweet marjoram, in equal quantities, with the addition of a chopped fresh bayleaf. Season with salt and ground black pepper, pile the cheese up in a dish, and leave it several hours before serving, to give the flavour of the herbs time to penetrate the cheese. This cheese has a lovely fresh flavour. It can be eaten simply with brown bread, or, with the addition of 2 or 3 tablespoons of grated Parmesan can be stirred into a dish of hot spaghetti or noodles.

Instead of lemon thyme and marjoram, chopped borage leaves give a very delicate and unexpected flavour of cucumber to a cream cheese.

PICNICS

PICNICS

Picnic addicts seem to be roughly divided between those who frankly make elaborate preparations and leave nothing to chance, and those others whose organization is no less complicated but who are more deceitful and pretend that everything will be obtained on the spot and cooked over a woodcutter's fire, conveniently to hand; there are even those, according to Richard Jefferies, who wisely take the precaution of visiting the site of their intended picnic some days beforehand and there burying the champagne.

Not long before the war I was staying with friends in Marseille. One Saturday night a picnic was arranged for the next day with some American acquaintances; it was agreed that the two parties should proceed in their own cars to a little bay outside Marseille, and that we should each bring our own provisions. On Sunday morning I and my friends indulged in a delicious hour of shopping in the wonderful market of the rue de Rome, buying olives, anchovies, salame sausages, pâtés, yards of bread, smoked fish, fruit and cheese. With a provision of cheap red wine we bundled the food into the car and set off, stopping now and again for a drink; so that we arrived at our rendezvous well disposed to appreciate the sun, the sea and the scent of wild herbs and Mediterranean pines. Presently our friends drove up and started to unload their car. One of the first things to come out was a hatchet, with which they efficiently proceeded to chop down olive branches, and in no time at all there was a blazing fire. Out of their baskets came cutlets, potatoes, bacon, skewers, frying pans, jars of ice, butter, tablecloths, all the trappings of a minor barbecue. Our reactions as we watched these proceedings were those of astonishment, admiration, and finally, as realization of the inadequacy of our own catering dawned, dismay. How wilted they seemed, those little packets wrapped up in rather oily paper; the olives which had glowed with colour in the market stalls of the rue de Rome looked shabby now; the salame seemed dried up and the anchovies a squalid mess. Miserably, like poor relations, we sat with our shameful bundles spread out on the grass and politely offered them to our friends. They were kind, but obviously preferred their own grilled cutlets and fried potatoes, and we were too embarrassed to accept their proferred hospitality. Presently they produced ice cream out of a thermos, but by now we were past caring, and finally it was their turn for surprise when they found we hadn't even provided ourselves with the means of making a cup of coffee.

Then there was the hospitable family I remember in my childhood; they owned a beautiful house and an elegant garden and were much given to out-of-door entertainments, pageants and picnics. On picnic days a large party of children and grown-ups would be assembled in the hall. Led by our host and hostess we proceeded through the exquisite formal Dutch garden, across the lane and over a fence into a coppice. Close on our heels followed the butler, the chauffeur and the footman, bearing fine china plates, the silver and tablecloths, and a number of vast dishes containing cold chickens, jellies and trifles. Arrived at the end of our journey, five minutes from the house, our host set about making a fire, with sticks which I suspect had been strategically placed by the gardener, over which we grilled quantities of sausages and bacon, which were devoured amidst the customary jokes and hilarity. The picnickers' honour thus satisfied, we took our places for an orderly meal, handed round by the footman, and in composition resembling that of an Edwardian wedding breakfast.

Since those days I have had a good many opportunities of evolving a picnic technique on the lines laid down by Henry James, 'not so good as to fail of an amusing disorder, nor yet so bad as to defeat the proper function of repasts'.

Before deciding upon the food, its packing and transport must be planned. (I am assuming for the moment a car-transported picnic.) Those who are lucky enough to possess an Edwardian picnic hamper, fitted with spirit lamp and kettle, sandwich tins and a variety of boxes and bottles, need look no further. These hampers may be cumbersome, but they are capacious and solid; an aura of lavish gallivantings and ancient Rolls-Royces hangs about them, and they are infinitely superior to the modern kind in which the use of every inch of space has been planned for you in advance. Insulated picnic bags are highly effective and useful.

As to plates and glasses, if I am going to have them at all I would prefer to have china plates and glass glasses, although it must be admitted that clear, colourless plastic glasses such as are used on airlines are more practical.

A spirit lamp and kettle plus a tin of Nescafé provide a hotter and fresher cup of coffee than any which ever came out of a vacuum flask. Iced coffee on the other hand can be transported in thermos jugs, and a large thermos jar filled with ice is a blessing for those who don't care for warm drinks, or who like to put ice into coarse red picnic wine.

As for the food, the buying and preparing of it always seem to me to provide half the fun. The possibilities are almost without limit. On the whole, though, I think that such elegant foods as foie gras and lobster patties should be excluded as they seem to lose their fine lustre when eaten out of doors, whereas the simpler charms of salame sausage, fresh cheese, black olives and good French bread (if you can find such a commodity) are enhanced when they are eaten on the hillside or the seashore. Sandwiches I rather like (George Saintsbury considered that venison makes the best sandwiches), but many people do not, so there must always be alternatives; thin slices of ham rolled round Frankfurter sausages, or Frankfurter sausages split in half enclosing a slice of Gruyère cheese are good ones. Remember that such delicious foods as jellied egg, duck in aspic, and so on aren't really ideal for long journeys on a hot day because the jelly (if it has been made as it should be) will melt *en route*; mayonnaise also has a dismaying habit of turning into a rather unappetizing-looking oily mass when the weather is hot. A cold chicken with a cream sauce is a better bid than a chicken mayonnaise. Cold steak and kidney pudding is fine picnic food, so is cold spiced beef, which cuts into nice slices. Cold escalopes of veal, fried in egg and breadcrumbs, make excellent picnic food provided they are very thin and well drained after frying. Hard-boiled eggs are time-honoured picnic food, so I always take a few, but they are not everybody's taste. Cheese seems to me essential for an out-of-doors meal; next to the salty little Mediterranean goat and sheep's milk cheeses English Cheddar or Cheshire, or Gruyère, are perhaps the easiest picnic cheeses. Some people like a rich moist fruit cake for a picnic, but I prefer a slab of the dryest, bitterest chocolate available (Terry's make a good one but the best is the Belgian Côte d'Or), to be eaten in alternative mouthfuls with a Marie biscuit. Apples and figs and apricots, because they are easy to eat and transport as well as being good in the open air, are perhaps the best fruit for a picnic.

The nicest drinks for picnics are the obvious ones. A stout red wine such as a Macon or a Chianti, which cannot be unduly harmed by the journey in the car; vine rosé (particularly delicious by the sea); cider, lager, shandy, Black Velvet; iced sherry and bitters. For a very hot day Pimm's No. 1 couldn't be bettered but involves some organization in the matter of cucumber, lemonade, oranges, mint, borage, and all the paraphernalia, and a thermos jar of ice is essential. An effective way to keep wine and mineral waters cool on a long journey is to wrap the bottles in several sheets of dampened newspaper.

TISSOT, JAMES, *Holyday,* c.1876.

For soft drinks the most refreshing are tinned grapefruit, orange or pineapple juice, and tomato juice. (In this case include the tin opener.) Delicate china tea, iced, with slices of lemon and mint leaves is admirably reviving. An early edition of Mrs Beeton asserts that 'Water can usually be obtained so it is useless to take it'. For the walker's picnic perhaps the perfect meal has been described by Sir Osbert Sitwell: 'the fruits of the month, cheese with the goaty taste of mountains upon it, and if possible bilberries, apples, raw celery, a meal unsophisticated and pastoral . . .'.

SMOKED COD'S ROE ⋄ SANDWICHES IN BROWN ⋄ BREAD

Make a paste of ¼ lb of smoked cod's roe, as described on page 35. Spread it on buttered wholemeal bread.

⋄ SMOKED TROUT OR SMOKED ⋄ MACKEREL SANDWICHES

Fillet the trout or mackerel (smoked mackerel, although not so well known, are cheaper than smoked trout, and excellent), spread buttered rye bread with a layer of horseradish cream and place the fillets of fish on top.

⋄ BACON AND LETTUCE ⋄ SANDWICHES

One cos lettuce; one large rasher of bacon for each round of sandwiches; a mustardy French dressing. Shred the lettuce fairly fine and toss it with the dressing without letting it get sodden. Cut each rasher of bacon in half and fry very lightly. Put a layer of lettuce on the buttered bread and the bacon on top.

⋄ PAN BAGNA ⋄

A Provençal sandwich which makes delicious out-of-door food. See the recipes on pages 38 and 39.

◇ *SHOOTER'S SANDWICH* ◇

'The wise, "at least among the children of this world", to use one of Walter Pater's careful qualifying phrases, travel with a flask of whisky-and-water and what I call a "Shooter's Sandwich". This last is made thus: Take a large, thick, excellent rump steak. Do not season it, for that would cause the juice to run out, and in grilling it keep it markedly underdone. Have ready a sandwich loaf one end of which has been cut off and an adequate portion of the contents of which has been removed. Put the steak, hot from the grill, and – but only then – somewhat highly seasoned, into the loaf; wrap the loaf in a double sheet of clean white blotting-paper, tie with twine both ways, superimpose a sheet of grease-proof paper, and more twine. Place a moderate weight on top, and after a while add other weights. Let the thing endure pressure for at least six hours. Do not carve it until and as each slice is required.

'With this "sandwich" a man may travel from Land's End to Quaker Oats, and snap his fingers at both.'

T. Earle Welby, *The Dinner Knell*, Methuen, 1932

I have sometimes made this sandwich and kept it in the refrigerator as an emergency store when packing, moving house, and at other times when, although too busy to cook, everyone needs good nourishing food. For such occasions, as well as for picnics and journeys, T. Earle Welby's recipe is invaluable.

◇ *FRENCH GARLIC LOAVES* ◇

Heat a couple of French loaves a few minutes in the oven. While they are still hot, split them lengthwise and spread each side with butter into which you have pounded one clove of garlic, some chopped parsley and a little salt. Put the two halves together, and when you get to the picnic cut them into slices in the ordinary way.

◇ *PRAWNS WITH WATERCRESS* ◇
DRESSING

For a seaside picnic it is nice to have some fish; in all probability you won't find it there, so take it with you. Buy the ready peeled prawns, put them into

273

a suitable jar, season with salt and pepper, and take in a separate bottle a generous quantity of French dressing made with lemon juice instead of vinegar, into which you mix a good handful of very finely chopped watercress.

✧ COLD SPICED SALT BEEF ✧

Soak a piece of salted silverside in warm water for half an hour. Make about a dozen incisions all round the beef into which you insert half cloves of garlic rolled in chopped fresh herbs; rub it all over with ground cloves and ground black pepper and put it into a pan with half a glass of red wine, enough water to cover, and thyme, bayleaves, marjoram, rosemary and an onion. Bring it to the boil, then cover it closely and put in a low oven until it is tender – about 1 hour and 20 minutes for two pounds of beef: but as the quality of salt beef varies considerably it is advisable to try it from time to time, for if it is over-cooked it will crumble to pieces when cut. When it is done, take it out of the pan and put it on a board, cover it with a piece of greaseproof paper and put a weight on it. Next day it can be cut into fine slices.

✧ FIGS AND CREAM CHEESE ✧

Dried figs are delicious for a picnic; agreeable to bite on at the end of a meal. Have them with a home-made sour milk cheese, very slightly salted, or little French cream cheeses.

✧ ORIENTAL PICNICS ✧

1
'When I was going through the course of Garrison instruction, and accustomed to long days out surveying, I was partial to a galantine made of a small fowl, boned and rolled, with a block of tongue and some forcemeat introduced into the centre of it. A home-made brawn of tongue, a part of an ox-head, and sheep's trotters, well seasoned, and slightly spiced, was another specialité.

'A nice piece of the brisket of beef salted and spiced, boiled, placed under a weight, and then trimmed into a neat shape is a very handy thing for the tiffin basket; and a much respected patron of mine recommends for travelling, a really good cold plum pudding in which a glass of brandy has been included.'

LUCKNOW ARTIST, *Indian Servant Carrying a Tureen*, c.1830.

2

'The traveller's luncheon basket, and that of the sportsman are analogous. A friend of mine with whom I used to walk the paddy fields adopted the plan of taking out a digester pot, previously filled with stewed steak and oysters, or some equally toothsome stew. This he trusted to his syce, who lit a fire somewhere or other, in the marvellous way the natives of this country do, and, as sure as there are fish in the sea, had the contents of the pot steaming hot, at the exact spot, and at the very moment we required it.'

Extracts from *Culinary Jottings for Madras*, 'Wyvern' (Col. Kenney Herbert), 1885

3

Charles Baskerville, the American painter, has described an Indian picnic given by the Maharajah of Jaipur, in 1937.

'Yesterday we spent the whole day picnicking . . . a lorry with lunch and bottles followed our car . . . one thing I particularly like about these outdoor luncheons is the cold dried fish. Besides the European food there are always some spicy Indian dishes . . . cold curry of boar's head (without the eyes) or peppery leaves of spinach fried in batter . . . of course a hamper of whisky, beer, gimlets, cider, and water is always taken along.'

4

My own experience of Indian picnics wasn't always quite so satisfactory. There was one in particular, a moonlight picnic near the Kutub Minar, the leaning tower near Delhi. There was nothing wrong with the transport, the food, or the moonlight; we had merely reckoned without the hordes of half wild dogs which are a familiar feature of Indian outdoor life. Scarcely had we time to draw the cork of a bottle of the Rhinegold Australian hock which we were lucky to get in war-time India than we were surrounded by nearly every dog in the province; literally surrounded. They did not apparently want food, or at any rate not our food; they simply formed a circle round us at a respectful distance and stared and howled.

First we pretended not to notice, then we shoo-ed them away several times. They returned immediately, with reinforcements, re-formed their dreadful circle, and howled and stared and sniffed again, until they forced us to get into our cars and return to the city, leaving them in possession of their ruin.

5

In Egypt the picnic season starts sometime in March, with *Shem el Nessim*, the 'smelling of the Zephyrs', a day which is kept as a public holiday, when the whole population goes out to eat in the open air and greet the first day of Spring.

An agreeable form of picnic in Cairo was the felucca party; on board a hired Nile sailing boat Arab servants would carry the food; there were copper trays of pimentos, small marrows and vine leaves stuffed with rice, large, round shallow metal dishes filled with meat and spiced pilaff, bowls of grapes and peaches and figs and melons cooled with lumps of ice, mounds of flat Arab loaves stuffed with a salad of tomatoes, onions and mint; there would be music and the wailing of Arab songs as the boat swung rather wildly about, the crew made Turkish coffee, and we drank the odd, slightly salty red Egyptian wine from the Mariut, one of the oldest wine-producing regions in the world.

✧ A PROVENÇAL PICNIC ✧

Ford Madox Ford has described (in *Provence*, Allen and Unwin, 1938) a Provençal picnic of heroic proportions; the scene was one of the beautiful *calanques* along the coast from Marseille, a beach accessible only in boats; the whole banquet was cooked on the spot, in huge cauldrons, beneath the umbrella pines. Sixty-one bottles of wine were consumed by sixteen adults and a shoal of children; half a hundredweight of bouillabaise, twelve cocks stewed in wine with innumerable savoury herbs, a salad in a dish as large as a cartwheel, sweet cream cheese with a sauce made of *marc* and sweet herbs, a pile, large enough to bury a man, of apples, peaches, figs, grapes . . .

✧ A BREAKFAST PICNIC ✧

'He [William Hickey's father] engaged one of the Nunnerys, as they are called, for which he paid fifty guineas . . . Provisions, consisting of cold fowls, ham, tongues, different meat pies, wines and liquors of various sorts, were sent to the apartment the day before, and two servants were allowed to attend . . . It was half past seven in the morning before we reached the Abbey. . . . We found a hot and comfortable breakfast, which I enjoyed, and which proved highly refreshing to us all; after which some of our party determined to take a nap in their chairs. . . . Their Majesties being crowned, the Archbishop of Canterbury mounted the pulpit to deliver his sermon, and as many thousands were out of the possibility of hearing a single syllable, they took that opportunity to eat their meal, when the general clattering of knives, forks, plates, and glasses that ensued produced a most ridiculous effect, and a universal burst of laughter followed.'

William Hickey's *Memoirs*, 1749–1782. Edited by Edward A. Spencer, 2 volumes, 1913–1918.

◇ *BILL OF FARE FOR A PICNIC* ◇
FOR FORTY PERSONS

'A joint of cold roast beef, a joint of cold boiled beef, two ribs of lamb, two shoulders of lamb, four roast fowls, two roast ducks, one ham, one tongue, two veal-and-ham pies, two pigeon pies, six medium-sized lobsters, one piece of collared calf's head, eighteen lettuces, six baskets of salad, six cucumbers.

'Stewed fruit well sweetened, and put into glass bottles well corked; three or four dozen plain pastry biscuits to eat with the stewed fruit, two dozen fruit turnovers, four dozen cheesecakes, two cold Cabinet puddings in moulds, a few jam puffs, one large cold Christmas plum-pudding (this must be good), a few baskets of fresh fruit, three dozen plain biscuits, a piece of cheese, six pounds of butter (this, of course, includes the butter for tea), four quartern loaves of household bread, three dozen rolls, six loaves of tin bread (for tea), two plain plum cakes, two pound cakes, two sponge cakes, a tin of mixed biscuits, half a pound of tea. Coffee is not suitable for a picnic, being difficult to make.'

From an early edition of *Mrs Beeton*

◇ *THE IDEAL* ◇

'Bright shone the morning, and as I waited (They had promised to call for me in their motor) I made for myself an enchanting picture of the day before me, our drive to that forest beyond the dove-blue hills, the ideal beings I should meet there, feasting with them, exquisitely, in the shade of immemorial trees.

'And when, in the rainy twilight, I was deposited, soaked, and half-dead with fatigue, out of that open motor, was there nothing inside me but chill and disillusion? If I had dreamed a dream incompatible with the climate and social conditions of these Islands, had I not, out of that very dream and disenchantment, created, like the Platonic Lover, a Platonic and imperishable vision – the ideal Picnic, the Picnic as it might be – the wonderful windless weather, the Watteauish landscape, where a group of mortals talk and feast as they talked and feasted in the Golden Age?'

Logan Pearsall Smith, *All Trivia*, Constable & Co., 1933.

TABLE OF EQUIVALENTS

❖ OVEN TEMPERATURES ❖

Gas	°F	°C		Gas	°F	°C
¼	225	110 very slow/cool		5	375	190
½	250	120		6	400	200 hot
1	275	140		7	425	220
2	300	150 slow/cool		8	450	230
3	325	160		9	475	240 very hot
4	350	180 moderate				

❖ WEIGHT AND LIQUID IMPERIAL AND METRIC EQUIVALENTS ❖

¼ oz	7 g	9 oz	275 g	½ fl oz	15 ml	11 fl oz	325 ml
½ oz	15 g	10 oz	300 g	1 fl oz	25 ml	12 fl oz	350 ml
¾ oz	20 g	11 oz	350 g	2 fl oz	50 ml	13 fl oz	375 ml
1 oz	25 g	12 oz	375 g	3 fl oz	75 ml	14 fl oz	400 ml
2 oz	50 g	13 oz	400 g	4 fl oz	125 ml	¾ pt	450 ml
3 oz	75 g	14 oz	450 g	¼ pt	150 ml	16 fl oz	475 ml
4 oz	125 g	15 oz	475 g	6 fl oz	175 ml	17 fl oz	500 ml
5 oz	150 g	1 lb	500 g	7 fl oz	200 ml	18 fl oz	550 ml
6 oz	175 g	2 lb	1 kg	8 fl oz	250 ml	19 fl oz	575 ml
7 oz	225 g			9 fl oz	275 ml	1 pt	600 ml
8 oz	250 g			½ pt	300 ml	2 pt	1.2 litres

❖ INFORMAL MEASURES ❖

dessertspoon = 2 teaspoons
liqueur glass = about 1½ ounces
glass (wine) = about 4 ounces
coffeecup = about 4–5 ounces
teacup = about 6 ounces
tumbler = about 6 ounces
breakfastcup = almost 8 ounces
gill = ¼ pint/150 ml

❖ IMPERIAL AND METRIC MEASUREMENTS ❖

¼ in	5 mm	3 in	7 cm	8 in	20 cm
½ in	1 cm	4 in	10 cm	9 in	23 cm
¾ in	2 cm	4½ in	11 cm	10 in	25 cm
1 in	2.5 cm	5 in	12 cm	11 in	28 cm
1½ in	4 cm	6 in	15 cm	12 in	30 cm
2 in	5 cm	7 in	18 cm		

INDEX

INDEX

LIST OF ILLUSTRATIONS